SCENES FROM PREHISTORIC LIFE

Francis Pryor is one of Britain's most distinguished living archaeologists, the excavator of Flag Fen and a sheep farmer. He is the author of seventeen books including *The Fens* (a Radio 4 Book of the Week), *Stonehenge*, *Flag Fen*, *Britain* BC, *Britain* AD, and *The Making of the British Landscape*.

FRANCIS PRYOR

SCENES FROM PREHISTORIC LIFE

From the Ice Age to the coming
of the Romans

HEAD
ZEUS

An Apollo Book

First published in the UK in 2021 by Head of Zeus Ltd
This paperback edition first published in 2022 by Head of Zeus Ltd,
part of Bloomsbury Publishing Plc

9 7 5 3 1 2 4 6 8

A catalogue record for this book is available from
the British Library.

ISBN (PB): 9781789544152
ISBN (E): 9781789544169

Typeset by Ben Cracknell Studios
Maps by Jeff Edwards

Printed and bound in Great Britain by
CPI Group (UK) Ltd, Croydon CRO 4YY

Head of Zeus Ltd
5–8 Hardwick Street
London ECIR 4RG

WWW.HEADOFZEUS.COM

In fond memory of Teddy Faure Walker
(September 1946–June 2018)

Contents

Introduction

Setting the Scenes

Scenes – Landscapes – Chronology

Modern archaeology can sometimes seem miraculous. It is transforming our understanding of what it would have been like to have lived in Britain and Ireland in the million or so years that human beings have occupied this land. We are discovering about daily life in the warmer interludes of the Ice Age and in the centuries that followed, and we are revealing undreamt-of information about the settlements, economies and lifestyles of the millions of people who led highly organized, civilized lives in the four millennia before Christ.

The more we learn, the more we realize that prehistoric* communities were extremely adaptable and were able to settle in a number of very different landscapes, some of which we might view, even today, as being quite challenging, if not actually hostile. This was done by keeping in regular touch with other, often quite widely separated, groups of people. Mutually agreed

---

* 'Prehistory' refers to the story of human cultural and economic life before the introduction of writing, and with it written records. It varies across the globe. In Australia, for example, prehistory ends with the arrival of Captain Cook in the eighteenth century. In Britain, the Romans introduced writing when they invaded in AD 43.

routes, which later developed into paths, trackways and roads, must have been a feature of the landscape from earliest times. Travel encouraged the spread of new ideas and it also ensured that human and animal bloodlines avoided isolation and, with it, inbreeding.

There has been a huge increase in archaeological activity since planning laws changed in the late 1980s. This has produced large regional data sets of sites, monuments and finds,* both excavated and still in the ground. These are now so vast that there is a danger that any overview of British and Irish prehistory would soon become swamped by facts and figures. In my experience, too many statistics tend to obscure general themes. So in this book I want to sidestep the detail and bring the people of prehistory to the fore: their beliefs, the way they lived their lives, how they acquired the essentials of existence, and how they interacted with those around them. If possible, I also want to glimpse these things both locally and across society as a whole. To achieve this I will have to focus on individual sites and landscapes. My emphasis will be on what it would have been like actually to have visited these places when they were inhabited many millennia ago. That way, I hope we will be able to capture something of the accelerating pace of prehistoric change.

I plan to cover the full time span of British and Irish prehistory, as we currently appreciate it, starting about a million years ago. During the earliest periods, the areas that were later to become the British Isles were often too cold to inhabit. As a consequence, survival of these very old sites is thin and fragmentary. Despite that, they have produced some remarkable finds, including the extraordinary discoveries at Boxgrove and Star Carr.† But the

---

* These are usually managed by local authorities and are known as Historic Environment Records (or HERs).

† Scenes 1 and 2, respectively.

pace of population growth, together with social and technological change, increased rapidly with the arrival of farming, shortly before 4000 BC.* These later four millennia will form the main chronological focus of this book.

But now I want to get a little more personal: archaeology, after all, is a humanity, not a hard science – and its practitioners are only too human. Our own lives inevitably colour our views of time: past, present and future. For about sixteen years I was a member of Channel 4's *Time Team*, a programme that was last broadcast in 2014, but which has acquired a flourishing afterlife on digital channels and on YouTube. *Time Team* was popular because it brought archaeology to life: it showed how people coped with both simple problems and enormous challenges. Above all else, it focused on the daily routines of living, whether in an Iron Age round-house or a Victorian millworker's basement kitchen. These filmed scenes, or snapshots, from the past painted a far more vivid picture than a broad overview. And that is what I am going to attempt to do in this book, but in words and a few photos.

Time Team worked because each episode was specific: we investigated a particular community, at a given time in a known landscape (and we went to great pains, through our on-screen specialist Stewart Ainsworth, to get that landscape right). I plan to follow those principles here. So each Scene will concentrate on a particular landscape or group of landscapes, and I will use information from individual excavations and surveys to recreate a story that captures some aspect of what it might have been like to have lived there at a given time in prehistory. This book cannot pretend to offer a comprehensive view of ancient Britain, but I hope it will convey an impression of change. From around 4000

---

* In many books, the less religiously specific term 'Before Common Era' (BCE) is used instead of BC, and CE ('Common Era') rather than AD.

BC, thousands of small communities slowly evolved towards the strong tribal kingdoms that were eventually to confront the invading Roman army. My intention is to open front doors, peek behind curtains, look into farmyards, fields, gardens and cemeteries where ordinary life was being lived. And there we will see how the pace of change was increasing as time advanced. By the final five hundred years before Christ, the broad sweep of the British landscape would have become recognizable to many people living today: roads, fields, farms and villages had replaced the forests, moors, heaths and open floodplains that dominated the view when the first farmers arrived in Britain, four millennia earlier.

Another reason why *Time Team* worked so well was that every programme was about the actual process of discovery. All of us on the Team were aware that viewers in millions of homes right across Britain were looking over our shoulders. I slowly came to understand that being present at the moment of discovery was what gave archaeology its special appeal to so many people. Indeed, the more I thought about it, the more I gradually began to appreciate that I was no different from the millions of viewers who used to join us every Sunday evening, in the three dark months after Christmas.

The actual filming was hard work, but great fun, too. I loved being there, on the spot, when something was revealed. It was far more profound than mere treasure hunting. In some strange way, the process of discovery made you part of the ancient world you were investigating. It happened many times: I would be working away and then, sometimes quite abruptly, I would realize I understood how or why something – often something quite minor – was achieved in the remote past: maybe shaping a stone, butchering a joint of venison or raking out a fireplace. And the evidence was right there, before my very eyes. For the first time in thousands of years I was looking at what some stranger had just completed, before he or she broke off for a meal, or went to bed for the night. That sort of discovery or realization is about far more than excitement alone: it's almost like I had acquired a feeling of intimacy or familiarity with a particular group of people, or a family, in the past; it explains why I still find many ancient sites and places so special.

My deep engagement with archaeology, as someone who both researches and tries to communicate the subject, has taught me that discovering new information about past human behaviour is far from a simple process. Something might appear blindingly obvious in one trench, but then open another one in a neighbouring field and, lo and behold, what seemed so simple in the first trench is actually quite different. So two ditches parallel in the first trench join together into a single ditch in the second. *So what?* I can hear sceptical readers mutter. It matters a lot if you had identified the two parallel ditches in the first trench as the edges of a road or trackway. Such ditches never come together. So some other explanation is needed.* Archaeology teaches one to keep an open mind; but, being human, I can assure you it is not always as easy as it sounds.

I have been a prehistorian for almost fifty years and I must confess I still find it difficult to grasp the scale and speed of landscape change over the centuries. At university we were taught about the analysis of ancient pollen grains and other scientific techniques that were starting to reveal how fluctuating temperatures and other climate changes were affecting forest cover and natural vegetation. Today these approaches are far more sophisticated and our understanding of environmental change over the past four million or so years, when the first humans emerged, is now extraordinarily detailed.[1] This

---

* We will see this in Scenes 10 and 11 when we discuss the Fengate Bronze Age droveways.

knowledge is great when one wants to write a textbook, or do research, but I don't find it very useful when I try to imagine what it would have been like to have actually lived in a certain place at a particular time. How, for example, did people see their surroundings? Were they frightened, or content? Did they view the prehistoric landscape as a hostile environment? And how did they cope with cold winters and other seasonal changes?

These were difficult questions and I soon realized they could not be answered simply by reading books and by doing conventional library research. They required additional personal experience that I didn't then possess. But having been brought up in the country by a farming family, and being a fairly practical sort of person, I decided to devote a major part of my life to the establishment and running of a small sheep farm. Shortly before we made that decision, we had revealed archaeological evidence for some of the earliest prehistoric livestock farming in Britain. I was concerned not just about the way these early farmers managed their animals, but how they related to their neighbours and to other communities in the region. And back then, that sort of information was only to be found out there in the real world. Books could help, but they never joined the various aspects of a farming life together: they never told a coherent story. And that was what fascinated me: I was deeply interested in, almost obsessed with, the way our prehistoric ancestors farmed their land and conducted their lives. I have discussed families and farming in other books.[2] In these pages, I want to examine how prehistoric people blended into – and in many cases changed – the places where they lived. It is only once I had done so myself, through my work as a farmer, that I came to realize how ancient communities could have altered their surroundings to accord with their social, economic and religious lives. This, in turn, has led me to appreciate the richness and diversity of their cultures. I can now understand, just a little bit better, how it was they could produce some of the beautiful objects that now adorn the display cases of our museums.

My journey into the world of practical farming began about twenty-five years ago, when we laid out the fields and paddocks of our farm in the Lincolnshire Fens, not far from the small market town of Holbeach. We built our house, two barns and a farmyard alongside a medieval drovers' road at the fringe of a rural parish, some 5 kilometres (3 miles) from the village. It was, and is, quite a lonely spot. In this open, flat landscape, the wintery gales blew in fiercely from off the Wash and the North Sea, which was less than 16 kilometres (10 miles) away. To cut these winds, we planted a wood of native British trees along the north-easterly edge of our land, but even so, for the first five years they seemed to freeze the muscles in my legs, arms, back and neck. Carrying bales and feeding sheep became something of a nightmare on the coldest days of January and February. At first, the eight-acre (3.25 ha) wood seemed to be growing very slowly. Indeed, after the first year, only a few plants had ventured to poke their leading shoots above the protection provided by their knee-high green plastic growing-tubes.

But then things started to happen. In the first two years the young trees established their root systems and then they began to grow. After five years, the trees were as tall as me. Soon after that, if I took a walk through the young wood, I could not be seen from outside it. Wildlife was returning to what had once been an arable 'grain plain'. And not just in the wood: molehills were appearing in the meadow where we cut hay for the sheep in winter. It took five years for the earthworm population in the soil to increase following decades of intensive arable cropping – and the moles were feeding on them. Anthills also started to appear in the meadow – and soon we saw them being pecked over by green woodpeckers. After twenty years, we had buzzards nesting in the trees. The place had been transformed, and in less than a single human generation. The experience of watching wildlife return and seeing natural pasture becoming established by grazing sheep has given me some inkling of what prehistoric farmers must have felt as they saw their clearings within the trees, or as they established their paddocks along the edges of river floodplains. It isn't just a feeling of security or of achievement. It's far more profound than that – and moreover it's something that can never be taken away. So I don't regret what some professional colleagues have seen as my 'diversion' into farming.

I'm a great fan of L. P. Hartley's *The Go-Between*, and his opening words – 'The past is a foreign country; they do things differently there' – are of course memorable. But they're wrong. Profoundly wrong. I believe that the past is an integral part of the present and we must use it if we are to cope with the challenges of the future. I do not see archaeology or history as being somehow irrelevant to modern society and its social and political concerns, because knowledge of the past – in all its many aspects – is the only way to inform our choices for the future. You cannot isolate just one aspect of life, be it politics, religion or identity, from the rest of human culture and experience. All must be taken together and viewed as a whole, in the social context of a particular culture or region. This applies as much to the past as to the present. If you respect the people of earlier generations, you will treat their descendants properly. In fact, I would go further: if you learn to love the past, you will do everything in your power to ensure there is a future. Having said that, you can never turn the clock back and return to an earlier state of being. There is always a danger that our view of the past becomes distorted by being looked at through rose-tinted spectacles. That is why phrases like 'let's make America great again' are so very misleading.

Time cannot stand still. This applied as much in prehistory as it does today. By definition, prehistory cannot be revealed by historians because there are no documents for them to study. So the first prehistorians had to work out how to date and age the various sites and objects that seemed to be earlier than the Romans. The first real progress was made by some Danish museum curators in the early nineteenth century, who were trying to make sense of their collections of tools and implements made from stone, bronze and iron, which they knew pre-dated the Roman expansion across northern and western Europe.[3] Roman writers were the first people to record early military and political history in these regions (which included Britain), mostly in the final two centuries BC. The rationalization of museum collections gave rise to the three-Age system of Stone, followed by Bronze and then Iron. It's a system that is essentially based on the complexity of the technologies involved.

The modification of stone to form a tool requires considerable skill, but needs little heat or other technological development. The production of metal from ore (a process known as smelting) involves the careful manipulation of fire, together with other chemical and physical measures, such as the control of oxygen and the addition of carbon. The first metals to be worked were copper and gold. In its physical characteristics, gold is halfway between stone and metal. It occurs in streams as a tiny shiny grain or pebble and can be worked without heat. Copper can be smelted from its ore at reasonably low temperatures, but is quite soft. Copper axes are only a slight improvement on stone. But when about 10 per cent tin is added to it, the resulting alloy, bronze, is very much harder and stronger. Bronze tools are usually cast using stone or clay moulds. Iron requires much higher temperatures to smelt from its ore and is very much harder than bronze. It is shaped into tools and weapons by repeated beating on an anvil and reheating, a process known as 'smithing'. The iron produced in a blacksmith's shop is known as 'wrought iron'. Cast iron, a hard alloy of iron and carbon, although invented in China in the fifth century BC, was not introduced to Britain until the time of Henry VIII, when it was used to make cannons.[*]

If time cannot stand still, people cannot live alone. Like all mammals, we humans require communities in which to grow up and raise new generations. Contrary to popular opinion, there have never been any truly migratory people who wander the Earth completely at random: anthropologists have shown that even shifting communities follow well-established routes that obey a set of recognized boundaries. And boundaries denote landscapes. Human landscapes are all about dividing up terrain to avoid conflict and to make the tasks of daily life run smoothly. In the hunter-gatherer societies that existed in Britain before the introduction of farming in the Neolithic era (c. 4000 BC), the divisions would have been between the hunting grounds of neighbouring communities. Other important markers in the landscape would have been the places where animals could drink water or give birth to their young, at certain times of the year. These areas would have been respected, because it would have been in nobody's interests to have hunted game to near extinction – as happened to the American bison by the late nineteenth century. By then, of course, the European-derived populations of the United States had lost all connection with their original hunting traditions. This explains why they completely failed to appreciate the irreversible harm they were causing. Their prehistoric precursors would not have made such elementary mistakes.

Ancient boundaries within landscapes were subtle and were not always marked in ways that can be identified by archaeology

---

[*] The first major cast-iron structure is the bridge across the Severn at Ironbridge, which opened in 1781.

– even with its modern, sophisticated geophysical techniques. Certain trees, for example, could have been marked for special attention; piles of brushwood and bonfires could have been lit at certain times of the year. Such boundaries could have served practical purposes to do with hunting and farming, but they could also have marked out areas that were regarded as special in some way: maybe grounds that were set aside for burying the dead or neutral places where people from widely separated communities could come together without the risk of conflict. Such places were often on hills or close by lakes or rivers, where the shades of the ancestors and other forces in the spirit world were believed to reside. Only quite recently have we begun to realize that locations where shrines of the Bronze Age were erected had been viewed as special for many millennia previously. A good example of this is the sacred spring at Blick Mead (*c.* 8000 BC), near the much later site of Stonehenge (2900 BC).* Some of the traditional paths and tracks of pre-farming landscapes would have survived into the Neolithic and later periods and it is very possible that many of the roads that we know were in existence prior to the Roman period – and are still in use today – have origins that extend back many millennia.

Owing to practical constraints, archaeologists usually work at quite a small, site-based scale: most prehistoric excavations will concentrate on a single monument, such as a burial mound (or barrow), a settlement or a hillfort. As a general rule, too, the older the site, the smaller the excavation. This usually reflects the fact that ancient sites rarely extend over large distances and the evidence they offer can often be very fragmentary. Post-Ice Age Mesolithic sites, for example, are famous for producing tens of thousands of tiny (smaller than fingernail-sized) flint flakes, known as microliths. To recover these, the soil has to be

---

* I discuss Blick Mead in Scene 4, pages 65–8.

carefully sieved – rendering a large dig impossible. But in certain circumstances it is now possible to work on a larger, landscape scale – even on quite early sites. And these are the projects that have produced the most extraordinary advances in our knowledge of prehistoric Britain, since the late 1960s and early 1970s.

When you examine how past communities adapted to, and often changed, the landscape around them, you can gain an appreciation of the power of long-term communal action: marshes can be drained, forests felled and field systems established. But these changes are not always predictable and no two communities will necessarily adapt to similar surroundings in the same way. Just like today, there seems to be no limit to the creative independence of people in the past. Some theoretical prehistorians believe that it can be possible to predict what you will discover in the ground, provided you have a thorough understanding of the climate, the environment and the population of a given region at a particular period in the past. But in my experience such predictions always fall well short of reality – and yes, they can focus one's attention, but they can also provide intellectual blinkers that prevent one from seeing a broader and more interesting picture. Reconstructing, through patient survey and meticulous excavation, a picture of the way that communities and regional economies changed as they gained a measure of control over their surroundings is essentially a creative process. Good archaeology requires imagination. Analysis on its own is never enough. So I hope that the Scenes that follow will provide food for thought and will dispel the myth that people in the past lived lives that were simpler and somehow less rich than ours. Nothing could be further from the truth.

There is a general perception that life in Britain before the coming of the Romans changed very little, if at all. People in prehistory are still seen as somehow primitive, and waiting to be 'civilized' by armies of incoming Roman soldiers and administrators. But when the three Roman invasions happened (two by Caesar in 55 and 54 BC and the final conquest by the Emperor Claudius, in AD 43), the Roman army, then the most efficient fighting machine on Earth, developed a good deal of respect for British military resistance.

By the late first century BC, many upper-class or elite Britons, and this applied most particularly in the south and east, were adopting Roman patterns of dress; we can tell this from the bronze brooches they wore. As we do today, they were also enjoying Mediterranean wine, food and olive oil; again, we know this from the pestle and mortar fragments from their kitchens and from pieces of ceramic amphorae – the ancient equivalents of large bottles or small casks. The first coins were minted in Britain several decades before the Claudian invasion. I strongly suspect that many educated Britons in the south would have spoken Latin fluently and would have visited the mainland of Europe frequently. There would probably have been daily ferry crossings of the English Channel.

Late Iron Age Britain was very different from the same place almost ten thousand years previously, following the final retreat of the last Ice Age; indeed, it was another world. Apart from the fact that Britain had yet to become an island, which finally happened around 6000 BC, the population was still very small and people lived off the land by hunting and gathering their food. During the ten millennia of post-Ice Age prehistory, the population of what was to become the British Isles rose from a handful of settlers who migrated north, following the retreating ice, to something around three million at the time of the Roman conquest. It was that steady, but relentless, increase in population that helped to inspire and fuel the growth of distinctly British cultures. Social and economic change would not have been as fast as it is today, but I think people would have been aware of it, especially in the later Bronze and the Iron Ages – from about 1000 BC. And that is why prehistorians have subdivided the three technology-based Ages of Stone, Bronze and Iron into Early, Middle and Late subphases. This chronology varies widely across the globe and is constantly being modified and improved.

Chronology forms the skeleton of prehistory. In the past it was estimated by the occurrence, for example, of later prehistoric tools on well-dated ancient Greek or Roman sites. But otherwise the dates were essentially a matter of informed guesswork. All of that changed in the 1950s and 1960s with the development, in 1949, of the technique of radiocarbon dating by the American physical chemist Willard F. Libby. Today there are many other techniques of science-based dating, some of which can be astonishingly accurate – if bark is present, tree-ring dating (or dendrochronology) can provide dates to the nearest three months. For example, the waterlogged circle of Bronze Age timbers known as 'Seahenge', from Holme-next-the-Sea in Norfolk, is known to have been constructed between April and June in the year 2049 BC.

Accurate dates are only a part of the story. Yes, they provide a reliable framework for the events of prehistory and allow us to weave them into a coherent story. They can even provide us with clues as to how people lived. If, for example, you know that a house was only occupied for a short time, you can make some accurate observations about what went on in various parts of the building; but if it was lived in by many families over several generations, the accumulation of debris makes it almost impossible to work out who did what, when and where. In prehistory, too much information can cause as many problems as a lack of it.

Radiocarbon dating was one of the earlier science-based innovations that helped to transform prehistory – and there have been many more since. There have also been huge advances in the way we can find and map ancient sites, from the ground, from the air and even from satellites. The study of genetics and DNA is causing us to revise many long and sometimes fondly held views about invasions and migrations. They help us answer the question: was it the movement of people or the spread of new ideas that brought us innovations such as farming, or the technology of metalworking? Often the answers turn out to be far from simple, or indeed predictable. As in life, questions often lead to further questions, rather than simple answers.

So prehistory is in a state of flux. Everything seems to be changing. Personally, I think that's something to be welcomed. In the early part of my career, in the 1960s and 1970s, some of the textbooks we used had been written before the war. There was a stultifying orthodoxy about accepted interpretations of European prehistory. But even then, a few iconoclasts had started to probe the foundations of the accepted wisdom, which believed that following the spread of farming from the Near East, everything new in Europe *had* to originate from that part of the world. During my student reading I would come across the Latin catchphrase '*Ex oriente lux*' ('Out of the East, light'), again and again. Prehistoric people in western Europe were seen as being incapable of thinking for themselves. But then radiocarbon dates showed that the notion of progress invariably drifting from east to west was a myth. Sometimes ideas and innovations spread in the other direction. So the theoretical structure that had underpinned European prehistory for the first half of the twentieth century came crashing to the ground.

Of course, prehistorians have been rebuilding it ever since. Even now, fifty years later, the process of reconstructing that mental structure is still incomplete. Sometimes we seem to be making progress, then some fresh revelation causes timbers to crack and a newly built part of the structure collapses before

Table showing the dates and principal events of British prehistory

Age	From	To	Notes
Old Stone Age (or Palaeolithic)	1,000,000 years ago	12,000 BC	Period ends with the close of the last Ice Age.
Middle Stone Age (or Mesolithic)	12,000 BC	4000 BC	From the end of the Ice Age to the arrival of farming.
New Stone Age (or Neolithic)	4000 BC	2600 BC	The age of early farming. The first barrows and ceremonial centres.
Early Neolithic	4000 BC	3700 BC	First farmers and earliest communal tombs.
Middle Neolithic	3700 BC	3000 BC	Main use of long barrows and causewayed enclosures.
Late Neolithic	3000 BC	2600 BC	Henges and passage tombs. Larger settlements. First field systems.
Early Bronze Age	2600 BC	1500 BC	The Age of Stonehenge. The period starts with two or so centuries of using copper. Bronze arrived later. Round barrows. Flat axes and daggers. Seagoing ships.

Age	From	To	Notes
Middle Bronze Age	1500 BC	1200 BC	'Domestic Revolution'. Round barrows and henges cease to be used. Rapiers and palstaves.
Late Bronze Age	1200 BC	750 BC	Population expanding. Settlements increasing. Field systems growing. First hillforts.
Early Iron Age	750 BC	450 BC	First smelting of iron. Big increase in pottery production. More standardized round-houses. Rapid expansion of hillforts.
Middle Iron Age	450 BC	150 BC	Distinctive styles of heavier pottery. Population, farms and settlements rapidly expanding. Fewer, larger hillforts.
Late Iron Age	150 BC	AD 43	Decline of hillforts. First coins and wheel-made pottery. Larger, town-like settlements and ports/trading stations.
Roman Period	AD 43	AD 410	A blend of British and Roman lifestyles, now known as Romano-British culture.

our eyes. Yes, we live in very uncertain times, but it's a creative uncertainty and that's a huge improvement on the unwavering complacency of earlier decades. I'm sure all of my colleagues would agree that today is a very stimulating time to be a prehistorian. Indeed, there are moments when everything and anything seems possible.

Today there is a growing tendency to view the past through a series of isolated windows that focus on specific events. There are many reasons for this, including the sheer quantity of historical information revealed by recent historical and archaeological research. However, I believe a broader approach is needed if we are to understand all the implications of this new work.

Many of these often difficult questions can best be approached by taking a long view. For example, the immediate cause of the First World War may have been the assassination of the heir to the Austro-Hungarian Empire in Sarajevo in June 1914, but that was only a tiny part of a complex, multilayered story involving not just political leaders but underlying international tensions and ultimately the rise and spread of industrialism and the need for more democracy and greater social justice. Archaeologists are used to taking long views of the past, largely because the evidence we work with tends to be less specific and, of course, precise dating is very much harder. So we are good at detecting how, for example, prehistoric houses evolved over the millennia and the way that isolated settlements slowly grew into villages and eventually into towns. This broad-brush view of prehistory makes excellent sense and helps to explain how the peoples and societies of Britain developed in the millennia prior to the Roman conquest of AD 43. But it also draws our attention away from the people behind the changes. Sadly, we know very few names, as these were pre-literate societies, but we do know that many people lived full and healthy lives: evidence for malnourishment is rare in prehistoric graves – people often survived into their fifties, and some into their sixties and seventies. The fine detail revealed in many modern excavations allows us to reconstruct moments in the distant past, even if we are not sure of their precise date. So we know, for example, how an Iron Age house was arranged and where people would have cooked, eaten and slept. Then sometimes new finds help us to learn even more. It's these unexpected discoveries that can bring a place to life and transform a muddy site into a vivid Scene.

Scene 1

Britain During the Ages of Ice
(900,000–500,000 years ago)

Happisburgh – Pakefield – Boxgrove

Shoreline cliffs are the town walls of an island. Like the White Cliffs of Dover, they can come to symbolize a nation's identity, yet they are strangely fragile: liable to collapse without warning. Their many layers record the passage of the millennia, but their massive monumentality can seem timeless. They are, however, geological features and as such they have obeyed the same physical laws that constrain the processes of soil growth, river valley sedimentation and erosion that are still shaping our world today. The principle that the past and present were governed by the same rules is known as uniformitarianism and it provides the basis for modern, science-based approaches to both geology and archaeology. It was initially worked out by the Scottish geologist James Hutton in the late eighteenth century and culminated in Charles Lyell's *Principles of Geology*, first published in 1830. This was to prove one of the most influential and important books on science of the nineteenth century – second only to Darwin's *On the Origin of Species* (1859), which also had a lasting influence on the growth and development of archaeology.[1]

I have mentioned the early history of archaeology because I

want to stress that it is more than just a technique for discovering exciting objects. In order to study the long eras before writing existed, the disciplines of archaeology and physical anthropology – using excavation, geological and geographic surveys, and other scientific analysis – are the only tools we possess if we want to understand the place and role of humans on this planet. And this applies just as much to the centuries leading up to the Roman conquest as to the two million or so years of the Ice Ages, when Britain was still an integral part of the European mainland and when the North Sea and English Channel had yet to form. The Ice Ages belong within the Pleistocene geological era, which ended around 10,000 BC when the climate grew warmer. The Pleistocene was followed by the Flandrian, or modern era, in which we are living today. Of course, we don't know for certain, but the Flandrian may well be followed by another cold spell in the future – if, that is, the production of too much carbon by mankind doesn't mess everything up.

In the earlier part of the twentieth century, archaeologists of these very early periods tended to view their sites as geological phenomena: there was massive attention to the most minute details of every layer in each cave. Inevitably, this approach became rather mechanistic: the people of prehistory (then popularly known as 'cavemen') were seen as predictable, behaving in certain ways as the climate and environment around them changed. But in the last fifty or so years, archaeological attitudes have become less prescriptive and we can now appreciate that Stone Age communities did far more than merely cope with their surroundings. These fresher approaches to the study of the remote past have in part been caused by some remarkable new discoveries, made not, as might be expected, in caves, but out in the open, where most Palaeolithic people lived out their lives.

Modern archaeology is a science-based humanity that sets out to reveal the way various communities interacted and how this in turn led to their rise, or decline. But you cannot do this simply by studying artefacts. You must also pay close attention to the landscapes where people lived: to changes in the local vegetation, forest cover, crops, livestock and diseases of humans and animals. Surprisingly, a place as geologically tranquil as Britain can be adversely affected by flooding, soil erosion and landslides – and even by cataclysmic events such as short-term climate change brought on by distant volcanic eruptions. It has recently been shown that Britain was seriously affected by a North Sea tsunami, around 6200 BC, just as she was becoming an island.[2] These wider, explanatory goals help to explain why archaeologists today try to take the broadest view possible. So they always study their sites and monuments within a landscape setting, even when the questions that interest them are straightforward and direct. For example, I am frequently asked: when was Britain first settled by humans? To answer that, we must first point out that the British Isles are a recent creation (hastened by that tsunami I just mentioned). I then go on to explain that the earliest settlers occupied land that later, very much later, became the island of Britain. By this point, my listeners often start to look fidgety: this wasn't the quick response they had expected. So let's cut to the chase and return to those coastal cliffs, not all of which are so ancient, or so massive, as the well-known ones near Dover.

Norfolk is notorious for its place-name pronunciation: some say Hunstanton, others, 'Hunston'; Garboldisham is often pronounced 'Garbolsham', but the craziest of them all is surely Happisburgh, known across Norfolk (and even into my part of Lincolnshire) as 'Hazebrough'. Its weird pronunciation apart, Happisburgh is best known for its tall stone lighthouse, the earliest surviving in East Anglia, which was built in 1790. Today it is painted in wide red-and-white bands that can be seen for miles out at sea, and indeed inland. The village also boasts a superb medieval church – a classic East Anglian 'wool church' – which also stands out in the landscape and might explain why it was deliberately bombed in 1940.³ My wife, Maisie, and I often head along the north Norfolk coast in the winter, when the hordes of summer visitors and second-homers have retreated inland. This is when the coastal villages of north Norfolk return to the county that created them and local people can venture out onto the now empty coastal roads. In our experience, churches, beaches and coastal pubs are at their atmospheric best in these colder months.

The seaside towns and villages of East Anglia have a charm all of their own. I have a particular fondness for the cliffs at the little village of Dunwich, in Suffolk, with their thick woods that allow tantalizing glimpses of the sea far below and to the east. The waves conceal the remains of Saxon Dunwich, Britain's best-known vanished town, capital of the East Angles, which was overtaken by catastrophic storms in the late thirteenth century. Further north, and across the county boundary in Norfolk, Happisburgh used to be a terrible place for shipwrecks – hence the huge lighthouse – but the many waves also caused damage to the foreshore, where the cliffs were formed from muds and Ice Age estuarine and river deposits. This material had accumulated quite rapidly along the course of one of the streams belonging to an early version of the river system that today we call the Thames. Many British river names have very ancient roots and the Thames is no exception: it is almost certainly pre-Roman, and derived from the Celtic word for 'dark one' or 'river'.⁴

And now I must make a confession: I'm a fully qualified archaeologist, as is Maisie, and we have walked along Happisburgh beach many times. But we never spotted the prehistoric riches that were lying at our feet. I blame the tides for not exposing them – but that's just my excuse.

A team of archaeologists had been examining the ancient river deposits at Happisburgh since 2005 and had revealed five sites with evidence for human activity dating back to the Old Stone Age, or Palaeolithic. One of these (known to the Happisburgh team as Site 3) was particularly important, as it revealed a series of sharp flint tools that had almost certainly been made and used locally.[5] The shape of these tools suggested that the site was far too old to be dated by the usual radiocarbon method (which doesn't work for sites older than about 50,000 years). Then, in May 2013, there was a remarkable and seemingly very lucky discovery. I say 'seemingly', because when you examine how new things are revealed in archaeology, you often find that 'luck' is more apparent than real: it conceals a lot of careful thought and planning. And that was certainly the case on Happisburgh beach, back in 2013.

Dr Martin Bates and his brother Richard were doing a complex geophysical survey of the old river deposits beneath the rapidly eroding cliffs. They wanted to find out more about their width, depth and history of accumulation and erosion over the centuries. The process involves the sinking of numerous electrodes, which are connected to various devices, including a computer. Once the electricity has been turned on, it takes about an hour for the data to be gathered and during this time nothing must be disturbed. So Martin and Richard took a stroll along the beach, which had just had much of its sand removed by a particularly severe storm. The washing away of the sand had revealed the undisturbed muds of the ancient Thames estuary that formed the bed of the beach. Normally such deposits are quite smooth and you can spot little streams and the remains of patches of reeds. But Martin's attention was immediately grabbed by the lack of smoothness. These muds were bumpy and disturbed.

I've seen similar 'bumpy' prehistoric deposits at Flag Fen and in the Severn Estuary and they closely resemble the churned-up mud of a farm gateway in winter, when sheep or cattle have just been driven through. The Flag Fen footprints were of animals alone, but those on the Severn were made by bare-footed people and they stood out immediately – just as they did to Martin Bates, at Happisburgh. The human footprints I'd seen at Goldcliff in the Severn Estuary had been made around 4700 BC,[6] at the end of the Mesolithic, but the ones at Happisburgh were to prove very much earlier. Following a quite complex process of scientific dating, we now realize that the estuarine muds at Happisburgh formed between 850,000 and 950,000 years ago. This was when the tools found in the nearby Site 3 trench were made and when the footprints were formed. We know from many studies of Ice Age pollen and other indicators that this was a time when the climate was getting colder, following a warmer phase in the Ice Age. Broadleaf woodland (oak, ash and elm) was giving way to more hardy pine forest. Soon, people would retreat to warmer places south of what was later to become Britain.[7]

I can remember being very moved by the fact that the more recent footprints in the muds of the Severn were made by men, women and children and when I visited the site I could imagine Mesolithic families out for a stroll along the foreshore. But what we now realize were the earliest footprints in Europe, at Happisburgh, were probably left by a family group who were out foraging for food along the tidal river. The people themselves would have been precursors of modern humans (*Homo sapiens*), most probably *Homo antecessor* (or 'Pioneer Man'). A close examination of the forty-nine identifiable footprints shows that they were left by a man, a woman (probably) and three children. There's no evidence for larking about. Nobody runs or jumps. It looks like they were slowly walking in one direction, but weaving around a bit, as one would, when on the lookout for edible plants, birds' eggs, eels – or whatever. That small family group could never have imagined that their walk along the river had left marks that, almost a million years later, have now been

1.1 A mass of footprints on the beach at Happisburgh, north Norfolk. They were preserved in the muds of an old course of an extinct river that flowed into the North Sea about a million years ago.

1.2 Close-up of the best-preserved footprint at Happisburgh. The impression left by the heel is deeper, to the right, and outlines of four toes can just be seen, to the left.

7

recorded for posterity. The actual footprints in the mud have long since been reclaimed by the North Sea.

I come from a Quaker family and many of my ancestors were either brewers, maltsters or bankers. Today, of course, 'banker' has almost become a term of abuse, but in the seventeenth and eighteenth centuries Quaker bankers came to be trusted because of their high ethical and moral standards. So they were very successful. By the same token, people had become distrustful of many brewers and maltsters, who often watered down or adulterated their beers. Again, the Quakers stepped in and re-established public trust and confidence in their products. One of the breweries my family was associated with was Truman's of Brick Lane, in East London, where I worked after graduating. It was here that I was trained as a beer-taster. And I have never lost that taste for a good cask-conditioned real ale. Some of the best ales in East Anglia are brewed by Adnams of Southwold, on the Suffolk coast, and over the years I often found myself heading there. One of the routes south from Lincolnshire, where I live, is via Great Yarmouth, then along the coast, following the A12 through the Suffolk Coast and Heaths Area of Outstanding Natural Beauty – which includes Dunwich (a few miles south of Southwold).

Just outside Lowestoft, the A12 passes through the coastal village of Pakefield. The name was familiar to me through the researches of another beer enthusiast, the late John Wymer. John loved a pint or two of Abbot Ale, brewed in Bury St Edmunds, near his home; he was also a keen gardener, kept ducks and played a mean boogie-woogie piano. All in all he was a lovely, humorous man, but he was also one of the world's leading authorities on the Palaeolithic. I remember once discussing John with a student on a dig. He found it surprising that a man with so many interests could find the time to be such a good prehistorian. Then I heard myself saying something that has stayed with me ever since: 'No,' I replied. 'You've got it wrong. He was a great prehistorian *because* he lived his own life to the full. Yes, prehistory is about facts and information, but it's mostly about people and you will never be able to understand the challenges faced by ancient communities if you've led a sheltered life yourself.'

John Wymer wrote many books on the Palaeolithic and excavated a number of classic sites. The last major research project he was involved with took place below the cliffs at Pakefield. The area had long been known to archaeologists and geologists of the Pleistocene because of the Cromer Forest Bed which forms the cliffs and underlies the beach there. The Cromer Forest Bed, formed between two million and half a million years ago, was well known to both Victorian and twentieth-century prehistorians and geologists for producing Pleistocene tree stumps and animal bones. Its various layers are a remnant of the low-lying plains and river valleys that once extended across what is now the North Sea basin, between Britain, Germany and the Low Countries. Geologists have given this landscape, which connected Britain and Europe in early post-Ice Age (Flandrian) times, the name Doggerland, after the Dogger Bank, a huge sandbank about 130 kilometres (80 miles) off the Yorkshire/Lincolnshire coast.[8]

It's odd the way places, like people, reoccur in one's life. I can remember spending a wonderful holiday at West Runton, a coastal village in the sand dunes near Cromer in north-east Norfolk. My small boy's memories of the early 1950s are like a time capsule: steam trains chugging along the coastal railway and Mosquitos (the Second World War planes, not the insects) towing targets that were shot at by anti-aircraft guns mounted along the foreshore – far more exciting than boring old sandcastles and picnics on the beach. Much later, I was to learn that West Runton has one of the best outcrops of the Cromer Forest Bed, which in 1990 revealed the bones of Britain's earliest and most complete mammoth.[9]

The discovery of ancient flint tools, or the waste flakes that result from their manufacture, is always exciting, but everything depends on how and where they are found. So-called hand-axes are the best-known stone tools of the Old Stone Age, or Palaeolithic. They come in a multitude of shapes and sizes, whose classification and definition have kept hundreds of students and academics in gainful employment for decades. Hand-axes were probably not hafted and used as tree-felling axes, but were multipurpose cutting, butchering and digging tools. They may even have served as a source, or core, for the removal of smaller flint flakes, with razor-sharp cutting edges. While hand-axes have grabbed most people's attention, the majority of flint finds on Palaeolithic sites have been far humbler: a selection of flakes and fragments, which show the tell-tale signs of human manufacture.

I first learned how to identify deliberately worked flints when I was a student at Cambridge. Superficially similar flakes can be naturally produced by sharp frosts, or when glaciers crush layers of flint and gravel beneath tons of slowly moving ice. But it wasn't until I returned home in summer vacations and started chipping* away at flints myself that I really started to appreciate the intricacies of flint-working. And believe me, flint-knapping techniques can be extremely difficult to master: so-called pressure flaking, for example, is done by pressing (very hard!) on the edge of a piece of flint with a pointed tool made from bone or antler. And you have to get everything just right – the angle of the tool, its distance from the edge of the flint and the actual pressure applied – if you want to successfully remove a pressure

---

* 'Knapping' is the word usually used to describe the process of flint-working.

flake. Arrowheads and other small, delicate items can only be made in this way.

Two local collectors at Pakefield appreciated that the best time to find flints and fossils was during winter, especially after storms had caused small landslides along the Cromer Forest Bed cliffs. They realized that it was important to be quite certain of precise locations: it wasn't enough simply to find things on the beach. You had to prove where they originally came from. Their foresight, patience and persistence was rewarded in 2002, when they found a deliberately knapped flint flake in the Cromer Forest Bed, in deposits that formed around 700,000 years ago. This led to excavations that have revealed a total of thirty-two flint flakes, including a core, a larger lump of flint from which flint flakes had been removed to make smaller, sharp-edged tools.[10]

Most students of archaeology get to handle Palaeolithic flints and you can still see many of them in museum cases across Britain. By and large they tend to be hand-axes and they're often quite worn and abraded – as might befit their great age. Often such flints have come from gravel quarries, where they were spotted by sharp-eyed workmen or collectors. I can remember looking for them in a local quarry where the gravel was being sorted into various grades: fine sand, coarse sand, pea grit, fine gravel, coarse gravel and so on. The coarsest heap of all was known as the wasters' heap, because the rocks and occasional fossil mammoth tooth or bone had no commercial value. I stood by the wasters' heap as it slowly accumulated, but apart from a couple of fragmentary mammoth teeth, I found nothing.

I was astonished by the freshness of the flints from Pakefield and Happisburgh when they were published in the archaeological press. You could tell they hadn't been rolled around in glacial ice or river water. They were as clean and sharp as the day they'd been made – and of course that is why they are so very important. But will we ever discover an earlier site in Britain? I suspect we might find somewhere that is just over a million years old, but I would be very, very surprised if anything turns up that's much older. And will I regret saying that? Heavens, no: I like to lay down a challenge.

Coastal sites like Happisburgh and Pakefield have revealed the very earliest evidence for human occupation in Britain, but they have preserved little evidence for actual in situ remains, where Lower Palaeolithic people actually performed some of the tasks of daily life. You might suppose that European evidence for such very early activity might have been revealed in a cave or a sheltered valley somewhere in France or Spain, but no: one of the earliest and best preserved has been found, excavated and fully published in England, just a short distance from the south coast, at Eartham Quarry, off Boxgrove Common, in Sussex.[11] I visited the site twice in the early 1990s, while it was being dug. It was an experience I have not forgotten. To be honest, I had never been to a Palaeolithic excavation before, and by the end of my first visit I was almost overwhelmed by what I had witnessed. It took such skill: it was slow and meticulous, yet at the same time *so* exciting.

There is something about watching while a student, with the most extraordinary care, concentration and lightness of touch, excavates a hand-axe from the trampled floor, where it was discarded or dropped some 500,000 years ago. It was the sheer age of the flint she was revealing that I still find so hard to accept. Indeed, that vivid memory of the young woman, completely and utterly focused on her demanding task, still manages to give me goosebumps. Quite rightly, she was completely intent on what lay at her arm's length: our group of twenty middle-aged, mostly male, archaeologists did not concern her. I also very much doubt whether she would have noticed the tower of an old brick-built windmill high on the chalk downland of Halnaker Hill, overlooking the quarry, to the north. I have always loved windmills, and for some reason this one caught my imagination. It has stayed there, ever since.

Halnaker Mill stands at the top of what half a million years ago would have been a seaside chalk cliff. Today, the site and quarry at Boxgrove is just under 10 kilometres (6 miles) as the crow flies from the coast at Bognor Regis. Geologists and archaeologists have been able to plot the course of the Pleistocene cliff for almost 32 kilometres (20 miles) through Sussex and into Hampshire. In places it survives some 6 metres (20 ft) high. At Boxgrove it runs along the north edge of the Eartham Quarry. I have worked in many gravel pits and almost always the sands and gravels are separated by sieving or washing, following bulk extraction of the unsorted ballast. But at the Eartham Quarry, things were different. Here, the sand and gravel pits were separate, but next to each other. This separation was entirely natural, but it took some working out: a lot of archaeological and geological thought had gone into unravelling the processes that led to those complex deposits.

When we arrived we were shown the base of the original Ice Age chalk cliffs, which survived a few metres high, but which geologists reckoned were originally 75–100 metres (246–328 ft) high. So they would certainly have been comparable to those at Dover, at 110 metres (360 ft). The sands and gravels were deposited in two distinct episodes during the Pleistocene. The sand formed first and represents a beach that extended about 50 metres (165 ft) from the base of the cliffs. This beach would have been regularly visited by Palaeolithic people on the lookout for nodules of flint eroding out of the cliffs. We know this because occasional thin flint flakes have been found there. These were probably debris that resulted from the making of hand-axes.

At this stage of the Pleistocene, the sea was gradually retreating. Soon, tidal sandbanks started to form south of the cliffs and these gave rise to shallow lagoons, where the water flowed more slowly. Slow-moving water hasn't got the energy to shift the larger particles – grains of sand and fine gravel. So these start to accumulate in the form of tidal mudflats. These lagoonal muds turned out to be an archaeological gold mine, because in dry periods, when tides were low, they would dry out – and you could walk across them. And yet the cliffs behind them were still an excellent source of flint for tools. So people came here to make, or knap, hand-axes for use elsewhere. Often, the flakes of the knapping debris occurred in confined V-shaped spreads, which modern experimental work has shown is the result of a flint-worker sitting or kneeling on the ground to shape a hand-axe. Most of the debris accumulates in front and to either side of him.

Many of the completed hand-axes at Boxgrove were removed from the site, but in one instance the knapper accidentally knocked the tip off an almost finished hand-axe. I can well imagine what he said when this happened. So he did what I would have done: he threw the broken end away in disgust, and dropped the now useless tool in with the rest of the debris. But he had come to Boxgrove to make a hand-axe and he couldn't leave without one. So then he made another one, which he must have done successfully, because he took it away with him when he had finished. It's not often that you get such a detailed glimpse of a moment in somebody's life, such a very long time ago.

Another, if anything even more extraordinary, prehistoric working area was revealed in the second quarry. This proved to be the site of the butchering of a wild horse, but most remarkably, the bone and flint debris that was so painstakingly excavated over many weeks seems to have been dropped there over just one day, half a million years ago. We don't know how the animal was killed because most of the meat bones had been removed, but I think it unlikely that it had been dragged to the Boxgrove foreshore for any distance. It's far more probable that it was butchered where it was killed. The animal was first skinned and then defleshed with hand-axes that had been sharpened with a single, oblique blow to one side of the tip. This technique, which requires great skill to master, leaves a razor-sharp cutting edge.

Once the meat had been taken away, the leg bones were then removed from the horse's skeleton and split open, by bashing with a large, rounded stone (which left distinctive impact scars on the bone), in order to remove the nutritious marrow.[12] The excavators closely examined quite a large area around the butchery site, where they revealed at least a dozen clusters of flint flakes, which marked places where hand-axes had been made. The way these were arranged around the remains of the horse clearly showed that the hand-axes were made on the spot, to be used specifically for the butchering process. But the excavators were able to take the story even further.

The dozen flint-working clusters were of two types. There were concentrations where the flakes were larger and there were anvil stones, on which the big flint nodules were held to have the initial preparatory flakes removed with rounded hammerstone pebbles, which were also still there. These flint rough-outs were then taken to other areas, where finer flakes were removed with hammers or punches of bone or antler. It seems likely that the two tasks were performed by different people: maybe younger, fitter men did the initial preparation, while more experienced flint-knappers did the final, more delicate work. Many of the hand-axes that had been used for the butchery had been abandoned and lay around the few remaining bones of the horse, which had clearly been picked clean by scavenging birds and animals, whose gnawing teeth had scraped grooves that overlaid the nicks and scratches left by the human butchers, perhaps just a few hours earlier.

So who were these people, these 'butchers of Boxgrove'? I won't go into the intricacies of dating Boxgrove, because it depends on such esoteric things as voles' teeth and whether they are rooted or unrooted. But the consensus of evidence suggests that the various lagoon deposits were laid down during a warm phase that pre-dated the largest glacial phase of the Ice Age, the Anglian – when glaciers reached as far south as London. The Anglian began around 480,000 years ago. So the human activities at Boxgrove were probably taking place around 500,000 years ago. I can still remember how astonished the archaeological world of the late 1980s and early 1990s had been by Boxgrove's revelations, which seemed to get better and better, year after year. By 1993, few of us suspected there was even more to come.

It was decided to open a small trench just north of the main excavations in order to work out the sequence of overlying and intercutting layers. The Pleistocene geology was known to be complex in this part of the quarry, with many of the deposits buckled and contorted by water action. Once they had been worked out, there were plans to extend the large-scale excavations into the new area. I've done such preliminary research myself and it can be a lonely and seemingly thankless task, being confined to a small trench, often in the winter when the main body of the student workforce is safely out of the way at university or college. I would now try to do such work with somebody else: problems are far easier to sort out in discussion than on one's own. But that isn't always possible. And that was the case at Boxgrove, where the small trial trench was being excavated by a local volunteer, Roger Pedersen. Shortly before Christmas 1993, Roger discovered the fragments of a large long-bone, which had been partially crushed and moved when the ground shifted, due to waterlogging. He immediately contacted the project's bone specialist at the British Museum, who suspected, as indeed Roger did, that it might prove to be human. And they were both right. The bone, a tibia or shin bone, was eventually shown to have belonged to a large man (or very large woman), aged about forty, some 1.9 metres (5 ft 11 in) tall, weighing about 89 kilos (14 stone).

An extended area around the spot where the shin bone had been found was excavated in 1994 and 1995, and it proved to be remarkably rich in both flints and animal bones. Most of these, including the human bone, were found in stream channels running along the base of the nearby cliffs. It would seem that these streams were where wild animals came to drink. These included red deer, horse, bison and rhino. Many of their bones bore the distinctive cut marks left following butchery with hand-axes. Again, as with the horse butchery site, many of the animals, especially some juvenile rhinos, had had their limb bones removed. Put simply, they took the best cuts of meat home with them. But it wasn't until the end of the 1995 season that they made another great discovery – in fact, something they had been hoping to find since Christmas two years previously.

Long-running, large-scale excavations tend to wind down, rather than come to a sudden and dramatic end. That way, you can ensure that all the records and notes are in good order and that all the finds boxes are correctly labelled and stored in the right racks and that tools are put away, properly cleaned and in good repair. But in my experience, Sod's Law then dictates that you make the most important discoveries of the entire season in those last few days, when many of the staff have left and when the people running the dig are feeling tired and are desperate for a few days off. And that's what happened at Boxgrove in 1995.

This time, the find was far smaller than the shin bone, but in many respects it was much more revealing. It was immediately recognizable as one of the two front teeth (incisors) at the centre of the lower jaw. It was found in the same stream channel, but a metre below it. And then, on the very last day of the dig, they found the other front incisor, just 1.5 metres (5 ft) away. Both were the same size, fitted together, and were from the same person. They were covered with quite a thick deposit of dental plaque, which indicates that Boxgrove Man's oral hygiene left a lot to be desired and that he would probably have started to lose his teeth quite soon. The two teeth also carried tiny scars left by flint implements. The best explanation for these is that he would regularly grip meat in his teeth, which he would then cut off the bone with a hand-axe. These scratches went in the same direction (from top left to bottom right), which suggests he was right-handed.

Unfortunately, the tibia shaft wasn't sufficiently distinctive to allow Boxgrove Man to be placed within any of the known groups of early people. But the two front teeth were far more informative. They were slightly larger than those of modern man, *Homo sapiens*, and could best be matched with a mandible (lower jaw) found at Mauer, near Heidelberg, in Germany, in 1908. This person belonged to a group of early hominins* known as Heidelberg Man, or *Homo heidelbergensis*, which preceded modern man and Neanderthal man (whom we will encounter in the next Scene). Boxgrove Man was large, with a distinctive under-cut jawline that lacked any chin. He would have looked different from modern man, but there are no reasons to suppose that he was markedly less able or intelligent: I would certainly feel very challenged if asked to produce such fine hand-axes and the organization of the landscape at Boxgrove seems far from random or chaotic. I'm in little doubt that these people possessed language and used it regularly in their daily lives.

There is an extraordinary depth and diversity to the landscapes hidden below the old shoreline at Boxgrove. They speak to me of

---

* The word 'hominin' refers to all members of the genus *Homo* – mankind. The older term 'Hominids' is broader and includes great apes, such as chimpanzees. australianmuseum.net.au/hominid-and-hominin-whats-the-difference

temporality and change and the impermanence of features and places that help us to fix our role in the world – and with it our individual identities. And even in the deepest depths of prehistory, people must have regretted the demise of a much-loved place. How would Boxgrove Man have regarded the shrinking lagoons and encroaching grassland, as sea levels declined? We tend to think that people in the past judged everything from a practical perspective: were certain changes going to benefit the occurrence of wild game, or the growth of cereal crops? But in reality, they would also have had an emotional response to any changes that were happening around them. Maybe they didn't possess language sophisticated enough to express their more profound emotions, but I strongly suspect they would have had songs and rhymes where feelings of sadness, happiness or longing lay just behind the words – and of course human eyes can express almost anything. But even when you feel at your lowest, things can change in unexpected ways; then, as now, the landscape can be full of surprises – which brings me back to that lonely windmill high on the ancient cliff at Halnaker Hill, above the Boxgrove quarry.

Halnaker Mill was built around 1750 and continued to earn its keep, taking advantage of the strong winds off the English Channel, until it was struck by lightning in 1905 – which put it out of action. The poet Hilaire Belloc, best known for his *Cautionary Tales for Children* (1907), was brought up in West Sussex and even owned a mill. He was clearly distressed by the state of Halnaker Mill after the lightning strike. He saw the abandoned mill as a symbol of the rural economy, which was then in decline, following the agricultural recession of the 1870s.[13] His poem *Ha'nacker Mill* has to be one of the saddest poems about landscape that I know. It includes lines like: 'Spirits that call and no one answers – Ha'nacker's down and England's done'.

But nothing is permanent in this world: things do change. England wasn't done. The mill survived the Great War and was restored in 1934 and again in 2004. Today it is in the care of the County Council. And taking a rather longer view, I very much doubt if even Hilaire Belloc could have imagined the extraordinary finds that were later to be discovered far beneath his feet, at the base of those long-buried cliffs, just a short distance to the south. The poem, the mill, the buried cliffs and the finds concealed below them are all part of the same story. Those rolling green hills have so much to teach us.

Scene 2

The Persistence of Caves: Life, Death and the Ancestors (30,000 years ago–600 BC)

Goat's Hole Cave, Paviland – Killuragh and
Sramore Caves – Robber's Den Cave

Archaeologists and prehistorians deal with real things and scientific data. On the whole, we tend to ignore those 'what if?' questions that can fascinate historians. I sometimes wonder, for example, to what extent British prehistory would have been altered if the Ice Age cold spells had been milder. This particularly applies to the final glaciation known as the Devensian (which lasted from *c.* 75,000 to 12,000 years ago). We have glimpsed what life was like during a warmer phase half a million years ago, but there can be little doubt that everything slowed down markedly during the centuries of ice when most or indeed all of Britain was abandoned for long periods.

Recent research has produced some remarkable insights into this remote period that has proved so difficult to interpret. This work has also revealed the extent to which our own understanding of life in the later Old Stone Age (or Upper Palaeolithic) can be radically affected by quite minor shifts in the way we interpret, and reinterpret, the evidence. I shall give one example and then we must move forward to a warmer climate and a steadily growing population. But first we must visit a remote cave in the Gower Peninsula, on the coast of south-west Wales. This was where early clergyman-archaeologist Dean William Buckland discovered the skeleton of the Red 'Lady' of Paviland, back in 1823.

You will have noticed that I described the body, discovered by Dean Buckland in the unusually named Goat's Hole Cave at Paviland, as the Red 'Lady'. I say 'Lady' because 'she' was in fact a man, about twenty-five to thirty years old. Modern science has since demonstrated that the bones are the earliest example of a modern human (*Homo sapiens*) yet found in Britain. The earliest modern humans evolved as a new subspecies in Africa, over 200,000 years ago.[1] The clergyman who discovered the grave in the Goat's Hole Cave was in many ways as remarkable as the bones he came across. His life, both actual and intellectual, tells us much about the spirit of the times and what it would have been like to have experienced the start of the profound shift from Creationism to science-based rationality.

Buckland was Dean of Westminster Abbey, a Doctor of Divinity, a leading theologian and Fellow of an Oxford college. He was also an eminent geologist and Fellow of the Royal Society. During a diverse and very unusual career, he revealed one of the first dinosaurs (which he named *Megalosaurus*) and announced his discovery when he became President of the Geological Society in 1824, the year after he found the Red 'Lady'. At this point in his life, Buckland was a firm believer in the Biblical Flood, which ended the first process of creation (including Adam and Eve's Busy Week, as I always think of it), and initiated the geological record. In other words, the geological story of Britain began with the Flood. Everything else had to come later; there was nothing before the Flood.

The bones in Paviland Cave had been stained red by being

sprinkled with ochre* immediately after burial. The body lay in a shallow grave and was accompanied by objects carved from ivory, including two bracelets, two dozen wand-like objects (maybe the rough cuts for beads) and a number of perforated sea shells, which could have fringed a leather cloak or been used in a necklace or earrings. The grave was at the same level as the bones of extinct mammals, such as mammoth, which Buckland believed could not have existed at the same time as humans. So he guessed that the red bones were those of a prostitute who had been buried very, very much later in historical times.

Buckland seems to have been rather eccentric. My student imagination was caught when I read in a book by my then professor, Glyn Daniel: 'Buckland was a very strange character and anecdotes about him abound – how he ate the heart of a French king in Sutton Courtenay Church, kept an orang-utang in his rooms at Christ Church [College, Oxford], and prepared for Ruskin's breakfast "an exquisite toast of mice".'† This made me smile because the room at Trinity College, Cambridge, where I first read that was directly below the small tower where Lord Byron kept his tame bear. Byron did so because dogs were not allowed in our college. I don't know what Buckland's excuse was.

Like all great thinkers, Buckland's ideas changed throughout his life.[2] He was firmly pro-Flood in 1823, but by the early 1830s his views had changed and he advocated a rather complex sequence of divinely inspired creative events that gave rise to the various animal species. He was later to become friends with Darwin on the latter's return to Britain, in October 1836, following his five-year voyage aboard the *Beagle*.[3] Meeting

---

* A natural stain derived locally from clay and oxidised (rusted) iron.

† Glyn Daniel, *The Idea of Prehistory* (Penguin Books, Harmondsworth, 1962), p. 35.

with Darwin, and other people of a like mind, caused Buckland to change his views further, and although he never became an evolutionist or indeed an atheist, as Darwin most probably did, he certainly set aside his belief in the Flood and recognized that much of Britain's most recent geology came about through the action of glaciers. But what are current views about the young man buried in the Goat's Hole Cave at Paviland? To answer that question, we must return to the rocky shores of the Gower Peninsula.

The land that borders the southern parts of Cardigan Bay, and especially the two promontories to the west (around Tenby) and east (the Gower Peninsula), is known to be home to about thirty sites of the Upper Palaeolithic, including many caves.[4] These lay immediately south of the ice sheets of the Devensian glaciation. I say 'sheets' because Ice Age glaciers were not permanent: they came and went, advancing and retreating as the climate changed. These changes can be monitored by taking cores of sediment and rock from lake- and seabed deposits and examining the successive changes in plant pollen they reveal. As anyone with hay fever knows, pollen is present in the air we breathe and some of it eventually falls to the ground, where it can be preserved if conditions – such as wet muds or growing peat – are right. The plants producing pollen reflect the climate of the time: arctic conditions favour miniature tundra species, pines prefer it slightly warmer and oak and ash favour even milder weather. Pollen found with evidence for human occupation shows, not unsurprisingly, that people chose to settle in new areas during warmer interludes, between glaciations.

Any interpretation of the bones in Paviland Cave must first establish their date. Buckland's idea that 'she' was buried shortly before the Roman conquest was challenged in 1913 when it was argued that the grave had to be contemporary with the material around it on the cave floor. Radiocarbon dates processed after the Second World War suggested that the bones dated to around 18,000 years ago, but archaeologists soon realized that the natural conditions in the cave meant that the bones had been contaminated by more recent carbon. This led to a reassessment, which indicated the bones were much older: 26,000 years old. The latest filtration techniques now suggest a more realistic date of about 30,000 years. These older dates are important because they show that the burial took place during a warmer spell immediately before the final glaciation of the Ice Age.[5]

Cartoons like *The Flintstones* were very funny and in many ways they were accurate, because they portrayed Fred, Wilma and their daughter, Pebbles, as humans who were no different from us. When I first witnessed their antics on television in the late 1960s I laughed a lot, but I also scoffed a lot: having just read archaeology at university. I was aware that their seemingly suburban social life would have been impossible. I ask you: cavemen with next-door neighbours like Barney Rubble? We all knew, or thought we knew, that our prehistoric forebears inhabited solitary, isolated caves in order to cope with the bitter cold and fend off marauding mammoths, wolves and bears.

The distribution of caves and other sites containing evidence for human occupation in the late Ice Age strongly suggests that people did *not* live in isolation. And nor did they just inhabit caves. There is also good evidence to suggest that the caves were occupied by bears and other animals when the humans moved away. The young man from Paviland had been placed in the ground with a fair amount of ceremony: apart from being sprinkled with red ochre and buried with fine ornaments, his head was missing and had possibly been deliberately removed. Big stones had been placed at the head and foot of the grave, which was accompanied by the bones of large mammals. The red ochre may have symbolized blood. It has also been shown that the red staining was thinner above than below the waist and almost absent from the toe bones. This suggests that the body probably wore a two-piece outfit, with shoes.[6] The grave had also been carefully aligned parallel with the walls of the cave – where there may well have been ceremonial paintings. These rites can be matched right across western Europe and they clearly demonstrate that ritual and religion played a major role in people's lives. But I have always been intrigued by something else about the place – which might foreshadow what was to happen very much later in prehistory.

The Goat's Hole Cave lies high above the beach and can only be safely reached when the tide is out. But in the Upper Palaeolithic this landscape was very different. Sea levels were much lower and a large dry and fertile plain would have extended from what is now the beach out into the Bristol Channel. So the steep edge of the Gower Peninsula would have been a sharply rising escarpment that must have dominated the flat landscape to the south. In later prehistoric times, such prominent features were often chosen as sites for burial mounds, hillforts and other monuments. This was probably because ridges of hills, steep valley sides and escarpments would have seemed very special to people who lived out most of their lives in the fertile plains below. Following the introduction of farming in the Neolithic period, around 4000 BC, these regions were soon occupied by farms, fields and villages. But in earlier times they would have been the lands where most of the wild game roamed and where rivers were slow and deep enough to fish. Farmers, hunters and their families going about their daily business must always have been aware of those hills looking down at them.

Today, we treat such features in the landscape as things of beauty: they are attractive views, ranging from gently rolling to steeply impressive. In wintertime they can seem threatening or dangerous, but they rarely enter our spiritual or emotional thoughts, except perhaps through poetry. But things would have been very different in prehistory. There is a growing body of evidence to suggest that people often considered certain landscape features, such as steep hills, springs, cliffs, waterfalls or rivers, as rather magical.[7] In broad terms, these remote places were seen as being on the edge of the inhabitable world. Archaeologists use the word 'liminal' to describe them.[*] Beyond the liminal zone lay the realms of the ancestors and the forces of nature that controlled not just the weather, but the passing of the seasons and the rising and setting of the sun. Liminal features in the landscape were often chosen for burials and ceremonial sites. There would have been many complex reasons for this, but essentially it was driven by the belief that they were gaining a measure of control. It was also a way of introducing supernatural forces into the operation and control of human societies. Only important people, from elite clans or families, would have been accorded the honour of burial in such a place as the Goat's Hole Cave. For all we know, the Red 'Lady' may well have been a Palaeolithic prince.

I have long been fascinated by the idea of 'views'. The notion of landscape as a source of aesthetic satisfaction is actually quite recent. People almost certainly revered or admired certain features in the landscape, such as the Goat's Hole Cave high in the cliff at Paviland on the Gower Peninsula. But they would probably not have regarded it as a 'view', nor one that was particularly beautiful. All of that was to come much later, probably in the late sixteenth century with the arrival in Britain of landscape artists from the Netherlands. The term 'landscape', which derives from the contemporary Dutch term 'landscap', meaning a painter's view, first appears in English in

---

[*] Liminal is derived from the Latin word for a threshold, edge or boundary.

the early seventeenth century.[8] So how did prehistoric people regard their surroundings, if not as landscapes? And the answer to that is very complex. Indeed, I'm not at all sure we will ever be able to answer it completely.

Recent research is starting to provide us with some interesting and unexpected insights into the way ancient communities thought about and regarded the landscape. What I still find surprising is that the relevant sites and finds are very early. Many date to the Mesolithic, the era of post-Ice Age hunter-gatherers. It used to be thought that there was very little continuity between the resident British population of hunter-gatherers and the farmers who came over to Britain at the start of the Neolithic period, around 4000 BC. But we can now appreciate that the situation was far more complex and subtle. One good place to think about the Mesolithic is Ireland, an island that was uninhabited before the arrival of the earliest post-glacial hunter-gatherers, just after 8000 BC.[9]

We might find it simpler to think about people's attitudes to their surroundings if we compare what was happening in a single category of site, through time. As we're thinking about the very beginnings of post-Ice Age prehistory, I thought it would be best if we continued looking at caves because preservation of the most ancient deposits can often be very good. I must also confess I had an ulterior motive, since all the cave sites in Ireland have recently been completely reassessed by the leading prehistorian Marion Dowd.[10] Her findings have been unexpected – and highly intriguing.

It will always be difficult to make meaningful estimates of Mesolithic population levels because the archaeological evidence tends to be quite slight: post-holes for houses are quite shallow and people generally avoided digging large pits, wells or ditches. Later transformations of the landscape have either hidden or destroyed many early sites. In Ireland it was the growth of huge areas of peat across the midlands and in Britain it was the massive intensification of gravel-quarrying and agriculture. Bearing in mind that these are bound to prove underestimates, about 900 find-spots of Irish Mesolithic material are known. These would suggest a Mesolithic Irish population of some 3,000 people – which is roughly the same as a modern small country town.[11] Some thirteen cave sites are known to have contained Mesolithic finds. These are spread across the country, from County Antrim in the north to County Cork in the south. As in Britain, Mesolithic burials or finds of human bones are very unusual in Ireland, where just seven are known – and of these, two, roughly a quarter, are in caves. As we know so little about burial practices in the Mesolithic, these two caves are very important. The evidence also suggests that both places were visited repeatedly in Mesolithic times.

Finds from Killuragh Cave in County Limerick suggest that it was occupied, used or visited for a very long time, roughly from 7000 to 1000 BC.[12] At first glance, this cave, which has two low entrances on very rough ground overlooking the Mulkear River, doesn't look particularly special, or impressive. It's situated in a limestone area, where numerous caves have been formed by the action of acid rainwater on the alkaline bedrock of streams, both on the surface and underground. Many of the caves around it haven't yet been investigated. So it isn't even unique. Yet it was repeatedly visited by prehistoric people for some seven millennia. There must have been a reason for this.

Archaeologists and prehistorians no longer seek single or one-off answers to explain how or why a particular site came into existence – especially if it then continued to be used or respected. The notion that Stonehenge was simply an astronomical observatory is now seen as ludicrous. But when it was first put forward in the late 1960s it resulted in a bestselling book, which led to many spin-off TV documentaries.* As archaeological ideas go, it was very profitable. As we will discover shortly,† we now take a far broader view, which takes in the complex landscape around the Stones, their journey from Wales to Salisbury Plain and many other factors. The new story is rather like the evolution of the monument itself; it is far from simple and reflects some of the varied and very human motives that led to its construction and frequent subsequent modification. Viewed in this light, Stonehenge has far more in common with a great medieval cathedral than a mere astronomical calculator.

As is the case with most Irish caves, the initial finds from Killuragh Cave were revealed by farmers, landowners and cavers, but rather unusually they led to two seasons of proper archaeological excavations, in 1993 and 1996. These produced no fewer than 250 human bones, but all of these were loose, individual finds; none were articulated, either as limbs or as complete skeletons. A small sample of these bones was radio-carbon dated. Three of them turned out to be Early Mesolithic (around 6900 BC) and could possibly have come from the same man. The three Late Mesolithic (around 5500 BC) bones were from two adults and one juvenile, but all were of uncertain gender. Four bones were dated to the earlier Neolithic period (around 3600–3500 BC) and these probably came from two individuals. The flat ledge leading into the main entranceway was the scene of a dog burial, beneath a pile of pebbles. One of the dog bones produced a radiocarbon date that closely matches the human ones. Most of the human bones from the Neolithic and Mesolithic period were found close by the main cave entrance and were probably originally deposited on the small ledge just

---

* Gerald S. Hawkins, *Stonehenge Decoded* (Dell Publishing, New York, 1965).
† See Scene 7, pages 128–44.

outside (where the dog was buried). We'll consider the nature of that 'deposition' in a moment. But now I want to move forward into the Bronze Age.

It seems that the way Killuragh Cave was used changed subtly at the very start of the Bronze Age (around 2400 BC). Human bones and other finds of this period were discovered beyond the tight entranceway tunnel, in a small end chamber. They included two Early Bronze Age human bones, which were radiocarbon dated to around 2000 BC; a dog and a pig jawbone were dated to the centuries just before and just after the start of the second millennium BC. A horse breastbone was found deliberately buried in the ground at the far end of the cave; this was slightly more recent, around 1200 BC. Finally, the interior of the cave also revealed nine sherds of Early Bronze Age pottery, belonging to three different urns, dating to around 2000–1500 BC. All these finds had been taken deep into the body of the cave.[13]

The second cave known to have produced Mesolithic human remains is very enigmatic: we know it exists, because we have finds from it and detailed notes from the caver who investigated it. We also know its name, Sramore Cave, in County Leitrim, and its approximate location, on the north side of Sramore Mountain.[14] The trouble is we can't actually relocate it, although we know for a fact that it's there – somewhere. And that, of course, says something about the nature of the cave: like Killuragh Cave, it's a bit shy and retiring. It certainly isn't high profile, prominent or in-your-face. This probably tells us quite a lot about the way these caves were viewed and may help explain how they were used.

According to the caver's notes, Sramore Cave is situated high on the mountainside, with panoramic views of the surrounding country, but it has a very restricted entrance (just 1.3 m x 1 m/ 4 ft x 3 ft), which leads into a narrow passage (0.9 m/3 ft high x 0.6 m/2 ft wide). Some 15 metres (50 ft) along the passage, near the cave's centre, cavers discovered three human bones from a man: a thigh bone, an upper arm bone and a lower jawbone. Given that the bones represent very different parts of the body, it seems likely that they originally came from a complete skeleton. Conditions in the cave were very cramped indeed. So it could very plausibly be argued that the human bones were carried into the cave as loose bones, maybe wrapped in bags. We just don't know for certain, because a proper archaeological excavation was impossible. The bones gave radiocarbon dates that showed the man had died shortly before 4000 BC. The earliest current dates for Neolithic farmers in Ireland are about 3850 BC, which is very slightly later than the Sramore Cave body. Having said that, such dates mustn't be taken too literally and I tend to share Marion Dowd's view that the man in the cave might well have witnessed the beginnings of farming.[15] It's a tantalizing thought.

The earliest bones from Killuragh Cave seem to have been deposited on the small platform just outside the entranceway. This rite continued into Neolithic times and probably has something to do with the process of excarnation in which flesh is removed, or is allowed to be removed (usually by carrion crows), from the bones, eventually leaving a clean skeleton. In many tribal societies the removal of the flesh is believed to represent the ascent of the soul into the Next World. In some communities the process of excarnation is seen as being sufficient of itself: the soul has moved to another realm, so the bones themselves cease to be important. This belief may have been current in Iron Age Britain, where loose human bones occur quite commonly on settlements, in pits and dumps filled with household debris and other rubbish. Having said that, many Iron Age communities also cremated their dead and there is abundant evidence for quite elaborate burial rites, especially in the higher echelons of society. Simple explanations rarely work when it comes to the disposal of the dead.

In many recent and ancient societies, the process of excarnation was seen as the first stage of the soul's journey into the Next World. Once cleansed of flesh, the bones would be ceremoniously transferred to the family tomb. This may have been what happened at the Early Bronze Age site known as Seahenge on the north Norfolk coast.[16] Seahenge consisted of a large upside-down oak tree, surrounded by a tall wall of close-set oak posts. No bones were discovered, but it seems highly likely that a body had been laid within the tree roots, to be defleshed by carrion crows, buzzards and other scavenging birds. The tall wooden wall would have helped to exclude foxes, badgers, wild cats and wolves, who would have torn the corpse apart. Once defleshed, the bones would have been carried just a few yards to be buried in a burial mound known as a round barrow, which we know was erected at precisely the same time as the Seahenge timber circle.[17]

The first evidence for taking human bones into the cave at Killuragh is in the Bronze Age, when bones may well have been carried from the platform outside the entranceway, where the excarnation had taken place, into the body of the cave, where they were placed, along with animal bones and man-made items such as pottery. These rites seem to have taken place on numerous occasions, over many centuries. They also appear to be part of an ancient but continuing and evolving tradition, whose roots go back to the earliest Mesolithic settlers. The continuity shown in the Irish caves from hunter-gatherers to Neolithic and Bronze Age farmers is remarkable. Yes, the rites changed, but never radically: the same places were used again and again. This suggests that many of the early farmers were probably direct descendants of people, like the man in Sramore Cave, who witnessed the arrival of the new way of life. We tend to think of farming as being entirely different from hunting and gathering, but as a livestock farmer myself I am in little doubt that managing animals, whether in the wild or safely enclosed in a field, is about experience and knowledge. These are things that hunters must also understand, especially during those times of the year when game is harder to find.

Today we have elaborate laws about hunting game, with closely monitored seasons when game such as fish or pheasants must be left alone to breed. Any hunter knows that the animals he hunts cannot just be wiped out, because he will need to rely on them in the future. So it seems probable that Mesolithic hunters would have protected watering holes and safe places for animals to raise their young. This almost amounts to a form of farming and may help explain how and why early Mesolithic hunters were able to domesticate dogs from wolves – which we know had happened by around 9000 BC.* I am also firmly convinced that hunter-gatherers effectively farmed certain plants, such as hazelnuts, whose bushes have to be pruned and managed in a very specific way if they are to produce the quantities of nuts that have been found on many Mesolithic settlement sites. So the shift to farming would not necessarily have been a traumatic process at the time it was happening – although its long-term consequences for the landscape were of course profound.

Shared beliefs in the power of the ancestors and other religious doctrines undoubtedly helped to maintain social cohesion when farming and other new ideas were introduced at the start of the Neolithic period, around 4000 BC. Although the remote caves where some of the ancient rituals and ceremonies took place continued to be venerated and remained much the same, the rites themselves were constantly changing. We tend to think of religion as being somehow fixed and immutable, but pause to reflect: yes, our cities, towns and villages are dominated by ancient cathedrals and churches, but would a medieval peasant identify with a modern service, which would be conducted in

---

* Dog bones are known from Star Carr, see Scene 3, pages 39–42.

English, not Latin, and might even be overseen by a woman priest rather than a man?

Recent discoveries in the ominously named Robber's Den Cave, high above the west coast of County Clare, provide us with a vivid picture of changing rites and rituals.[18] In 1989 the cavers exploring the Robber's Den Cave would have been aware that they were in a landscape that had been very important in the Bronze Age. The Burren is today an Irish National Park and nature reserve best known for its glaciated 'karst'* landscapes, where the underlying limestone lies at the surface. The exposed, bare limestone does not favour luxuriant plant growth, but those that do grow there are hugely varied and find their sustenance in pockets of soil preserved between the slabs of the limestone pavement. But we know from pollen analysis† that this would have been very different in early post-Ice Age prehistory, when yew and pine trees would have provided protection against the strong and persistent winds off the Atlantic. Tree roots held the soil together and allowed other grasses and plants to thrive.

During the Neolithic and Early Bronze Age, the light, fertile limestone soils of the Burren attracted early farmers because they were far easier to plough than heavier clay land. So the trees were cleared, and when that happened, the light soil, which had previously been held in place by their roots, began to erode. By the end of the Bronze Age (i.e. in the centuries leading up to 500 BC), the soil had grown too thin to allow trees or shrubs to re-establish themselves – and the open, rocky Burren had been created. Today, of course, it is cherished by ecologists and botanists, but Bronze Age farmers would not have shared their enthusiasm while their crops dwindled and it became increasingly difficult to earn a living.

---

* 'Karst' is borrowed from German, where it refers to limestone Alpine landscapes.

† See Scene 8, page 152.

The Burren had enjoyed an all-too-brief period of prosperity in the Bronze Age, during the second and early first millennium BC. We can see this in the numerous Bronze Age sites that still cover the landscape. The upper, hard limestone plateau contains many wedge-shaped burial mounds. Below this was a more sheltered plain, which is liberally dotted with evidence of settlement, including a fort-like enclosure, a dozen settlement or farming enclosures, several house sites and a number of so-called burnt mounds.

These strange sites occur across the British Isles and consist of a heap of burnt stones, often covering a wooden tank, made from planks or a hollowed-out tree (I can think of one example from the Fens that actually made use of an old dugout canoe). There have been various explanations for burnt mounds. Some people think they were Bronze Age saunas, but others – and they have good evidence to back them up – think they were ancient mash tuns.[19] For readers who have never worked in a brewery, the mash tuns are where the hops, malt and water are boiled together in the first stage of brewing beer. Personally, I prefer that explanation – but then I confess, I'm biased. But I also believe there was more to them than just being baths or breweries. Burnt mounds are often located close by other ceremonial sites in places in the landscape that were seen to be liminal – on the edge – in some way. In the Fens, for example, they often occur in pasture close by permanently waterlogged ground.

The entrance to the Robber's Den Cave was located in a steep cliff, which modern cavers have to climb using ropes. This cliff was at the boundary of the fertile plain with all the Bronze Age settlement remains and the sparse limestone plateau above it – where the tombs occur. So it could be seen as a way into another realm. Entering the cave was not an easy process and, once inside, the passages were extraordinarily narrow. But somehow Late Bronze Age people carried the corpse of a woman aged over thirty-five into the deepest part of the cave. Here she was laid on the ground, together with two decorated stone rings, which were placed, one on top of the other, alongside her skull. A radiocarbon date suggests that this happened in the centuries around 600 BC. The fact that the woman's body was disposed of with such extreme difficulty suggests either that she had transgressed in some way or that she was a religious person – perhaps the equivalent of a hermit nun – who had made the cave her personal spiritual domain. Either way, she must have been a very special person. And of course we only know about this because we have found her bones. It's hard for us to imagine all the different ways in which ancient caves might have affected – and enriched – the lives of ordinary people.

This exploration into the Irish caver's world has taken us forward into the later Bronze Age, but now we must return to the Mesolithic and the centuries that followed the end of the last Ice Age. We will descend from the dramatic uplands of western Ireland and cross the sea to the low-lying river floodplains of East Yorkshire. It was in unspectacular regions like these that the majority of the population lived out their lives. The various landscapes of the British lowlands were the places that would be most affected by the arrival of farming and the massive growth of population that would accompany it. These were dynamic times that would have an enduring influence, not just on the shape of the landscape, but on the developing character of modern European society.

Scene 3

Inhabiting the Post-Glacial Landscape:
Living on the Plains (9000 BC)

The Vale of Pickering – Glacial Lake Flixton

I have lived for most of my life in the British lowlands and I have found they have a quiet charm all of their own. But when I was young I was desperate to get away, to experience something less dull and more stimulating. So in August 1962 (during what was known as the first 'cod war' with Iceland) I sailed on a North Sea trawler to the Icelandic coast; then in my 'gap' year I spent time in southern Spain and Venice; eventually I took up residence in Toronto, on the shores of Lake Ontario. After nine very happy years spent living in Canada, but digging in England, I came to my senses and laid aside the carbon my seasonal transatlantic commuting was adding to the environment. I could not run away from the reality that I was British and have always loved life in the English countryside. I had been brought up in rural north Hertfordshire and by the late 1970s I had become convinced that, far from being dull, the English lowlands had actually exerted a very profound influence on the person I had become.

Although they have quite strict rules of good behaviour for young people, traditional British rural communities are also kind and tolerant. And by my late twenties I was beginning to appreciate how much they had to offer. Now, in later life, I find I am taking a longer view: were such values just a phenomenon of the past few centuries, or can they be found earlier in history – maybe even in prehistory? Of course, this is all pure speculation, based on what can best be described as a 'gut feeling', as there are few hard facts to support me. I think it's especially important to imagine, in a world that now seems to be becoming increasingly self-centred and intolerant, that there are other, kinder, ways of living.

Knowing what I know now, I think I would feel quite confident if somehow I were to be transported back to the Middle Ages, the Bronze Age or even the Neolithic. Farming communities have always had to confront the diverse problems thrown up by nature and the weather. They lived in settled villages, surrounded by fields, meadows and woodland, and we know that families formed the basis of their social systems. Given the presence of these familiar elements of life, I believe it's much simpler for modern western people to feel a sense of kinship with more recent rural communities – and by 'recent' I am extending my chronology back a mere six thousand years, to the arrival of farming around 4000 BC – than with those who lived in earlier periods of history.

But what about those preceding million or so years (give or take the odd millennium) of British prehistory, when people hunted or gathered their food from the natural world around them? Was *all* their time spent chasing after food, or did they have leisure for other things? Had I been writing this in the 1950s, I would probably have been very pessimistic about life in pre-farming times: I would have written of sparse populations eking out a frugal existence from resources that were often threatened not by global warming (as they are today), but by approaching episodes of ice. So were the lives of these small groups of nomadic hunter-gatherers *really* nasty, brutish and short? To answer that question, we must first think about the nature of the archaeological evidence.

Throughout my professional life, I have been grateful that the university authorities linked the two subjects of Archaeology and Anthropology together so closely for my degree. Students of archaeology were constantly reminded that the subject of our study was *Anthropos*, the ancient Greek word for mankind, or humanity. As archaeologists, we were being trained to reach into the past through finds made on excavations and surveys. Sometimes these were big and spectacular, more often they were scraps of pottery, tiny flint flakes or pieces of bone. We also made use of science: everything from molecular biology to geophysics, but it was all part of a larger plan, to reveal the lives of ancient people – men, women and children. So the objects we discovered were always a means to an end. They were never an end in themselves – which is what distinguishes archaeology from treasure hunting.

As you work your way further back in time, the quantity and often the quality of your evidence decreases. This is the inevitable result of natural processes, such as floods, glaciers and just the day-to-day erosion of nature: food decays, cloth and skins are attacked by fungi and moths, wood is eaten by woodworm, wet- and dry-rot; even pottery and flint can get crushed underfoot or be shattered by fire and ice. To make our task harder, people living a very long time ago lacked most modern technologies. The earliest assuredly recognizable humans (hominins) evolved in Africa around five million years ago.[1] And yet fire only seems to have been discovered about half a million years ago.[2] Even if fire can be pushed back to a million years, that still leaves our ancestors without cooked food or warmth for some four million years. Of course, this doesn't mean that they were ill-informed or stupid in any way at all: it merely highlights just how difficult it is to achieve such changes. It is perhaps worth remembering that men and women with the intelligence of an Einstein or a Newton were still being born every few generations and even with their input people were unable to make what we can now appreciate was one of the first great technological step changes. So was this an age of stagnation, when nothing happened?

Recent research in Africa and elsewhere has revealed that even in the earliest millennia of human existence, things were constantly changing. Finds from the few sites we know about have revealed that tool shapes were evolving and that weapons, hunting and butchery practices never stood still; these observations further suggest that language and communication skills were improving – and as communication improved, we would also have seen parallel developments in family, social and religious life. We have seen glimpses of such developments in the Irish prehistoric caves, but can they also be detected in the open country where people actually lived out their lives? Again, recent research has produced some very exciting new information. It is time to come down from the hills and see how the Ages of Ice have subtly changed the modern landscape.

Geology teaches us that the massive power of an expanding glacier is capable of resculpting hills and valleys. I first learned about this at school and I well remember visiting the Scottish Borders in Dumfries and Galloway, where I was entranced by the shape of the glaciated valleys with their distinctive U-shaped profiles, scraped to perfection by centuries of ice.[3] Maybe they lacked the powerful, dramatic impact of vertical cliffs and escarpments, but to my eye their gentle, graceful form was somehow more human and less threatening.

Glaciers can also alter the landscape in more subtle ways. As the ice progresses along a valley, it scrapes the ground and the earth, pebbles, rocks and boulders it removes are pushed ahead of it – much like a bulldozer. This advancing bank of loose material is known as a moraine. Eventually, the glacier will have to stop. Usually this happens when it reaches the coast, a wide plain, or when the climate starts to grow warmer. When the glacier stops advancing, the ice melts and the moraine it was pushing is immediately stranded. Geologists have named these glacial banks 'terminal moraines'. Quite often, glaciers start to retreat before they reach the end of a river valley or floodplain and in these instances the terminal moraines can permanently block or impede the flow of streams and rivers in the rapidly forming post-glacial landscape. Often, water accumulated behind these terminal moraines, giving rise to glacial lakes.

The traditional view of the resettlement of Britain following its abandonment to ice and tundra has always been very uncertain, largely because we have lacked the information we needed. It was assumed that the climate warmed gradually and that there was a prolonged period of several millennia when people made occasional summer visits in warm years. As time passed and the weather grew warmer, a few groups dared to stay for longer, but the emerging island of Britain, which was still firmly joined to the continent, remained a very open, treeless place, devoid of natural shelter. So small groups of hunters eked out a meagre livelihood by keeping constantly on the move, following the few herds of reindeer and other game they depended upon. It doesn't sound very pleasant.

The real story began to emerge when climatologists, geologists and palaeo-environmentalists started to turn their attention to the details of how and why our climate changed in the millennia leading up to and into the Holocene – the post-Ice Age era. Subsequently, of course, we have witnessed how these various natural changes have been greatly accelerated by carbon emissions brought about by the rise of modern industry from the mid-nineteenth century.* The new research convincingly demonstrated that climate change wasn't always a smooth and gradual process. Instead, there were spikes and troughs that didn't always last for very long. But sometimes they did.

One of the clearest examples of a rapid, long-lasting change took place over some fifty years around 9600 BC.[4] It was during this time – maybe a short human lifetime – that the climate of northern Europe warmed by some ten degrees Celsius, before it levelled off. Subsequently, it has wobbled or changed from time to time, growing a little wetter and colder at the turn of the first millennium BC.[5] In historic times we see this in the cooler phases, sometimes dubbed the 'Mini Ice Ages' of the sixth and seventh centuries AD and in the so-called Mini Ice Age of 1645–1715, when the River Thames froze in London.[6] Such phenomena, however, were local rather than regional and often had clear causes, such as the aftermath of volcanic eruptions. This new appreciation of the speed and scale of post-Ice Age warming coincided with a number of important archaeological discoveries. These new sites and finds have caused us to rethink the story of early human resettlement of what was quite rapidly becoming the island of Britain.

For many people, the appeal of upland or mountainous landscapes lies in what one might term their 'unchangingness': they are massive, humbling monuments to the past. In certain respects I share this view, but I also have to confess that the archaeologist deep within me feels rather frustrated, as I stand and stare down the dished sides of a once glaciated valley: it all seems rather unchallenging, because it's there, in front of you – in-your-face, as it were. And besides, we know for a fact that people have never inhabited remote upland landscapes in

---

* The term 'Anthropocene' has been proposed for this era, but there is still no general agreement about when it should begin.

appreciable numbers. I would far rather get in my car and drive down to the plains surrounding the hills, because these are the places where the archaeological problems – and opportunities – lie. These landscapes have been changed enormously by the numerous communities that once inhabited them.

The modern county of Yorkshire is perhaps best known for its picturesque Moors and Dales – the landscapes of *Wuthering Heights* and the stories of the farm vet James Herriot and other flights of creative imagination. A certain amount of attention is still paid to the valleys and lowlands where the factories and workshops of the mill towns of the eighteenth and nineteenth centuries heralded the rise of the industrial era. But the part of Yorkshire that sometimes seems to have slipped off the map is the low-lying plain that separates the rolling hills of the Yorkshire Wolds, which form the south-eastern part of the county – the old East Riding – from the steeper uplands of the North York Moors. This plain is the Vale of Pickering and it has been well known to archaeologists since the 1950s. Today, much of the Vale is threatened by intensive agriculture, land drainage, housing and factory development, but research in the second half of the twentieth century has revealed an extraordinary wealth of earlier and later prehistoric remains, together with some of the best-preserved Roman, Saxon and early medieval villages and farms in Britain. It is a rich, fertile and gentle landscape of enormous old-fashioned English charm. It is rightly famous for things that really matter: for traditional beers, cheese and, of course, fish and chips.

In pre-glacial times, the Vale of Pickering was drained by earlier versions of the River Derwent, which flowed out of what, much later, became the island of Britain, between the modern coastal towns of Scarborough (to the north) and Filey. In the final stages of the last Ice Age, however, a large glacier deposited a substantial terminal moraine right across the Vale, just inland from Scarborough. So today the River Derwent follows an entirely new course, southwards, through Malton, eventually joining the River Ouse just east of Selby – a long way to the south. But at the point where the natural drainage was blocked by the terminal moraine, a large glacial lake began to form. This lake (now dry) has been named Lake Flixton by archaeologists and geologists and its shores contain some of the most important, and ancient, prehistoric sites in northern Europe.

The extent to which lowland landscapes have been changed by the hand of man has fascinated me for a long time and many of the most important processes can be clearly seen in the Vale of Pickering. But perhaps the most important point to stress is that the natural, untouched landscape of Britain was never particularly simple, nor straightforward. In the past, historians would write about Britain reverting to deep forest when the Romans withdrew in the early fifth century. These dark, brooding woodlands somehow gave an added spooky feel to the Dark Ages, those four centuries prior to AD 800 when the political organization of the emerging kingdoms of early medieval Britain became apparent. Modern scientific evidence has clearly shown that although there were changes in land use when the Romans withdrew, there is no evidence for spreading forests; indeed, in some places woods were actually cleared to provide grazing for sheep and cattle. That is one of the reasons why the term 'Dark Ages' has been abandoned in all academic writing about the period.*

The landscape that might have confronted the earliest post-Ice Age settlers in Britain was seen in a very similar way: essentially, it was thickly wooded and fairly impenetrable. Between the two world wars, botanists using the newly developed technique of pollen analysis began to show that the blanketing forests were

---

* The term 'Migration Period' has replaced it.

something of a myth. Yes, there *was* extensive tree cover, but it was by no means impenetrable, as it was largely composed of birch, willow and poplar – all 'pioneer trees' that are the first to grow in previously open landscapes and require much light for their characteristic rapid growth. The slower-growing trees of the new woodland, first ash, followed by oak, elm and beech, can grow in deeper shade and will eventually come to dominate a mature, established wood. But this took time: centuries, even millennia.

Recent changes to the British landscape have been very profound, too. Glacial Lake Flixton has vanished and if you didn't know it had once been there, I don't see how you could have spotted it as you drove through it. Yes, there are a few clues for the sharp-eyed, especially if, like me, you enjoy spotting sluices, pumping stations and other tell-tale signs of modern drainage. The drainage of Lake Flixton mostly took place in the nineteenth and twentieth centuries and centred on the straightened and embanked artificial River Hertford, which makes a Fenman like me feel remarkably at home, but which does not sit quite so happily in the gently undulating landscape of the Vale of Pickering.[7] Thanks to that terminal glacial moraine blocking its natural outfall into the North Sea, the River Hertford has to flow backwards, from east to west, towards the similarly reversed course of the River Derwent.

Whenever I'm travelling up to visit friends and family in Yorkshire I always try to go via Hornsea, which lies on the North Sea coast, about 24 kilometres (15 miles) north-east of Hull. Immediately inland, to the west of Hornsea, is Hornsea Mere, a shallow glacial lake that would have been closely similar to Lake Flixton. Today, Hornsea Mere is protected as a place of environmental importance, because of its natural vegetation, which is astonishingly rich and diverse.[8] Botanical evidence preserved in the peats clearly demonstrates that the same could also have been said of Lake Flixton, prior to its drainage.[9] And of course thriving and varied plant communities attract game, wildfowl and, in the lake itself, fish and eels. Lake Flixton would have been nothing short of a natural larder.

3.1 A view of the glacial lake Hornsea Mere, in Holderness, Yorkshire, some 16 km (10 miles) north-east of Hull, close to the North Sea coast. In early post-glacial times, the lakeside woodland would mostly have been composed of birch, poplar and willow.

New archaeological sites tend to be discovered either from the air, usually by planes (but increasingly by drones), or on the surface, using geophysics, ground-penetrating radar or sometimes simply by slow and methodical field walking. Nowadays such work is most often carried out by professionals working either for academic research projects or commercial clients, who need to assess the land they are proposing to develop – usually for quarries, roads or housing. But in the years after the last war, money for academic research was very scarce and commercial developers did not require archaeological clearance from local planning authorities. And this is where the unpaid 'amateurs' came in – and I deliberately use the word in quotes, because in the vast majority of instances their methods and approaches were highly professional. John Moore, a local enthusiast from Scarborough, was a fine example. He was a modest man and his name is still not as widely known as it should be. His discoveries in the Vale of Pickering were to have a profound effect on the subsequent development of British and North European prehistory.

In 1947, Moore and other enthusiasts set up the Scarborough and District Archaeological Society.[10] Moore was interested in the peaty landscape of the Carrs, which had formed behind the terminal moraine between the small town of Seamer, to the north, and the rural village of Flixton, to the south. Researching peaty landscapes can be challenging, largely because the peats themselves are often very deep and effectively conceal whatever lies within and beneath them. So he decided to conduct an auger survey. Most augers are rather like giant corkscrews that you screw into the ground to the depth of the screw's length, and then pull out. Once out of the ground, you can examine the soil or peat on the spiral auger blade and remove any fragments of wood, flakes of flint or pieces of bone. You then carefully clean the blade (putting the heap next to the soil from the previous auger 'bite', usually on a plank or piece of old plastic guttering) and return to the hole for another bite. And another (it can be back-breaking work!). Eventually the auger hits the rock, clay or gravel lying below the higher, softer layers and the person, or people, working the screw can feel the change through the metal: gravel, for example, has a distinctive 'gritty' feel and the screw suddenly becomes easier to turn. If there's clay below the peat, the auger immediately becomes much harder to twist.

Screw augers or simple metal probes work well in most places where the ground below your feet is likely to contain pebbles, bands of gravel or fragments of preserved wood, such as the famous 'bog oaks' of the Fens. But in certain landscapes the deposits are finer, and often softer, too. The Carrs region of the Vale of Pickering is one of these places, and here it is possible to employ a more subtle and highly effective type of auger. These augers have to be pushed into the ground and if you are doing the job by hand you'll need the assistance of at least one, and preferably two, hefty and fit young men. These augers contain a long chamber with a door that is closed by a twist. When the auger is withdrawn from the ground, this chamber contains an undisturbed sample of the ground deep below the surface. I have always felt the excitement of the moments when the door protecting the sediments is opened and there, before you, are fresh deposits from the ancient past. They even smell more like lakes than the dry peaty soils of the modern field. You can clearly see the 1- or 2-millimetre-thick layers of winter flood-clay that formed each season on an extinct lakebed, over ten thousand years ago. Such samples are of great interest to palaeobotanists, who can reconstruct a very precise picture of the changing vegetation through time. And of course they also allow samples to be taken for accurate dating, by radiocarbon or other techniques.

In 1948, the year after he had helped set up the Society, John Moore took a small group of fellow enthusiasts out into the Carrs to do an auger survey. Over the following years, this patient and disciplined research revealed the outline of the long-vanished glacial lake. As my own research team was to learn very much later in the Fens, you cannot hope to discover what might lie beneath peats and other wetland deposits by simply using one approach. You have to be prepared to walk along muddy dykes and ditches on the off-chance that you might spot something on their sides; and when isolated 'islands' appear through the peats (there are three main ones in Lake Flixton) then you must carefully examine their surfaces, especially around the edges, as that is where you are most likely to find evidence for past settlement. This sort of research has to take place at different times of the year: freshly ploughed or tilled fields are rarely productive, but allow two or three weeks of frosts to break down the topsoil and make it crumbly and suddenly you can spot the often quite tiny fragments of flint, bone or pottery that were deposited there in prehistory. They stand out brightly, because frost and rain have washed them clean.

John Moore had long been interested in the peaty landscapes around what he was later to call Lake Flixton. Back in 1947, before he began his survey with his new archaeological society, Moore had found a small flint blade in one of the new ditches that had just been dug to help drainage and to mark out field boundaries. It was a small flint flake of a very distinctive type, known to archaeologists as a microlith. Microliths took much skill to make and were produced during the Mesolithic period from just after 10,000 BC, at the conclusion of the Ice Age, until around 4000 BC, which saw the start of the Neolithic period and with it the introduction of farming, the first pottery and new techniques of flint-working. Microliths were often used to make tooth-like barbs for wooden or bone fish-spears, arrowheads and suchlike. They changed a great deal through time and archaeologists love to produce huge, highly detailed academic papers about them. I've tried flint-working myself, and I can appreciate how much skill it took to produce a microlith, but I have to confess that I find the intricate details of their changing sizes, profiles and shape less than completely fascinating. Having said that, such things have to be studied (if not by me), because it isn't merely the devil that lurks in the detail. The more we learn about the little things in ancient lives, the greater will be our understanding of those larger, more important ideas and beliefs that motivated people not just to eat and work, but to get up in the morning and to love their homes, their families and life in general.

Modern archaeology is increasingly drawing on science and scientific techniques. Hardly a day goes by when I don't read about some new discovery about human genetics and the origins of ancient communities in far-off places. Close microscopic studies of the working edges of flint tools, for example, can reveal fascinating details about the way people butchered their meat and prepared their vegetable food. But neither genetics nor microwear can tell us anything about the motivations that led people to move from one place to another, nor why they chose to eat or avoid certain foods. Somebody has to step back from the detail and attempt to paint a broader picture that might mean something to interested people living today – otherwise all the detailed research will have been in vain. This is where the concept of landscape archaeology comes in.

Even today, media coverage of new archaeological discoveries tends to be very localized and site-specific. Totally inappropriate parallels are drawn to link a new find with something well known from the past: if I had to think of a parallel for a briefly occupied, waterlogged Bronze Age site in the Cambridgeshire Fens, it would *not* be a long-lived, stone-built Roman town. And yet that was the place chosen by the BBC as a comparison. I suppose it made a good headline: 'Britain's Pompeii' (try googling it). Personally, I think it undersold the site because it made it sound like a freakish one-off discovery, whereas the reality was that it was the result of more than half a century of patient archaeological research. And that research is ongoing. I am certain there are many more similar – and maybe even better-preserved – prehistoric sites waiting to be revealed in the Fens around Must Farm.

Archaeologists have long known that readily identifiable 'sites' – usually places where people lived or buried their dead – are just one component in an ancient landscape. If you want to understand what motivated people to live and work in a particular settlement, you must try to discover how it fitted into the fields or hunting territories that surrounded it: who owned or controlled what land; how they sold or exchanged food, gifts and commodities; whether they lived in peace or tension with their neighbours, and what the burial or cremation of their dead can tell us about their spiritual lives and beliefs. These questions can only be addressed if we move beyond sites and look at an ancient landscape as a working, evolving and, yes, living entity. And this was something John Moore appreciated. He realized that those first flints he was discovering would only begin to make sense if he understood something – anything – about the landscape in which they originated.

So John Moore walked around the edges of Lake Flixton, which had formed in the lower-lying parts of the gently undulating Vale. He was looking for places where early Mesolithic people might have settled. You can clearly spot the lake edges today: the area that would have been lake is now black peaty topsoil – rather like a giant growbag – whereas the edges are formed by low sandy or gravel banks and mounds that were originally raised by passing glaciers. Where the banks rise steeply, the contrast between the dark peats and the much paler sands is quite sharp and easy to spot, but where the sides slope more gently it becomes harder to decide precisely where the actual dry land begins. But with time, you develop quite a good eye, which is important because the edges of the lake were where prehistoric people chose to settle. So you've got to be able to spot such shoreline areas accurately.

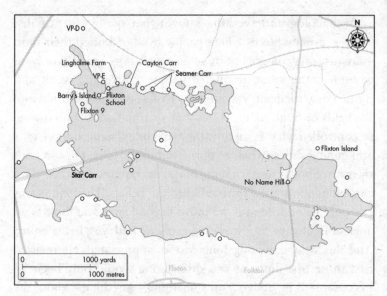

3.2 A map of glacial Lake Flixton as it would have appeared in early post-glacial times, around 9000 BC.

John Moore's initial research revealed the outline of Lake Flixton, together with at least three areas that were producing early post-glacial flints and were therefore potential Mesolithic settlements. One of these sites, which Moore labelled Site 4, turned out to be of international importance. In the early 1950s it was excavated by a team from Cambridge University and became well known as Star Carr.[11] The latest excavations there (by York University) have revealed a settlement of some fifteen houses. We cannot tell how many would have been occupied simultaneously, but it seems entirely possible that the community consisted of several families and that it was occupied for some two to three centuries, sometime around 9000 BC. The settlement has revealed hearths, meat bones and evidence that food was prepared and consumed in and around the small, roughly circular single-family houses.

Star Carr also provided evidence for shaman-based religion, in the form of several spectacular antler headdresses. Some seventy years of research in and around Lake Flixton is continuing to plot its islands and shoreline in extraordinary detail, but rather surprisingly, no other substantial settlement sites like Star Carr have yet been revealed.[12] There are, however, many indications that some of the twenty-four smaller sites around the lake and on the islands were occupied for shorter intervals than Star Carr itself. Some were visited repeatedly and there is good evidence that they were visited for specific purposes, such as preparing and consuming food. Others seem to have been used very differently: for producing flint tools (using high-quality flint brought in from outside the area); in other areas, people worked red-deer antlers into tools or sharpened flint axes for woodwork. Maybe these were smaller, perhaps temporary, settlements or campsites for people from Star Carr as they went about their daily tasks of hunting, fishing and gathering food.

These varied activities give us a clear impression of the way people would have perceived Lake Flixton in early prehistory. In a word, it would have been their territory: they controlled it. But such control would not have been absolute and it would have changed not just through time, but with the pattern of the seasons, as game and other resources became available. Of course, we can only guess at this early stage in our investigations, but what we see as 'the woodland' around the lake would have been viewed as a number of different environments, such as feeding and drinking areas for game, good land for felling trees and coppicing and maybe holy places that were reserved for the spirits of the ancestors. It all had pattern and purpose. It was never unstructured. So we must drop any idea that the early inhabitants of post-glacial Britain wandered around like lost souls. Wild game was plentiful and there is now good evidence for the use of specialized digging-sticks to find edible roots.

I would be surprised if somewhere as large as Lake Flixton was home to just one major settlement, so it's important that research should continue. But it must take place on a sufficiently large, landscape scale, because we will never understand how early post-glacial communities lived in Britain if we don't study a range of settlement types.

I'm sure that the people who lived around Lake Flixton were familiar with neighbouring communities, both on the higher land around the Vale and on the river floodplain to the east and west as well. These relationships would have been different and would have changed through time. It has taken us over half a century to begin to understand the diversity, richness and complexity of early prehistoric life around just one extinct glacial lake. But in some respects, research has only just started.

There are few other areas in Britain that have been as intensively studied as the region around Star Carr. But there is one notable exception. It lies much further south, in the county of Wiltshire, and it owes its fame to a huge stone monument that was constructed at least a millennium after the close of the Mesolithic. Thanks to some extraordinary recent research, all of it on a landscape scale, we are now beginning to understand some of the very ancient beliefs that after several millennia may have inspired people to construct a hauntingly enigmatic and enormously complex stone monument on the dry limestone landscape of Salisbury Plain. Stonehenge is starting to reveal the secrets of its origins.

Scene 4

From Wood to Stone on Salisbury Plain (8000–3000 BC)

The Stonehenge Car Park – The Avenue – Blick Mead Spring – Stonehenge

The archaeological evidence for the Mesolithic communities that inhabited Britain in the millennia following the Ice Age is remarkably slight. This is doubtless a result of the passage of time, but it must also reflect the fact that people tended to live in naturally fertile lowland areas, where food plants, fish, wildfowl and game were plentiful. Sometimes their houses were quite light, but often they were well built, if modest by later prehistoric standards, and so far we have not discovered evidence for larger public buildings, nor for religious and other places where neighbouring communities would have come together. To make matters worse, these slight remains have been damaged, or obliterated altogether, by later activities, such as farming and gravel extraction. The archaeological damage caused by deep ploughing and subsoil drainage in the past fifty years has been truly devastating.[1]

The arrival of farming in Britain just before 4000 BC also witnessed a sudden increase in the building of collective tombs under large barrow mounds, followed by the construction of communal meeting places and shrines, starting with the causewayed enclosures.* Although it may have taken two or three centuries to gather pace, this apparent explosion of construction was in marked contrast to the Mesolithic tradition, evidence of which – in the form of burials, for example – remains very hard to discover. But the seeming scarcity of built monuments in Mesolithic times should not be confused with a lack of veneration for special places, as indeed the early use of caves in Ireland so clearly demonstrated. More recently, evidence has emerged for the recognition that certain landscape features were seen as sacred or special as early as 8000 BC, or possibly even earlier. This leads me to believe that the inhabitants of Star Carr† would probably not have regarded the shores of their own Lake Flixton as just a source of food and fuel. I am sure that, in their minds, the waters of the lake would have been imbued with depths of spiritual meaning – whose richness and diversity we would find it hard to imagine, given our own reliance on rational explanation.

The traditional archaeological view of the great Neolithic and Early Bronze Age monuments of Britain is that they were innovations that came from overseas, with the introduction of farming. And although there may be much truth in this, we are now starting to realize that the new sites were often positioned in areas of the landscape that had long been considered special. There is also growing evidence that many of the beliefs enshrined within the new sacred tombs and enclosures had elements that echoed earlier practices and ideas. And one of the best places to view what we now know was a changing, dynamic relationship between people, shrines and landscape is the area around the most famous site of them all: Stonehenge.

Every prehistorian must have at least one unwritten book about Stonehenge inside his or her head. Wisely, because it's a

---

* See Scene 5, pages 78–81.
† Which we visited in the previous Scene, pages 54–5.

site that everyone has strong views about, most people don't take the trouble to put their ideas on paper.* This interest and controversy has given the site and the landscape around it new life and relevance, which I have to confess I find very moving.

Recent research has generally focused on the remarkable ancient landscapes that surround and form the setting for Stonehenge.[2] Indeed, it is probably fair to say that these landscapes are an inseparable part of the monument: not only have they revealed where the workforce who erected the great stones once lived, but they have also provided us with clues as to why the region was chosen in the first place. Modern technology has played a huge part in these studies, with everything from precise geological identification of the various stone sources to ground-penetrating radar, geophysics and even drone surveys.[3]

As I read yet another revelatory story about the site, I often wonder to what extent all this attention on one place is affecting our view of British prehistory: the people who built and worshipped at Stonehenge certainly produced some remarkable structures. But we also know for a fact that there were hundreds of other henge sites – some made from wood, others from stone – right across the British Isles, and most of them were similarly surrounded by rich, so-called ritual landscapes, where people processed along ceremonial routes, buried their dead and regularly came together to celebrate. I don't believe that Stonehenge was unique. Yes, it was probably the most significant monument in Neolithic and Early Bronze Age Britain, but there were many others, too. Stonehenge is revealing the extraordinary richness and complexity of life between 3000 and 1500 BC, both in Britain and across the Channel in western Europe, with which there were many close ties. Stonehenge came to prominence some five thousand years

---

* Although I have: *Stonehenge: The Story of a Sacred Landscape* (Head of Zeus, London, 2016).

ago, but we now know that its roots almost certainly extended back another three millennia.

Early indications of the antiquity of Stonehenge came when the landscape was first studied in any detail, in the decade following the First World War. The use of aerial photography as a means of closely observing enemy trenches during that conflict had led to huge improvements both in plane stability and camera technology. The result was a famous book, *Wessex from the Air*, published in 1928.[4] In their preface, the authors admit that both the camera (an Ica Type F.K.1 German Service Pattern) and its lens (a 4.5 Zeiss Tessar) were German, bought from the UK government Disposals Board shortly after the war. *Wessex from the Air* revealed many sites for the first time and showed the extraordinary archaeological richness of Salisbury Plain. At the time it was appreciated that some of the sites surrounding Stonehenge had to pre-date it by many centuries. Today, we realize that was just the start of the story.

The next major step was unplanned. Stonehenge had always been a tourist attraction and in the era that immediately followed the Second World War, when income was short and money was still quite tight, it was decided to expand visitor facilities there. In 1966 work began on the expansion of the car park just across the road* that used to pass directly by the Stones, to the north. Before the construction work began, archaeologists were given the chance to excavate the land and they discovered a straight line of three quite widely, but evenly separated post-holes.† The posts had been partially charred (supposedly in the belief that this would prolong their life) and the charcoal, which was identified as pine, was radiocarbon dated. The dates fell between 7000 and 8000 BC.

---

* The old A344 (now closed).
† A hole dug to receive a post. Quite often these will preserve a post 'ghost', a darker stain in the soil left by the long-decayed post.

In 1988 the car park was further extended and another pine post-hole was revealed. It was to one side of the alignment of the original three posts, but most probably belonged to the same monument or structure. Again, the new post was dated to 8000–7000 BC, a long time span that suggests the posts had been replaced over the centuries. The early date for the posts would help to explain the use of pine, which is a hardier tree than oak and which we know was able to grow well in early post-Ice Age times. All four posts were also quite large, with diameters of about 75 centimetres (2½ ft) – roughly that of a modern telegraph pole. This would be very large for a Mesolithic fence or building. Their use in a defensive screen can be ruled out because of the wide gaps between them – and besides, the ground in this part of Salisbury Plain is flat and would have been impossible to defend without a major earthwork of some sort – usually a deep ditch and wide bank. So what was going on?

When no obvious practical purpose for a possible structure presents itself, archaeologists tend to reach for their explanation of last resort, namely 'ritual', or religion. And that seems to be the best explanation for these very early and quite massive pine posts. Presumably they marked out or formed part of a temple or shrine of some sort, but having said that, we should remember that throughout history Christian churches were important meeting places for local people, so the Stonehenge pine posts may also have served a communal, or social, role.

Another clue to the possible importance of the Stonehenge area was revealed by archaeologists in the 1960s, although nobody grasped its significance at the time. That didn't happen until almost half a century later, when a new generation of archaeologists re-excavated the earlier trench. They didn't find any significant new objects. They just looked at the old evidence from a different perspective. And what they revealed was amazing – and yet thoroughly convincing.

***

Many of the most famous ancient sites, such as Stonehenge, had often been over-investigated by archaeologists, especially in the mid- and earlier twentieth century, when there could sometimes be a rather cavalier attitude to the prompt writing of full reports. Sometimes they were also rather lax about establishing archives and samples from their excavations for future generations to study and re-examine. As a result, the authorities who now control access to such sites have become loath to grant permission to excavate undisturbed ground, even to well-established professionals. Their usual way out of this dilemma was to grant new researchers permission to reopen an old archaeological trench, rather than start a fresh one in virgin ground. And this was what happened to Professor Mike Parker Pearson and his team on the Stonehenge Riverside Project when they were looking for somewhere to excavate near the Stones, in 2008.

The old trench that Mike and his team chose to reopen had been excavated in the 1960s across the full width of the Avenue, near the Heel Stone, one of the great stones that marked out the ceremonial approach to the main monument. The Avenue was probably a formalization of a previously established processional way, which led up from the River Avon, then turned south-east to approach Stonehenge from the north-east. It was marked out by banks and ditches on either side and was constructed just after 2400 BC. The Avenue's final approach to the Stones followed the alignment of the mid-summer and mid-winter solstices (the longest and shortest days of the year).* Stonehenge itself is arranged to respect this north-east–south-west alignment, which is fundamental to the organization of this complex site.

---

* The word 'solstice' is derived from two Latin words: *sol*, meaning sun, and *sisto*, meaning to stand still.

When the Riverside Project reopened the earlier trench, they discovered a series of deep natural fissures in the underlying chalk bedrock.[5] These parallel cracks in the rock lay on precisely the same alignment (NE–SW) as the Avenue. At first they looked very much like plough scratches, or even the narrow ruts left by cart wheels. But on closer inspection they turned out to be far too deep. In my experience, most plough scratches or wheel ruts are very rarely more than 15 centimetres (6 in) deep and 7.5–10 centimetres (3–4 in) wide, but these proved to be about 50 centimetres (18 in) deep and 30 centimetres (1 ft) wide. Mercifully, the deep grooves had not been fully excavated out by the earlier archaeologists and this meant the deposits within them were undisturbed. So they were closely examined by the Riverside Project's soil scientist and geologist, who came to the firm opinion that they were entirely natural. Normally, archaeologists are looking for early evidence of human action, so such a result would be very disappointing. But in this instance they were delighted.

Soil can take a long time to form, especially on rocky outcrops, such as chalk and limestone, and in cold conditions such as those at the end of the Ice Age. This was a time when many of the soils of Britain had been worn very thin. Trees and shrubs had been decimated by the freezing temperatures and the open landscapes were very prone to erosion because there was no plant cover to fend off the winds. The hidden network of fine fibrous roots that holds the soil together in modern gardens, woodlands and pastures had almost completely vanished during the Ice Age centuries – and such things take time to recover.

With most of its soil removed by natural erosion, the solstice-aligned natural cracks in the exposed chalk of Salisbury Plain filled with rainwater and melted snow. During the bitter temperatures of night, the ice froze and expanded with enormous force. This pushed the chalk apart and at the same time it shattered its surface, giving rise to the deep parallel grooves, which are simply following the natural bedding planes that were originally laid down when the chalk was formed on the seabed, back in the Cretaceous era, about a hundred million years ago.

Soils take a long time to become established and they were quite slow to accumulate when the climate grew suddenly warmer at the end of the Ice Age. So the very first people who moved onto Salisbury Plain would almost certainly have been able to see the dark lines of soil filling the tops of the grooves into the chalk. In summertime these natural grooves would have been partially screened by growing grasses and wildflowers, while in winter the soil would have been more bare and dark. The contrast between the two solstices could not have been greater. And then as time passed and the soils grew thicker, the grooves slowly vanished from view. But they had done their work: they had helped to inspire successive generations of people to treat this landscape as very special.

You might have noticed that I said the grooves 'had helped' to inspire. The more we learn about prehistory, the more we are starting to appreciate that ancient beliefs were as convoluted and complex as our own religious doctrines are today. In the post-war decades, experts – and not always archaeologists – were convinced that sites like Stonehenge could be simply 'explained' by one thing alone. Thus *Stonehenge Decoded** revealed the site to have been a sophisticated astronomical observatory; a 'Neolithic computer'. The problem with this view was that it assumed that prehistoric people had a modern science-based and analytical attitude to the solar system. Yes, they were indeed highly skilled in predicting solar events – possibly even lunar eclipses[6] – but these observations were made not to explain the

---

* Gerald S. Hawkins, *Stonehenge Decoded* (Dell Publishing, New York, 1965).

movement of the sun, moon and stars, so much as to link life on Earth with worlds beyond the horizon, which many would have believed were populated by the spirits of the ancestors. Perhaps the astronomical side of Stonehenge might be better explained in terms of astrology – or something akin to it – rather than modern astronomy or computer science.

The precise positioning of Stonehenge can probably largely be explained by those solstice-aligned grooves in the subsoil. But would they have been enough to have inspired so many people to treat such a large area as special for so very long? Of course that's an unanswerable question, but as I have already suggested, sacred landscapes can sometimes be shown to owe their sanctity to more than one unusual occurrence – and recently we have learned that Salisbury Plain is part of this tradition. It was concealing yet another unexpected secret.

The ancient site of Blick Mead lies just 2.75 kilometres (1.7 miles) to the east of Stonehenge, on the edge of the valley of the Salisbury Avon.* The site came to public prominence because it lies just south of the A303 and would be directly threatened if that road were to be widened, enlarged or buried within a tunnel. The archaeological excavations at Blick Mead have been quite small in scale, but they have involved both academic archaeologists and many local volunteers. It is a fine and continuing example of community archaeology.

Blick Mead lies just outside the ramparts of an Iron Age fortified site known as Vespasian's Camp, which was probably constructed around 500 BC.[7] Modern research into Blick Mead began in 2005 and has mainly been concentrated around the Blick Mead freshwater spring. Research into early maps and

---

* Avon is the Celtic word for 'river'. There are six River Avons in Britain.

estate records has shown that although the area has had at least two ponds, presumably fed by the spring and maintained there to water livestock, there has been little disturbance of the ground below the modern surface. Excavations around the spring have further revealed extensive evidence for Mesolithic settlement in the area, starting around 8000 BC (when, incidentally, the grooves near Stonehenge would still have been visible), and continuing through to the onset of the Neolithic period, in the early fourth millennium BC.

The sheer abundance of struck (i.e. worked) Mesolithic flints found at Blick Mead is remarkable and suggests that this was not a briefly occupied, one-off settlement. By 2018, the excavation had revealed a total of 30,608 Mesolithic flints.[8] People returned repeatedly to Blick Mead for some four millennia and they must have been aware that groups of hunter-gatherers had been there previously – simply because of the accumulation of debris on the surface. Very often the supposedly 'random' migrations of nomadic bands of hunters follow quite closely defined routes. This helps to avoid conflict with other bands living in the area. It also reflects the fact that game tends to move seasonally and certain areas become harder to exploit in certain seasons. So it is entirely feasible that Blick Mead could have provided a temporary base to several hunter-gatherer communities at different times of the year.

Examination of the many animal bone fragments found at Blick Mead has revealed that about 60 per cent were from giant wild cattle known as aurochs. These huge animals can provide sufficient meat to feed about 200 people and it seems inconceivable that they would have been hunted down and killed merely to provide food for a small family-sized band. Radiocarbon dates suggest that aurochs were being hunted for almost two millennia, from 6650 to 4722 BC. There is also evidence for long-distance travel. A piece of Welsh slate had been fashioned into a tool type found widely on the Weald of Kent, and known as a Horsham point. Analysis of the chemical composition of the enamel of a tooth from a large, Alsatian-type dog found here showed it had spent much of its life in eastern England, possibly even from as far away as the Vale of York.

The site has also produced evidence for at least one probable house, which had been constructed in the shallow hollow – known as a 'tree-throw pit' – that is left when a mature tree is blown over in a gale. There was also good evidence that part of the pit had been built up with local pebbles. Finds from the pit suggest that it was occupied sometime in the late fifth millennium BC – in other words, very shortly before, or actually during, the transition into the Neolithic and the new era of farming.[9] Sacred places such as Blick Mead would have helped provide stability in what might otherwise have proved turbulent times.

Springs are known to have been important to prehistoric people all over the world, but not just for practical reasons. They were widely understood to provide more than just a supply of drinking water for people, game and domestic animals. Water was seen as a reflector of images and thence a mirror on, and symbol of, life itself. But disturb the tranquil surface and the image distorts, breaks down and vanishes. So water can also become a symbol of death and of the time and process of dying. Below the surface is the realm of death itself and perhaps other worlds and dimensions, inhabited by the powers of nature and the spirits of the ancestors. In many societies, offerings of prized possessions were placed into the waters near springs when somebody died. These were very special places indeed. But the stream and ponds at Blick Mead possessed another, very unexpected and highly unusual secret that would have marked them out from all other sacred springs.

As anyone who regularly buys bottled water knows, spring water can vary hugely in taste and purity. This is not just caused by the rocks and geology alone. The waters from the Blick Mead spring include a naturally occurring red alga known as *Hildenbrandia rivularis*, which has the remarkable ability to stain flints and stones lying on the beds of the seasonally flowing stream and nearby pond. But the colour of the stain is truly extraordinary: a pinkish-reddish-turquoise, whose tint and intensity will vary according to the strength of sunlight and shading.[10] The staining is likely to have been even more marked in Mesolithic times, when levels of water flow would have been higher and would have discouraged the less colourful competing algae that are present in the water today. Given the often rather dreary greys, creams and browns of most flint nodules, the algal-coated stones from the Blick Mead ponds are more than just startling. Even to modern eyes, the bright colours appear truly miraculous, but to the Mesolithic gaze, they must have seemed to be imbued with an extraordinary, deeply spiritual quality.

Stonehenge is by far the best-known Neolithic site in Britain, if not in Europe, and the more we investigate its origins and construction, the more extraordinary it becomes. The coloured spring at Blick Mead and the glacial cracks on Salisbury Plain were most remarkable and were regarded as very special by contemporary Mesolithic communities; but interest in the area continued – indeed grew – in the subsequent Neolithic period. However, it was the movement of large stones that really seemed to fire the modern imagination, especially in the decades following the last war. This was also the time when the Loch Ness monster acquired a new life and I wonder whether both were seen as antidotes to the rather drab world of the 1950s.[11]

The stones in question were not the huge monoliths and lintels that give Stonehenge its distinctive form and shape; these are made from sarsen, a locally occurring rock. The distinctive bluestones (which, despite their name, have a greenish tinge when freshly quarried) are very much smaller than the sarsens that surround them; the larger sarsens weigh about forty tons, the bluestones closer to four. It had been suspected for some time that the bluestones originated outside the area, but it was not finally proven until 1923, when their geological source was shown to be in the region around the Preseli Hills of south-west Wales.[12] But how did they get there?

The earliest archaeological theories favoured the use of rafts and the emphasis was entirely on practicality. All explanations to do with the movement and erection of the stones at Stonehenge were treated as engineering problems. In other words, what was the simplest and most efficient way of achieving a particular task? But we have no reason whatsoever to suppose that prehistoric people thought in such a way. Again, as with the axe 'trade', we were imposing modern ways of thinking on people who lived in a very different world, a long time ago. Certainly we know that prehistoric people were capable of performing some remarkable feats of construction, but we must not assume that they were obsessed with speed, cost-effectiveness and efficiency in quite the same way as we are. We will discover shortly that when it comes to the movement of bluestones, we must be very careful indeed before we jump to the 'obvious' conclusions.

The ultimate practical solution to the movement of bluestones from Preseli to Salisbury Plain – a distance of over 225 kilometres (140 miles) – would be natural. In other words, they weren't moved by people, but by glaciers, during the Ice Age. Indeed, there is a known and named glacier, the Bristol Glacier, a branch of the much larger Irish Sea Glacier, that moved large quantities of ice from the Irish Sea to the south and east. The glacier scoured out the Avon Gorge and could possibly have moved pieces of bluestone from Preseli to Salisbury Plain.

The idea of transportation by an Ice Age glacier gained much popular support following the publication of a paper in the highly influential scientific journal *Nature*, in 1971.[13] I recall the controversy this caused in the archaeological world but I, in common with most of my colleagues, remained decidedly unconvinced. Having said that, archaeology gave the theory a very fair hearing and in 1991 a long and detailed pro-glacier paper was published in the leading journal of prehistory.[14] And even that failed to convince many of us.

It was also about this time that evidence began to emerge that Preseli bluestone was being quarried in south-west Wales by the Neolithic communities there. And despite the glacial theory, there were still no discoveries of unworked bluestone anywhere in the Stonehenge area. By contrast, natural, unworked rocks of sarsen stone occur widely across Salisbury Plain and the surrounding area, where they are often known as 'grey wethers',* because of their slight resemblance to sleeping sheep.[15]

Then in 2003 the Stonehenge Riverside Project got under way. The approach of its archaeologists was much broader. They were interested not just in bluestones, but in how the many components of Stonehenge came into being and how they related to the nearby River Avon and to other, slightly less well-known prehistoric sites, such as the neighbouring henges at Durrington Walls and Woodhenge. The Riverside Project has given rise to further research, much of it devoted to the source and movement of the bluestones, and this has been accompanied by a series of geophysical and aerial surveys that have given us a much better picture of the complexity of the prehistoric landscape around Stonehenge. To describe this work as exciting is missing the point. I suspect we will be pondering its implications for many

---

* 'Wether' is the term that is still used to describe a castrated male sheep. Most meat lambs are wethers.

generations – and of course this will inevitably stimulate further research. And even then, I doubt if we'll ever understand this remarkable place fully.[16]

The new research has forced prehistorians to abandon many of the rather simplistic, mechanistic suppositions we had previously made to explain how ancient people performed certain practical tasks. We had always assumed that because there was a large natural waterway, the Bristol Channel and the Severn Estuary, between Preseli and Salisbury Plain, people would have made much use of it when moving the bluestones. But that fails to take into account the underlying motives that inspired ancient communities to transport the stones in the first place. If it was just a matter of acquiring cheap rock for an unimportant structure then yes, a raft would probably have been the right decision. But Stonehenge was never a cheap structure and besides, people were building it for very complex social, historical and spiritual reasons. So we shouldn't simply assume that the bluestones would have been moved in the most efficient, cost-effective manner. That would be rather like suggesting that the Queen should have travelled to Westminster Abbey by bus for her coronation: quick and cheap, yes, but not entirely appropriate to the person, or the occasion.

In the final three decades of the twentieth century, growing prosperity gave rise to an increasing number of so-called rescue or contractual excavations, in which land was excavated ahead of commercial development, for roads, houses, industrial areas and gravel quarries. There was also an upsurge in university research, much of it funded by European sources. This new work showed that the Neolithic population of Britain and north-western Europe was much larger than had previously been supposed and that the landscape was more fully developed and integrated. It became clear that, quite early in the Neolithic period, the new farming settlements did not sit in lonely isolation within small clearings in vast tracts of ancient forest. People tended to settle in naturally open or lightly wooded landscapes and then they would start to clear even more land for arable and grazing, as the community expanded.

It soon also became apparent that the growing number of Neolithic and Bronze Age farms and settlements kept in regular touch. There are, for example, close similarities in the styles and motifs of pottery decoration right across Britain, from southern England to Orkney and the Highlands. Houses too, were closely similar and recent research has shown that live animals were often moved many hundreds of miles. So by the early fourth millennium BC, regular communication between different communities was an essential component of social and economic life. To have worked effectively, this would have required a mutually agreed network of roads, tracks and navigable rivers. Many of these routes would probably have marked out and run along the edges of tribal and community boundaries. In other words, the landscape was rapidly becoming partitioned and developed. Such landscapes, however, only work well if the settlements within them remain on good terms and the people communicate regularly with each other. And this is where ideology and religion entered the picture.

While the glacier/human debate about the Stonehenge bluestones was in its final stages in the late 1990s, one or two archaeologists began to wonder whether the stones had been moved from south-west Wales by water, as was still commonly supposed, or by a different route, overland. By this time, too, there was a growing body of evidence that the movement of people, objects and livestock was not just about trade and exchange but was an important way of maintaining peace and social cohesion. Very often these exchanges took place during important ceremonies to do with the main 'rites of passage' in peoples' lives: at birth, marriage and death. As today, these were occasions when people from many regions would have come together for a family and community gathering.

If this theory is correct, then it makes little sense to transport something like the bluestones by sea, as the whole point of moving them was to allow everyone in the areas they passed through to see and admire them. So the stones' journey was part of much larger ceremonies. It was about coming together to show communal appreciation and respect. I would imagine the passage of a bluestone through a settlement might have been rather like the journey of a medieval king or queen's corpse from the place where he or she died to their eventual final resting place, in Westminster Abbey. The surviving Eleanor Crosses of eastern England (named after Eleanor of Castile, wife of Edward I) are a good example of this. These fine monuments are found from Lincolnshire to Hertfordshire and were erected by Edward I between 1291 and 1295 to mark the overnight resting places of his wife's body, on her last journey to London.[17] I wouldn't be at all surprised if there weren't similar monuments, probably erected by local people and maybe made from wood or fired clay (so they are unlikely to have survived), in the various places where the bluestones might have halted on their journey (or journeys) to Stonehenge.

The latest work carried out by Dr Mike Parker Pearson and the Riverside Project team has convincingly proven that the bluestones were moved overland from Preseli and probably once formed the walls and roof of a chambered tomb* that was transported block by block all the way to Salisbury Plain, where the stones were used at Stonehenge and at a newly discovered site, which they named Bluestonehenge, built on the Avenue, the ceremonial routeway from the River Avon.[18] We can only guess at the emotions people experienced, as a procession or succession of bluestones slowly passed through their communities, but I

---

* Latest research shows it was a stone circle, not a tomb.

strongly suspect they were profound. I can remember as a child the feeling of awe, mixed with fear and wild over excitement, as on 2 June 1953 I watched Her Majesty's magical golden coach pass through a wet and gloomy Trafalgar Square on its return from the coronation service in Westminster Abbey. I will never forget that day. I suspect the witnesses of the bluestones' journey south towards Salisbury Plain would have treasured similar memories for the rest of their lives, too.

As we can see from the debates surrounding the movement and route of the bluestones, prehistorians have had problems getting inside what one might call the 'mindset' – the way of thinking – of Neolithic and Bronze Age people. We have had to rethink our interpretations at a very profound level and we must be very careful not to make another set of patronizing assumptions: prehistoric societies were not simpler than ours are today. The people were certainly less technologically advanced than us, but that does not mean that their imaginations were less developed or creative.

Take buildings as basic as a house, or a place of worship. Today, the two are completely separate and the way people behave in each is entirely different. We still regard churches and places of worship as special in many respects. Whatever our beliefs, or lack of them, most of us appreciate that structures like Stonehenge and certain great cathedrals possess numinous* qualities that transcend daily life. Nobody knows what might lie behind the 'magic' of these places and I suspect it will always defy rational analysis; but when I visit them I can feel it – and that's enough for me. I have no wish to destroy it by seeking explanations. I leave that for people who have had the misfortune never to have experienced such things. I cherish the fact that, for me, it's there – and out of reach – far beyond truth or meaning.

---

* 'Other-worldly', mystical, a power or force beyond rational analysis. From the Latin word *numen*, meaning divine presence, deity.

Scene 5

Hunters Become Farmers (from 4000 BC)

Fengate – Etton and Windmill Hill –
Clava Cairns – Tomnaverie

The introduction of metalworking in the centuries just before 2500 BC is often seen as one of the biggest developments in prehistoric Britain – and it certainly was profound, with very long-term effects that continue to impact our lives today. But was it such a big deal at the time? We're now starting to understand how metalworking arrived in Britain and we are also learning more about the people from the continental mainland who introduced it. With hindsight, we can appreciate that these newly arrived technologies were to have a lasting effect on British prehistory. But to what extent did they alter the way that most people led their daily lives? We know, for example, that houses remained the same as before, as did farmyards and domestic animals (cattle, pigs, sheep/goats*), all of which were domesticated at various times, much earlier. Burial rites did change somewhat, but corpses continued to be placed under barrows, much as before. If you want to find a period of change that profoundly affected all aspects of people's daily lives, you have to turn the clock back a further

---

* I use the term 'sheep/goat' because it is extremely difficult to distinguish between the bones of the two species.

millennium and a half, to 4000 BC. This is the period that saw the introduction of farming and, with it, the birth of the Neolithic (or New Stone Age) period.

In the mid-twentieth century, before the invention of radio-carbon dating, archaeologists had to construct time frames for prehistory using key events that could be given a reasonably precise date in calendar years BC. Very often these events involved the known ancient civilizations of the Near East, together with a few clues that could be provided by geologists and other specialists working with pollen cores, lakebed deposits and tree-ring dates.

Using this sometimes rather flimsy framework of dates and events, prehistorians were able to reconstruct a picture of prehistoric Europe, which showed how the idea of farming spread from its Eurasian origins in and around modern Iraq, and then north and west into Europe. They were even able to define certain routes followed by the earliest farming communities: west through the Mediterranean, or up the River Rhône, or overland north of the Alps and so on. It was very often seen as the spread of an enlightenment – a new way of living that was much superior to the earlier style of hunter-gathering. Books and articles on the subject sometimes included the Latin phrase '*Ex oriente lux*' ('Out of the East, light') – a term that was first used to describe the spread of religious beliefs from the Near East. In many respects, the spread of farming was seen in a similar light.

And then facts began to muddy the crystal-clear waters. New radiocarbon dates showed that the process had taken place rather earlier than previously thought and there was evidence that some of the innovations supposedly introduced from the Ancient Near East had actually moved in the other direction. Many of the new types of religious and ceremonial monuments that appeared in western Europe during the Neolithic – such as chambered tombs, stone circles and stone rows – had been developed locally, and had then spread eastwards. We used to believe that farming took more than a millennium to diffuse from southern England to northern Scotland. We now realize the spread was very much faster: probably no more than two centuries.[1] It is quite clear that the introduction of farming was a far more complex process than we had previously supposed.

The first farms appeared in southern Britain in the century before 4000 BC. Current evidence would suggest that they were introduced by new arrivals, but we cannot rule out the possibility that some may also have arisen through the spread of an idea, or new knowledge. However, DNA and other biological research indicates that most of the population of Neolithic Britain were arrivals from the continent, probably via Spain and Portugal, following several generations of migration westwards, along the shores of the Mediterranean. But a word of caution is needed. The latest study is based on analysis of bones from sixty-seven Neolithic individuals across Britain.[2] That's not a huge sample, and there is also a possibility that the bones in question, most of which came from special places, from chambered tombs, barrows, causewayed enclosures and caves, might be skewed to favour the upper echelons of society. Six samples of Mesolithic bones were analysed and these had strong similarities with Mesolithic bones from continental Europe. They were also distinctively different from those of the Neolithic farmers. So what happened? Was the indigenous British Mesolithic population and culture simply wiped out by the newcomers? Or did they survive to influence the development of later prehistoric societies?

Coming from a farming family myself, I have long been intrigued by those first farmers and how they would have behaved in the British landscape. Then in 1982 I was given – or rather acquired – the opportunity to excavate a so-called causewayed enclosure, just outside the little hamlet of Etton in the lower

Welland valley, on the edge of the Fens near the Lincolnshire/ Cambridgeshire border. Causewayed enclosures were built and used in the centuries around 3600 BC. They consist of a ditch, or series of parallel ditches that were dug around a plot of land where communities in the region held regular gatherings. The area of land in question was in the River Welland floodplain and the site was located within a now extinct meander of the old river, which has long since been straightened and canalized behind high flood banks. But you could see quite clearly on aerial photos that the ditched enclosure had been set to one side of the slightly rising ground within the meander.[3] I can remember thinking that this was rather odd, as they could easily have taken in the whole of the meander, with very little extra effort. Had they been constructing an Iron Age fort, three millennia later, that's precisely what they would have done.

The more I thought about the positioning of the enclosure, the more I became convinced that it had been deliberate. But why? I tried in vain to come up with a rational explanation, but none occurred to me. Instead, I found my thoughts were often returning to another, and far better-known, causewayed enclosure at Windmill Hill, near the magnificent Wiltshire henge at Avebury. The author of the definitive report on the pre-war excavations of the site describes the positioning of the enclosure as crowning the hill 'lopsidedly'.[4] And when you visit the site, the lopsidedness becomes even more apparent. As I just mentioned, this off-centre positioning is in stark contrast to Iron Age hillforts, which are famous for the way they often seem to crown a hill: in effect, the ramparts, the ditches and banks of the fort capture the hill and dominate it, just as the placing of a crown on an English monarch's head symbolizes that the new king or queen may be chief among all citizens, but is still subservient to God.[5] It seemed to me, however, that causewayed enclosures were sending out a very different message.

Very often, the simplest explanations are the best and when you see something dissonant or somehow 'unnatural', such as the off-centre positioning of causewayed enclosures, it must conceal truths about ancient attitudes to the landscape. It seems to me that the modern approach is Us First: obstacles are there to be bridged or tunnelled through; rivers are straightened; bogs and swamps are drained. In the Middle Ages, it was all about God. So hills and plains were dominated by the soaring towers of magnificent cathedrals. Even as early as the Iron Age, the spectacular positioning of hillforts was used to proclaim a particular tribe's dominance of a given landscape. But Neolithic attitudes still owed much to the Mesolithic hunter-gatherer communities, who had to live in greater harmony with the plants and animals around them – and on which they depended for their survival. They seem profoundly different: less arrogant, perhaps. In my darker moments, when I see pictures of farmers burning the Amazon rainforest, and am depressed by the state of the world's deteriorating climate, I sometimes think back to 4000 BC: could we have done things differently? What if we had retained more of our hunter-gatherer traditions – would we be living in greater harmony with nature? Maybe – but we didn't.

Farming is essentially about modifying and harnessing different aspects of the landscape to provide a reliable source of healthy food. It has never been about complete domination: the landscape must work *with* farmers, not *for* them. Recent research suggests that the first farmers in Britain grew cereals and kept a few livestock. Essentially, this was small-scale subsistence farming. But after a few centuries, people in different areas adapted to the landscapes where they lived and farmed. In the Fens, for example, livestock became increasingly important because of the abundance of pasture, especially in summertime when water levels dropped and flocks of sheep and herds of cattle were able to graze the lush meadows. In other regions, such as river valley floodplains, fertile gravel soils were ploughed to grow crops, while areas of damp or upland grazing were selectively used at different times of the year. In many places, these more specialized forms of farming were able to expand beyond the subsistence or family-sized unit to become larger and involve more people. Eventually, from about 2000 BC, the earliest field systems began to appear, replacing the more open patterns of grazing (which were probably never truly unbounded, and would have involved informal agreements between neighbouring communities).

Having set up a small farm myself, I know only too well that the process of specialization requires a degree of humility. If you want to be successful, you cannot just impose your farm on a landscape without making concessions to it. And often, the simplest way to discover what your particular soils are best at growing is to ask a few local people. I was told, for example, that our sticky clay-silt soil grew excellent grass and clover, but was far too heavy for potatoes. And they were *so* right: every season the maincrop potatoes from my vegetable garden are honeycombed by hungry slugs, which thrive in the damp ground in high summer. But you can get away with first and second early varieties, as long as you harvest them by early August.

Attitudes to landscape are about far more than the practicalities of farming or hunting. Just find yourself caught outside by an unexpected severe storm and you will soon discover how gales, rain, snow, thunder and lightning can show who's in charge. By the same token, experience a clear dawn over Salisbury Plain or a blazing Fenland sunset and you will glimpse moments of transcendent peace. So I don't see the arrival of the first farmers in Britain as a prehistoric version of cinema's Wild West, with incoming cowboys fighting hostile natives. Indeed, the distribution of Early Neolithic and Mesolithic settlement sites in the Fens is almost identical. So even if the two groups were genetically different, it seems that they shared the same knowledge about the best places to settle and establish their communities.[6] This suggests that the two groups were in regular contact and there is no archaeological evidence to indicate that there was active hostility between them – although it should be said that all archaeological remains of what one might term 'the contact' period just before 4000 BC are slight and very hard to identify. The more we are learning about the period, the more it would seem that the relationship was flexible and probably very complex.

Because the builders of sites like Etton and Windmill Hill must have had a close relationship with the landscape in all its aspects, practical, agricultural, spiritual and emotional, I am in little doubt that the 'lopsided' positioning of the two enclosures was both carefully considered and deliberate. The simplest explanation is that they did not want their enclosures to be seen to crown or dominate the hill or landscape features on which they were built. This interpretation of their builders' underlying motive would in turn suggest that human communities believed they were subservient to the powers behind the landscape: the sun and the passage of the seasons, which were closely tied to more local effects such as storms, the flooding of rivers, the growth of plants and the availability of fish, game and grazing. The emphasis on elaborate tombs from the start of the Neolithic would suggest that the forces who controlled these great powers would have been reached through the ancestors. Given this world view, it is quite understandable that they did not want their enclosures to dominate certain prominent places that had probably been regarded as spiritually special for a long time.

We live in a world where big is beautiful, where spectacular location and grand design guarantee many visitors, great reviews and commercial success. In a culture where braying politicians are becoming the norm, we forget that there have always been other, quieter ways of doing things. I have long considered restraint to be a sign of strength – albeit inner strength – not weakness, which is why I have long been fascinated by the mundane and everyday in prehistoric life. Of course, we can never be certain, but I think it probable that most ordinary people in later prehistoric Britain had never visited Stonehenge or Avebury and if they had, they would have been told to wait behind the bank and ditch that surrounded those great henges; the inner area would have been a very holy place, reserved for important individuals on special occasions. So how did ordinary people satisfy the need, which we all have from time to time, to experience the numinous or to seek emotional comfort and consolation in times of personal crisis? Were there prehistoric equivalents of parish churches or non-conformist chapels? Rather surprisingly, the answer to that question is a firm Yes – indeed, we know of hundreds of them. In my view, they are one of Britain's hidden treasures and should be *far* better known. More to the point, they have revealed a huge amount of information on how they were built and used and about the rituals that took place within them.

Small henge-like shrines of the Neolithic and Early Bronze Age survive in many places across the British Isles. Quite frequently they were located in liminal places that were deliberately removed from settlements. But this was not always the case. In a very few instances, such as Seahenge,* we can make reasonably well-informed estimates on the numbers of people that would have attended the ceremonies (or ceremony) that were held there. At Seahenge, for instance, the 'congregation', including bystanders, might have been as large as 200–250 people – the size of a large country funeral today. In other instances, where the monument shows clear evidence for repeated reuse, the congregations would

---

* See Scene 7, pages 121–33.

have been very much smaller – maybe one or two families and perhaps a couple of dozen people. Indeed, the more research I have done, the more convinced I have become that these shrines were in many important ways the prehistoric equivalent of present-day places of worship.

Two particularly important groups of small prehistoric ceremonial sites survive in north-east Scotland and these provide a superb example of what one might term an ideological landscape. Few other places in Britain can boast such high-quality preservation and completeness.[7] Archaeologists love to categorize everything they find: it's part of the process of imposing sense and order onto the seemingly random assemblage of sites, finds and vanished landscapes that we reveal every year in our excavations and surveys. The sites in question are known as Clava cairns and recumbent stone circles and they occur on the northern slopes of the foothills of the Grampian Mountains, east of the Moray Firth, roughly between Inverness in the west and Aberdeen on the east coast. The Grampians are a presence – I am tempted to say a brooding one – to the south, but the landscapes where the sites occur are generally lower-lying, situated along river valleys and amid rolling hills. Today the area is characterized by numerous small towns and villages, linked by a complex network of roads and lanes. It is not the stereotypical Scottish Highland landscape of steep slopes, grouse moors and lonely castles. It was almost certainly quite densely inhabited in prehistoric times, too.

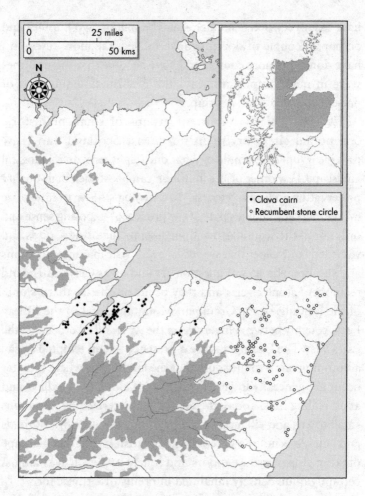

5.1 A map of north-east Scotland showing the distribution of Clava cairns and recumbent stone circles.

I don't want to get bogged down in too much detail, but I must first briefly explain the main characteristics of the two types of monuments: Clava cairns and recumbent stone circles. At first glance, it seems quite simple. The names say it all: cairns are mounds or heaps of stone, whereas stone circles are arrangements of single standing stones. Most cairns occur in upland areas of Britain, where they often formed part of funerary monuments. Their role was essentially the same as that of the soil or turf forming the mounds of barrows in lowland Britain, which concealed and protected bodies, coffins and cremations. Some upland cairns, known as clearance cairns, concealed nothing and may well have been used as boundary markers. Clearance cairns were probably heaped up when the surface of the land was cleared of stones to make fields or meadows.

I mentioned clearance cairns because they illustrate one of the largest challenges that archaeologists working out in the field have to face. If you're looking at drone images or conventional aerial photos, you automatically achieve a sort of remoteness or distance that makes certain decisions seem much simpler. Take those clearance cairns, for example: from the air they'd look very different – far more haphazard and random – than the far more carefully arranged and structured cairns over a burial monument or within a stone circle. Sometimes, of course, the seeming clarity provided by an overhead, aerial view can be misleading, but then that's archaeology: always full of surprises. But on the ground, nothing's ever simple and that's because you can see the site in its full context, including background views, neighbouring outcrops of rock, thickness of soil cover – even changes in surface vegetation – all of which can provide useful clues. And the situation gets even more complicated when you start to excavate.

Conventional archaeological maps display the prehistoric monuments of north-east Scotland in the two distinct groups that can be seen in the map on page 84. Viewed from the surface, there do indeed appear to be two quite distinct types of monuments: the more cairn-like Clava cairns to the west and the very characteristic recumbent stone circles to the east. Indeed, the carefully shaped and placed cairns and recumbent stones, with their two characteristic upright flankers, stand out prominently and make the distinction of the two groups seem very straightforward. I won't go into the details of how the two groups of sites have been dated, as the evidence is both rather thin and also convoluted and complex.

Archaeologists have also become increasingly aware of the hazards inherent in many forms of modern dating techniques. Take radiocarbon, which measures the way organic material such as charcoal decays through time. The technique – the science – is becoming more and more accurate, but it still depends entirely on the context of the material being dated. Take oak charcoal as an example. Oak has always been the main timber for buildings, simply because it's very strong, hard and its heartwood is quite rot-resistant. It's also a great firewood, when dry, and was often used in domestic hearths and in pyres, where much sustained heat is needed to cremate a body. Oak grows quite slowly and trees used to form the larger timbers – not just in buildings, but in timber circles and other ceremonial structures, such as those found beneath cairns and barrows – may easily be two hundred years old. So if an archaeologist finds a piece of oak charcoal in, say, the remains of a pyre, it could pre-date the cremation by two centuries – or even more if the wood was taken from an old structure or building. This is one of the reasons why modern archaeologists tend to be a little wary of oak-based radiocarbon dates quoted in reports of the 1950s, 1960s and early 1970s. Since then we have become more aware of the problem and generally look for younger oak samples for radiocarbon dating. You can determine the age of a piece of wood by looking at its size, shape and the curvature of its growth rings.

The dating of Clava cairns and recumbent stone circles has depended quite heavily on oak-based radiocarbon samples and much of the work was carried out in the mid-twentieth century. This was also a time when archaeologists often applied an interpretational framework that was based around the theory that new ideas gradually diffused – spread – from one place to another, rather like an infectious disease such as the Black Death. In certain, very broad instances, this idea works. The concept of farming, for example, spread from its origins in Iraq and the Middle East, around 8000 BC. By 7000 BC it had crossed the Aegean to Crete and from there it spread in two directions: north-west through central Europe and west, through Italy and the Mediterranean, arriving in Britain shortly before 4000 BC.[8] All of that seems fairly clear, but the simple idea of gradual diffusion breaks down when one examines the process in greater detail. Take the disease analogy. This works well if you plot the spread of, say, plague across a large inland area, such as continental Europe, but different models must be applied when it comes to maritime trade, where infected sailors can, and did, carry infection across seas and oceans in a very short time indeed. It all depends on the scale one wants to work at. Viewed very broadly, the diffusion model fits well, but seen at the local level, different explanations are needed. And this brings me back to those sites in north-east Scotland.

The once fashionable idea of diffusion was often applied at too small a scale. It ignored, for example, the fact that even in the later Neolithic, farmers needed to acquire new bloodlines for their sheep and cattle from distant farms, to avoid inbreeding. I think it was for this reason that there were regular contacts, for example, between people living around Salisbury Plain and others as far north as Scotland. Similarly, there were contacts between Bronze Age communities in the Fens and in north-west England. Such long-distance contacts might also help explain how and why the stone axe 'trade'* developed so readily. The developed societies of later Neolithic Europe were bound together by a system of

---

* Described in the first section of the next Scene.

roads and tracks that aided communication and helped provide boundaries between different communities. So ideas, and indeed diseases, wouldn't have gradually 'diffused' from one group of people to another; instead, they would have jumped quite rapidly, and especially after communal gatherings, for example weddings and funerals, when people from quite widely separated farms and settlements came together. So if we are more cautious about oak-derived radiocarbon dates and no longer assume that ideas simply 'diffused' from one community to another, then it becomes far less straightforward to date and sequence the Clava cairns and the recumbent stone circles simply on their appearance.[9] A more detailed approach is needed, one that involves excavation and new surveys to acquire fresh and reliable evidence. Fortunately for us, such a study exists. It was carried out by a team led by an old friend and colleague, Professor Richard Bradley.[10] For my money, it is one of the most imaginative prehistoric landscape projects undertaken in recent years.

Archaeological research is never straightforward, for the simple reason that it has to take place in the real world. This means that inevitably any conclusions and observations that may be made can be heavily influenced by practical constraints. Early in my own career my team discovered a large, deep ditch that we had good grounds to suspect was pre-Roman, but for practical reasons we weren't able to examine more than a short length of it. As so often happens, it was also near the end of the dig and we didn't have the money to continue any longer. We needed a good story to tell the people who had funded us – and which would help guarantee future excavations. So I announced that the ditch was part of a prehistoric defensive system. The idea was plausible, and was well received, even if I personally had my doubts. The following season, when we were able to open up much larger trenches, we proved beyond any doubt that the big ditch wasn't anything to do with defence, but actually formed part of an elaborate four-thousand-year-old (Bronze Age) field system. So the truth was more exciting than my short-lived fiction, which arose because of the non-archaeological constraints we were then facing.

I mentioned that short fable from my past (and any archaeologists who have ever achieved anything worthwhile will have similar tales to tell) to illustrate the extent to which practical considerations can colour or curb the interpretation of archaeological fieldwork. In that example, we were facing constraints of space, time and money, but the sites we were investigating were all below ground and were about to be destroyed by the development of a large industrial estate. Researchers into sites like the Clava cairns and recumbent stone circles face very different obstacles. Almost always, such sites are listed under Ancient Monuments legislation, which is designed to assure their survival into the future. This means they are protected against developers and others who would demolish them. However, archaeological research can also harm them, so sensitive, and often very difficult, decisions must be made by the officials who are charged with their care. These curators, as they have come to be known, would also be aware that archaeologists, especially in the mid-twentieth century, had a terrible reputation for excavating, and then not publishing the results of their work.[11]

I think it was the late great Sir Mortimer Wheeler (who published everything he dug) who said that without full publication, excavation is merely methodical destruction. How right he was – and that's why curators are somewhat loath to allow researchers to dig trenches into intact and protected ancient monuments, such as the Clava cairns or recumbent stone circles. But they also know that without more knowledge, we won't realize the true importance of such sites. In order to carry out further archaeological investigation of a site or monument, it may, for example, prove necessary to enlarge the protected area – defined by the wonderfully archaic-sounding word 'curtilage' – that surrounds Scheduled Ancient Monuments.[*] Were they not politically hot potatoes, such enlargement should have been effected years ago at places like Avebury, Stonehenge and the foreshores of the River Thames as it passes through London.

Bearing in mind similar curatorial and practical constraints, Richard Bradley and the team decided to concentrate their efforts on three recumbent stone circles, all with splendidly evocative names: Tomnaverie, Cothiemuir Wood and Aikey Brae. In addition, they carried out large-scale field walking (where the ground surface is closely examined for flints, pottery, bone fragments and any other evidence for ancient activity) around Tomnaverie and Cothiemuir Wood. Such surveys aren't always a lot of fun to do (especially if finds are rare and the weather is wet!), but they often play a key role in explaining how and why certain monuments were placed where they were.

Tomnaverie was chosen as the principal excavation and I shall concentrate on it here, because the meticulous work carried out there revealed fascinating insights into the way it was used, and how people would have regarded it some four and a half thousand years ago. Professor Bradley's team were allowed far greater freedom to excavate this protected monument because the stones of the outer stone circle had been disturbed in the not-too-distant past. The disturbance had been caused by a neighbouring stone quarry, whose working face was immediately alongside the site. So one of the aims of the dig was to make good the recent damage and restore the site to its original condition.[12]

---

[*] Curtilage was originally used to describe a small paddock or yard attached to a larger building.

The site at Tomnaverie consisted of two principal elements: a circular cairn, whose edges were clearly defined by a substantial kerb of closely set larger stones, and an outer circle of even larger standing stones. The kerb of the inner cairn was approximately 15 metres (50 ft) in diameter. The recumbent stone and the most southerly of its two flankers lay to the south-west, in what was plainly a slight extension to the outer stone circle. The northern flanker to the recumbent stone lay nearby and was accurately repositioned by the excavators. This superb photograph (fig. 5.2), taken at night during the excavation, shows how the recumbent stone and its two flankers frame a view towards the distant hills. It is hard not to think that this beautiful nocturnal vista would have been enjoyed by the people who built and used the site, and that the dramatic nature of the views from it was one important reason why the stone circle was erected here. Were they looking towards the realms inhabited by their ancestors, or were they thinking about their own journey through life? Whatever their thoughts might have been, the recent research project leaves little doubt that their religious and social worlds were closely united. Enduring beliefs, monuments and a profound sense of place would have provided communities with the inspiration to continue and the motivation to avoid conflict with their neighbours. The more we research, the more we realize that these were not simpler societies in a less complex world. Indeed, we underestimate them at our peril.

The excavation at Tomnaverie revealed a far more complex monument than had previously been supposed.[13] It proved to be larger, with an overall diameter of 23 metres (75 ft) rather than 17 metres (56 ft). It was also one of the first archaeological field projects to use digital photography as part of its survey. In an excavation involving thousands of rocks of different sizes, together with loose rubble, the position of every stone was potentially crucial; so accurate digital plans were essential

5.2 A view across the portal of the stone circle at Tomnaverie with the recumbent stone and the two flankers at either end. On a moonlit night the stones frame the moon over the mountain of Lochnagar, some 30 km (19 miles) to the south-west.

and they helped the team untangle the site's complex history of construction, modification and later reuse.

The earliest evidence for activity consisted of a low mound, mostly within the topsoil buried beneath the rocks of the cairn. This mound was made up of burnt soil, a mass of broken-up pieces of charcoal and numerous small fragments of burnt human bone. Burnt human bone almost invariably means a cremation pyre, as human bodies take a lot of heat and fire to burn off the muscle, and particularly the fat, to get down to the bones beneath. Bodies found in most accidental house fires are rarely, if ever, cremated. Funeral pyres aren't just bonfires, either: they are carefully constructed from dry wood and must burn with real intensity for at least an hour and a half to cremate a corpse thoroughly. Cremated bones are very distinctive: they lose their resilience and become white and brittle; soon they break up into tiny pieces. So that shallow mound of cremated bones and charcoal is telling us that the low hill, which was later selected for the stone circle, was already a special place where funeral pyres were built.

Today, we tend to see cremation as a reasonably inexpensive way of avoiding the cost of a coffin, gravestone and permanent grave. But many communities in the world still see it in a more traditional light, as a process by which the soul is released from the body by the flames. Because of these beliefs, funeral pyres were often placed close by rivers or in special places thought to have had ready access to those realms beyond the world of mere mortals, where the souls of the ancestors dwelt in perpetuity. This might help to explain why the site at Tomnaverie crowns a low mound that rises quite prominently from the otherwise gentle, rolling landscape around it – and why it has such striking views of the distant mountains, which may well have been seen as special places for the ancestors. Ironically, the steep working faces of the modern quarry, which so nearly destroyed this remarkable site, actually increase its prominence. Its restoration is therefore symbolically important because it demonstrates that conservation and imagination can triumph over the needs of commerce. We must never forget that ancient sites have modern relevance, too.

The first phase of the monument that was then built over the pyre area was a platform-like raised stone cairn of about 15 metres (50 ft) diameter, which was carefully edged by large kerbstones and a drystone wall. Initially, this cairn seemed circular, but on closer inspection the team could see that it had been laid out in a rough polygon with some eight sides. A very similar arrangement of about eight wooden 'panels' was observed at the slightly later (2049 BC) timber 'circle' at Seahenge. This segmented pattern would suggest that both sites may have been constructed by workers from a number of different communities or families.[14] All the people involved were clearly motivated by the same concept of the sites' general layout and both monuments have their broadest segments or panels along a south-west–north-east alignment. The narrow entranceway through the oak uprights at Seahenge was from the south-west, which is precisely where the recumbent stone and its two flankers were placed at Tomnaverie.

The cairn at Tomnaverie was far more than just a flat heap of stones. Within the cairn, and reaching about halfway to the centre, was a series of spoke-like smaller walls, which further subdivided the mound into another twelve or so segments, whose layout resembled slightly uneven slices in a round cake. This might hint at two levels of organization, the 'cake slices' lying within the larger group represented by the outer segments. Maybe this arrangement reflects a social structure in which families formed part of wider tribes or communities. The arrangement of the 'cake slice' walls was more prominent and therefore easier for the excavators to discern towards the north-east, i.e. towards the 'back' of the monument (if the slightly later recumbent stone can be assumed to have been its front). The excavators were also able to discern another arrangement of curved drystone walls that were clearly a part of the cairn and would have helped to provide structural stability, but they were not essential. More likely they were part of the monument's overall design as, like the radial 'cake slice' walls, they would have been clearly visible in the top of the cairn. They provide hints that there was more to the belief system behind these monuments than the simple lunar and solar alignments suggested by the layout of henges or the south-west–north-east alignment. We must be careful not to oversimplify in our search for explanations. Medieval churches were indeed aligned east–west, towards Jerusalem, but the belief system underlying Christianity was, and is, vastly more complex and subtle.

We are given further glimpses of complexity in the colour of the stones used at Tomnaverie. Stonehenge is famous for its bluestones, dragged there from the Preseli mountains of South Wales. By contrast, the excavators at Tomnaverie found that the builders there had deliberately selected stones of a red hue for the cairn and its kerb. This colour contrasted markedly with that of natural stone outcrops nearby. As a general rule, the colour of stonework often fades with time (the Stonehenge bluestones are today a drab brown), so we must assume that the reds at Tomnaverie have also faded. A paler, more sparkly, quartz rock was selected for the part of the ramp that extended around the cairn's kerbstones; this was clearly intended as a support or revetment, to prevent them leaning outwards.

The second main phase of building at Tomnaverie is represented by the outer stone circle of twelve uprights and one horizontal, recumbent, stone. The holes to receive these were clearly cut through the stones and soil of the ramp that supported the cairn's kerb. So they have to be of a later date. The outer stone circle may have been slightly later than the cairn, but it was clearly intended to form a part of it – and a very important, final part, at that. The recumbent stone and its flankers had been moved by quarrymen, possibly as late as the 1920s, but they hadn't moved them very far and in the process they had simply lifted them out of the ground, or rolled them over, without causing disturbance to the rest of the site. So the two sockets that held the flankers could be recognized and excavated. The same went for a shallow depression that accommodated the underside of the recumbent stone. With these clues to guide them, the excavators were able to replace all three stones with considerable precision.

Excavation of the flanker sockets and the recumbent stone's foundations revealed that the kerb of the central cairn had been disturbed during the erection of the two flankers, but the damage had been made good and the kerb had been modified to veer slightly outwards to join up with the flankers. The result was a seamless join that proved beyond any doubt that the slightly later stone circle had always been intended to form part of the earlier monument.

The excavations revealed a detailed plan of the stone circle. The upright stones were arranged in six pairs, starting with the two flankers on either side of the recumbent stone. The pairs of stones comprising the main circle were arranged on either side of a central axis that ran south-west–north-east through the centre of the recumbent stone. The pairs of matching stones on opposite sides of the circle were unevenly spaced, with narrower spacing towards the rear of the monument, on the other side of the circle from the recumbent stone. The stone pairs were matched for size and were graded in height, being larger towards the recumbent and smaller towards the north-east and the rear of the circle. With one exception, the uprights of the stone circle were made from the distinctive red-coloured stone that matched the colour of the cairn's kerbstones. The exception was the recumbent stone, which was in white quartz and was clearly selected to stand out.

Close inspection of the stonework revealed that the builders of the stone circle had been at pains to match the uprights to the shape and size of stones used to form the central cairn's kerb. Again, there are symmetries both across the circle and within the different panels of the kerb. Structure is apparent everywhere. The framing of the Deeside mountain of Lochnagar, some 32 kilometres (20 miles) to the south-west, between the two flankers of the recumbent stone, when seen from the centre of the circle, was clearly deliberate. This view would never have framed a rising or setting sun, but it would have caught the position of the setting moon, every eighteen and a half years.[15] This layout, together with the use of red stone and the distinctive, pale and slightly glistening surface of the quartz recumbent, suggests that Tomnaverie was probably intended to be used at night. And of course there is something very special about night-time rituals and ceremonies.

Midnight Mass might be one thing, but imagine being here at Tomnaverie in moonshine, with the white light reflecting off the coloured stones. Those stones would also have affected the acoustics of the place, muffling some sounds, but amplifying what was being said, sung or chanted within the stone circle. We noticed the powerful muffling and enhancement of sound in the reconstruction we made of the Seahenge timber circle – where the effect was intensified by the release of tannic acid fumes from the recently split oak timbers surrounding us.[16] The fires that we know were burned at many cairn sites might well have included scented herbs. The combined effect of these various elements on people's senses – sight, smell and hearing – must have been profoundly moving.

I think the most remarkable conclusion of the excavation is that the sequence of building at Tomnaverie was carefully planned. Richard Bradley puts it succinctly:

> It seems that the entire sequence recovered by excavation was conceived by the builders from the outset. The successive elements were fitted on to one another in a predetermined order until the process reached its conclusion. Little was left to chance and the nature of the monument was not altered radically from the moment of its inception.[17]

On current evidence, it would appear that the site was first built and used in the twenty-fifth century BC. People returned to it as a place to bury cremated remains almost a millennium or so later, in the Bronze Age, sometime around 1600–1400 BC. I've already hinted that the development and chronology of these sites in north-east Scotland has fascinated prehistorians for a long time and I won't attempt to unravel the complexity here. Personally, I suspect it would prove a pointless exercise, because it is quite clear from the research already undertaken that cairns and recumbent stone circles have many features in common, but they also differ regionally and between individual monuments. If, as Richard Bradley suggests – I believe convincingly – the development of Tomnaverie was carefully planned from the outset, then this tells us much about the way communities in the region behaved towards each other.

For a start, nobody sat in impoverished isolation. These communities were in regular touch with one another and the slightly different development paths of the ceremonial monuments they built for themselves reflected their identities and aspirations. I live in a Fenland parish, where the nave of the once quite large parish church collapsed in the seventeenth century, leaving just a small part of the chancel to the east and the tall bell tower to the west. Between them is open ground. I suppose that, as Lincolnshire parish churches go, it is less than exciting. But if anyone were to dare to propose rebuilding the nave, I'm certain the local population would rise up in open rebellion. Our funny-looking church is now part of our identity: the land was soft, the building collapsed, but we continue – undaunted. Such expressions of communal togetherness make sense only in regions where the landscape has slowly evolved and where the different farms and settlements are in close communication. They are symbols of success, aspiration, ownership and identity. But to return to our theme, what about those recumbent stones – what did they symbolize?

The two flankers must surely hold the clue. Doorways must always have stout posts, if the weight of the roof or the floors upstairs are not to force the walls apart. So we can assume that the flankers represent doorposts and the recumbent stone is a symbolic blocking of the entrance to the shrine within. Presumably it was lowered into place when the monument's construction was finished. It marks it out as a very special sacred place, housing the spirits of the ancestors. Doubtless that is why it continued to be revered long after its completion. I'm sure such sealed-up monuments would have been seen as symbols of local pride and identity for a very long time. Indeed, that is why it is so very pleasing that Tomnaverie has at last been restored to its former glory with accuracy and sympathy. And of course, when we ourselves visit such sites, we should acknowledge that we are respecting very much earlier traditions. It never hurts to be humble.

Scene 6

From Stone to Bronze: Stone Quarries and Special Places (4000–2500 BC)

The Pike O'Stickle, Langdale – Orkney Islands

History happens as a series of interconnected events: one thing leads to another and there are inevitable consequences. If, for example, you had been living in Leicestershire on 22 August 1485, you would probably have learned very quickly that a nasty battle had just been fought in a field outside Market Bosworth. Soon, everyone in England would become aware that King Richard III had been killed there. Most people would also have been aware that the battle potentially marked the end of the long-running Wars of the Roses. In a short time, everyone would grasp that the new king, Henry VII, represented the start of another royal dynasty, the Tudors, but nobody could possibly have appreciated that the change also effectively marked the end of the Middle Ages. The English Midlands would then go on to play an important role in the move away from a closed feudal system towards the more open, owner-based enterprises that would ultimately lead to the industrialization that was to play such an important role in the birth of the modern world. Just fifty years ago, this process was generally seen as a very welcome step that brought with it great social and economic benefits.

Today, we are better able to appreciate that it also had major disadvantages, some of which could prove to be an existential threat to the modern world that it helped to bring about. So what we are seeing here are long-term processes and short-term events, both of which can be interpreted in very different ways.

The changes that marked the big steps of prehistory – represented by the Three Age system of Stone, Bronze and Iron – belong to the more general, long-term category. In common with most other enduring processes, they weren't recognized as such when they actually happened: people didn't wake up one morning to discover they had left the Stone Age and were now living in the Bronze Age. We saw in the Introduction that the Three Age system wasn't conceived until two millennia later, in the early 1800s, when Danish museum curators were looking for ways to catalogue their collections of ancient stone and metal objects. And make no mistake, it was a very important breakthrough, because it provided much-needed structure to our understanding of the remote past. Today, we can show both how and when these important technological and social developments actually happened in the pre-literate world; but at the same time, we should not let them dominate our understanding and appreciation of what it would have been like actually to have lived in prehistory. The spread of farming or the arrival of bronze would certainly have had an effect, but it would not have overshadowed all other aspects of life. So in this Scene I want to consider how two very different groups of people would have thought about the landscape and their roles within it, starting in the Neolithic and then moving into the Bronze Age.

In the modern world, obsessed as it is with wealth and material possessions, 'treasure' is usually portrayed in our newspapers, newsfeeds and television sets as gold. But I clearly remember the moment I discovered my first real treasure and it wasn't gilded and it didn't glisten. I was searching through the loose earth at the bottom of a Neolithic ditch on a site in the flatlands of the lower Welland valley, in north Cambridgeshire. I was about to empty my bucket into the wheelbarrow when something strange caught my eye. It had been raining on and off all morning and in my muddy hand was a small piece of stone, slightly larger than my thumbnail. At first sight I had thought it might have been a struck flint flake, which is why I was looking at it, but a quick glance immediately told me it wasn't flint – an impression that was confirmed by its feel and texture, which was very slightly grainy. Flint is always as smooth as glass. But something else was making me hesitate. If it was just a piece of stone, its colour was very odd. Most of the stone you find in the gravel subsoils of eastern England tends to be either rolled flint pebbles, or weathered fragments of ironstone, or limestone from the hills of the Midlands, further upstream. These pebbles tend to be rather drab greys and browns. But the piece in my hand was a quite distinctive green colour. Then I turned it over and suddenly I knew what I had just found – and had so nearly thrown away.

I was right about it being a struck flake, because you could clearly see where it had been given a sharp whack, probably with another stone. The side that had detached was the rougher one that I had just been feeling with my fingertips. The other face, which had formed the outside of the piece that had been whacked, was absolutely smooth. One glance confirmed what I had guessed already, that this flake had been struck off a polished stone axe. The polishing of stone to form axes, hammers, archers' wrist guards and bracelets was an innovation that appeared in Britain in the early part of the fourth millennium. It probably arrived with other new techniques, such as weaving and pottery-making, when the first farmers came to Britain, at the start of the

Neolithic, just before 4000 BC. A piece struck from a polished stone axe was certainly exciting – and I was delighted with what I had found – but I would hardly have described it as something to 'treasure'. So I put it in a finds bag, which I carefully labelled with all the details of its find-spot, and took it over to the Finds Shed.

Outside the Finds Shed the man in charge, David, was carefully washing pieces of flint and pottery. He then placed them in plastic seed trays (we had bought their entire stock from a local garden centre) and – on those rare occasions when we were blessed with hot summer sun – put them out to dry. I dipped the piece of axe in water and then borrowed David's soft brush to remove some of the clay that was still sticking to it. As soon as it was clean, the colour – a distinctive, almost Lincoln green – stood out strongly, as did the very fine texture of the rock. I had seen many such axes in numerous museum cases right across eastern Britain, from south-east Scotland down to Yorkshire, Lincolnshire and into north Norfolk.[1] Technically, the fine-grained stone is an epidotized greenstone, which is essentially a rock that has been transformed by volcanic heat and pressure.[2] This transformation millions of years ago gave the stone its characteristic colour and firm, even texture, which makes it easy to shape, yet tough and resilient when used as an axe.

The quality of the greenstone and its highly distinctive colour is remarkable, but rather like the spring at Blick Mead,* the source of the rock used to make the distinctive greenstone axes is very unusual, if not unique. We now know the source of the greenstone was in very spectacular scenery high on the side of the Langdale Pikes in the Lake District of north-west England, where a distinctive pointed Pike, the Pike O'Stickle, has been revealed as the quarry where it was mined. The actual quarry was high on the Pike, but it is likely that rocks would also have been taken

---

* Which we described in Scene 4, pages 65–8.

from the scree further down the slope. The Langdale stone 'axe factory', as these identifiable quarries came to be known, was just one of many, with others distributed across western Britain from Scotland, into Wales and south to Cornwall. Further south and east, flint was the major raw material, and although it is harder to identify with absolute precision, quarry sites are known along the chalk downs of the south and, of course, in Norfolk, where some of the shafts and galleries of the Grime's Graves flint mines have been excavated and are open to the public.[3]

I put the words 'axe factory' in quotes because of the way we tend to regard factories today: as places of work alone – and often rather dull, routine, production-line work, at that. But such a description wouldn't have applied to the highly skilled Neolithic craftsmen who first acquired and selected the stone, and then fashioned axes from it. The reason I say this with some confidence is the special way that polished stone and flint axes were treated.[4] Some particularly fine examples, such as a superb jadeite axe from the peat bogs of the Somerset Levels, had clearly been placed in the ground, as offerings.[*]

Polished stone axes are also frequently found in Neolithic graves, but complete axes – and fragments like the one I had the great pleasure of discovering – can often be found at other ceremonial sites, such as the causewayed enclosures of the earlier Neolithic, where I believe it likely they were being sharpened or reshaped. Like many of the activities that took place within these enclosures, this work might have happened during ceremonies centred on clans or families – maybe after somebody had died, or in the autumn when the harvest had been safely gathered in and communities were preparing themselves for the colder months of winter. Polished flint and stone axes would have been the treasured possessions of senior individuals, but they would

---

* See the Sweet Track, Scene 8, pages 155–64.

6.1 The Langdale Pikes, Cumbria. The 'Stickle, site of the Neolithic axe stone quarry, is the sharp peak immediately right of the central valley. The lake in the foreground is Blea Tarn.

also have signified the means of gathering fuel – which in itself would have represented warmth and survival, especially for children and older members of the village. It would be a mistake to think that any object in prehistoric life could be explained in purely functional terms – just as mobile phones today are about far, far more than mere conversation.

The 'trade' in stone axes has been studied in great detail, ever since geologists developed microscopic techniques that could pin down with a fair degree of precision the sources and quarries of the rocks used. This work began before the last war and gathered pace in the 1950s and 1960s. Generally speaking, these studies viewed the axe 'trade' through the eyes of a modern market economist – hence the use of terms like 'trade' and 'axe factories'. Then in the late 1960s there was something of a revolution in prehistory, leading to what at the time was labelled the New Archaeology.[5] In hindsight, of course, it probably wasn't *that* new, because most of the theories it advanced had already been propounded by social anthropologists and others. But it did mark a very welcome shift away from a view of the past that was in many ways very predictable and not very exciting – and was mostly based on economic laws of supply and demand. Social anthropologists have known for a long time that large numbers of successful societies do not follow these principles; such societies perceive life very differently and in a variety of ways, many of which cannot be simply explained.

The human imagination certainly played an important part in shaping the way that objects were perceived in Neolithic societies, which were growing in number and becoming more settled. The houses and communities of the early farmers were far larger and more robustly built than those of their hunter-gatherer forebears – even though, thanks to sites like Star Carr,* we now appreciate that these could be substantial and permanent structures. The new way of life also demanded that the landscape should be partitioned and managed to avoid conflict between different families and communities – and eventually these boundaries would find more permanent expression with the appearance of the first field systems. Farming and a more settled lifestyle allowed – indeed, they required – more objects to accumulate: querns, or corn-grinding stones, baskets and jars for storage, spindles and looms for weaving, mallets and hammers, ploughshares and, of course, axes. These utilitarian objects were accompanied by purely decorative items, such as carved chalk drums, bracelets, earrings and beads. These first farmers also brought with them techniques for controlling heat and for firing clay. The first pottery was quite plain, but soon bowls and jars appeared that were highly decorated and some of the finest axes, such as those made in jade, must surely have been more than just tools.

---

* See Scene 3, pages 54–6.

Again, there is a danger of viewing these ancient objects through modern, classificatory eyes: we see things as either utilitarian (which increasingly means disposable) or decorative/non-functional. This way of appreciating objects lacks the richness and imagination of the past. We can only guess at what the motifs on a Neolithic pottery vessel would have symbolized, but rather like the elaborate patterns on a Scottish Victorian fisherman's knitted sweater, they would have looked very attractive, but would also have proclaimed to other seafarers and members of the fishing community the wearer's identity: his family and his port of origin. Even the most beautiful designs can be about more than just decoration.

The huge increase in the number, quality and variety of 'things', of movable objects, in a Neolithic household allowed people to express new ideas and to enhance older beliefs with new layers of imaginative interpretation.[6] The power of certain places, long seen as sacred or special, could now be re-expressed and recreated in the homes and farms where people actually lived. And this, I am firmly convinced, is one of the main reasons why so many greenstone axes from Langdale (the Pike O'Stickle) are found on the other side of the Pennines, in eastern England, right down to the Lincolnshire/Cambridgeshire border, to the causewayed enclosure at Etton,[*] where I found that small axe fragment. I should add here that it was by no means unique: the site revealed twenty-four pieces of polished stone axes, mostly from Langdale, including two almost complete examples.[7] These distinctive green-tinted axes were fine-grained and were undoubtedly effective as tools, but they were also thought to be endowed with something spiritually special that originated high on a mountain in the Lake District.

---

[*] See Scene 5, page 78.

We can only guess what that spirituality was about. I have visited Langdale and on a cloudy day the Pike O'Stickle can appear to vanish and then return as passing clouds briefly envelop it. It could be seen as being on the edge, the boundary, of the Earth and the sky.[8] Like those earlier caves, it too was liminal.* Again, we can only guess what added power this liminality from so far away gave to those axes from Etton, but they seem to have been used and placed in the ground in a variety of ways, ranging from family-based celebrations and ceremonies to the completion of certain, probably important, tasks. This suggests that their significance was seen as broad, rather than specific, and would help explain why so many were 'exported' from west to east. Again, it is worth briefly pausing to reflect.

Our excavations at Etton were quite substantial, but I am sure we did not find all the axe fragments that were in the ground. The original total may well have been several hundred. And these were just the survivors, as many more would have been washed away and eroded over time. Most would have been taken back home by the people who attended the ceremonial gatherings at Etton. Indeed, it seems very likely that the ceremonial exchange of items such as greenstone axes was one of the activities that would have taken place in causewayed enclosures. In prehistory there was no such thing as a market economy. Produce, objects and livestock were not traded for currency in the way they are today. The exchange of such items was more about the repayment of various long-standing family debts and obligations. Younger households paid tribute to older generations and people of lesser rank gave gifts, or tributes, to those higher up the social tree. An individual could express his or her success by the generosity of their gifts. Wealth was to be displayed and expressed, not

---

* See Scene 2, page 27.

hoarded, Scrooge-fashion. I could imagine the wide eyes of an elderly tribal chieftain and the gasps of the people attending the ceremony, as he was handed a large Langdale axe by a kneeling, but very ambitious young cousin. The fact that the older man would probably have been too arthritic to have used it was of course irrelevant: it was the gesture that counted.

Modern houses have become very compact, functional and comfortable. Digital technology is playing an increased role in the way we inhabit and service them. Lawns and gardens are becoming quite rare and when they do survive, they are often tiny. Vegetable gardens – the last remnant of self-sufficiency in a corporate world dominated by supermarkets – are increasingly unusual. Thank heavens that allotments are making something of a comeback and are no longer mostly inhabited by elderly men tending their late-season chrysanthemums.

The idea of the house as something functional – to be built, bought and sold, with or without a mortgage – has come to dominate our perception of domestic space. I have been as guilty of this as anyone, but I believe archaeologists and prehistorians have put too much effort into thinking about the technology of building.

We have assumed that ancient houses were built like those of today – as weatherproof boxes for living in and raising families. So we have been very anxious to work out where people ate, slept and prepared their meals. It's all about what happened where – and we have discovered a great deal. But revealing where people slept or prepared their food makes little sense if we don't also try to appreciate what it was that motivated them to get out of bed every morning.

I began to appreciate that prehistoric people thought very differently about the buildings they inhabited when I first visited

Orkney, when doing research for my general book on British prehistory, *Britain BC*. To say that my eyes were opened would be an understatement: what I discovered there was to transform my view of prehistory.

I had done as much reading as I could manage before I arrived in Orkney and one recurrent theme had caught my attention: circles and circularity – round barrows and stone rings. Back in the 1990s, new research was suggesting that the circular layout of many British prehistoric round-houses had something to do with the daily cycle of the sun and the passage of the seasons. It was a very general or broad conclusion and I liked it, because as an active farmer it chimed very well with what was then dominating my life: the seasonal recurrence of lambing, hay-making, shearing and regular trips to livestock markets. Days, weeks and months featured a repeated succession of actions that we were striving to do better and more efficiently each time, but the cycle – the ceaseless repetition – was fundamental to everything. And it seemed very reasonable to me to suggest that prehistoric people – who depended far more on farming than we do today – should have tried to enshrine this circularity in the shape of their houses, tombs and sacred places. It was the observed and experienced fact of regular, predictable repetition that provided hope that the process – and with it life itself – would continue into the future. That is why I, in common with most prehistorians, have never seen circular places such as Stonehenge as being mere calendars that record the passing phases of sun and moon. I believe they were about far more fundamental principles that lay behind the passing of time and the very act of living – which I suspect is what they have in common with the great churches and cathedrals of the medieval world.

As the principles underlying the circular places of the prehistoric world were so profound and all-encompassing, it should come as no surprise that they found expression in many, apparently unrelated ways. At first glance it might seem difficult to relate landscape to the passage of time and the cycle of the seasons. After all, landscapes don't change: they remain static. But of course the plants and animals that inhabit them do grow, flourish and die, with the changing of the seasons. Furthermore, the sun and moon rise and set against the horizon, which can be dominated by cliffs, hills and mountains, and these can be used to mark the changing season.

Even in a flat landscape, such as the Fens where I live, you can track changing day length against trees and other landmarks. When I sit down to breakfast every morning – and this especially applies from October to March – I note the rising of the sun as it shifts southwards in autumn, and northwards in spring. It reaches the centre of our rose pergola at the winter solstice (usually 21 December). It then appears to hover around the same spot for at least a week – as if unable to make up its mind – before it very slowly starts the New Year's journey back towards the north. I have never been surprised that prehistoric people regarded the winter solstice with such respect: if the sun did indeed fail to make its spring journey, they knew their crops would fail and life would end. Such fears must have been very real indeed – and shared by everyone.

Like most prehistorians arriving in Orkney, I was thinking about the big issues that were then dominating the subject: how Neolithic communities would have perceived time; the importance of the summer and winter solstices and why certain places in the landscape were regarded as sacred. But what surprised me and stirred my imagination profoundly were the glimpses I obtained there of a rather different, more intimate world, where I could see that big underlying beliefs – their world view, you might call them – did indeed underpin the layout and construction of their sites and buildings, but that there was far more to them than that.

For a start, the simple split between sacred and domestic places that we take for granted today often didn't apply: features from people's homes, such as cupboards and dressers, could also be identified inside communal tombs; conversely, houses frequently included altar-like structures in prominent positions, often facing the front door. The arrangement of sites in the landscape also showed this contrast between general principles and local choice.

Major sites were aligned across the landscape, but their individual layouts could be idiosyncratic. It was as if there were indeed controlling authorities, but these provided guidance rather than rigid authority. Family units clearly played a fundamentally important part in Orcadian prehistoric life, not just in the arrangement of individual sites of all kinds, but probably too in the selection and control of the people in authority, who made the larger, strategic decisions.[9] Tribally based societies are arranged around family ties and obligations and I think we can see this in Orkney, where the stones used to construct prehistoric sites are starting to reveal unexpected new information about the lives of the people who erected them, some five thousand years ago.

Any visitor from mainland Britain to the Orkney Islands will immediately be struck by the rarity of trees. They do survive in some places, but generally only in very sheltered locations. The best evidence indicates that, in warmer post-Ice Age times, trees returned to Orkney and were able to become established in the soils that had gradually accumulated there. However, the return of human communities in post-glacial times led to the felling of trees for fuel and timber. The tree-felling could have involved the pulling-over of the tree and the cutting of the roots. This works well in shallow soils and prevents any subsequent regrowth. Alternatively, trees were cut down and the removal of their canopy allowed winds and rain to get to the soil to both dry and wash it, thereby removing much of its nutrition and bulk. Under such conditions, the re-emergent shoots could not have thrived for very long. Once felled, the tree roots eventually died and were unable to hold what remained of the soils in place, given the heavy rainfall and strong winds from off the Atlantic Ocean that are (still) such a feature of the region. The lack of soil made it harder for new seedlings and saplings to become established and, as a result, most of the tree cover vanished.

The scarcity of wood and timber on Orkney must have caused its growing prehistoric communities many practical problems, especially with regard to fuel for their fires, but people are adaptable: peat can be dried and heather burns well. We also know that the high-tidelines of the islands' many beaches were often strewn with driftwood, much of it originating on the far side of the Atlantic, following winter storms. Firewood was one thing, but good-quality timber for building was a far bigger problem. And here the islands' natural geology came to the rescue in the form of a hard sandstone that occurs widely across the islands, just below the surface. The stone is quite easily split and can be used much like timber to provide shelves and shuttering, although not beams. In chambered tombs it can be worked to form roofs, using a technique known as corbelling, where one slab is placed over another, but jutting out in a stepped pattern, to form a kind of arch or dome. Most British prehistoric houses were built from wood and clay, so that all that survives of their actual structures are stains and marks left by posts that have rotted in the ground. In Orkney, however, the picture is very different. The hard stone with which they are built means that the islands' prehistoric houses have survived in remarkably good condition. Some of the houses feel as if their inhabitants have only just moved out.

In 1999 the outstanding preservation of prehistoric sites on Orkney's largest island, Mainland, was marked by the award of UNESCO World Heritage status.[10] The award was undoubtedly partly the result of a big upsurge in research from the 1980s, when a number of important new sites were discovered. This research also provided fresh information about the sources of the stones used in the great stone circle with the memorable name: the Ring of Brodgar (or Brogar). It's worth noting here that Norse or Viking settlers from Scandinavia had moved into Orkney in considerable numbers by the ninth century AD and they adopted many of the prehistoric sites, giving them Norse names, such as Brodgar. They also left graffiti behind, the best of which are in the tomb at Maes Howe. My personal favourite, carved alongside a sketch of a slavering dog, reads: 'Ingigerth is the most beautiful of all women'.[11] There was plainly far more to Vikings than invasion and conquest alone.

It is striking how many permanent settlements occur close by large tombs and stone circles on Orkney's Mainland. Elsewhere in Britain, the more substantial henges and other shrines are mostly confined to so-called ritual landscapes, which are often positioned in liminal areas away from fields and farms. The standing stones for the Ring of Brodgar were transported to the site from quarries near the settlements occupied by the people who erected and then used them.

It would be a great mistake to assume that life in Neolithic Britain was somehow homogeneous. There were certainly broad similarities in the way that tombs, henges and even houses were arranged, but these were not seen as rigid – to be adhered to at all cost. In Orkney, for example, the divide between houses where people dwelt and the ritual or ceremonial places, where they worshipped, could be remarkably fluid. The best-known houses on Neolithic Orkney are undoubtedly those at Skara Brae, a site that was first revealed, on the western side of Mainland, before the war. Today, it's very well displayed and they've made an excellent replica house that you can enter. I'm normally rather doubtful about attempts to reconstruct the past, as they're often very predictable and usually reflect what the modern guardians of the monuments think their visitors would like. To judge by open days at British medieval houses and castles, people in the Middle Ages spent 90 per cent of their time jousting, which I don't think very likely. The Skara Brae replica successfully avoids all these pitfalls.

However, to get the best impression of what an enclosed prehistoric space would actually have felt like, you could not find anywhere better than the chambered tomb at Maes Howe. I am so grateful that history has allowed this astonishing monument to survive more or less intact. It has had some restoration work done, but that's only to be expected, especially given Orkney's somewhat turbulent history.

Maes Howe (or Maeshowe) was located near the centre of the great cluster of prehistoric sites on Mainland. It is within comfortable walking distance of the two best-known Orcadian stone circles, the standing Stones of Stenness and the Ring of Brodgar – but also to two rather unexpected – and recently discovered – sites, which I'll mention shortly. But first the tomb itself.

Maes Howe belongs to a tradition of tombs known as passage graves, which probably originated in Brittany. It was built in the later Neolithic, shortly after 3000 BC, and consists of a long entrance passage that leads into a central hall with small side cells for burials. In common with the other great passage grave from these islands, Newgrange, in Ireland, the long entrance passage faces south-west, precisely towards the midwinter sunset. On that day, light shines down the 12-metre (40 ft)-long passageway and illuminates the central chamber.

Rather like the cathedrals and churches of our own times, many prehistoric tombs and shrines have complex histories. When you enter Maes Howe, for example, you will notice the huge upright stones at the corners of the main hall – these most probably formed part of a pre-existing stone circle, now built into the tomb. It's also very probable that an earlier Neolithic settlement lies in the ground beneath the floor. The attention to detail evident in all the Orcadian sites, whether houses or shrines, suggests strongly that they were visited and used at regular intervals; people would have been intimately familiar with them. It also suggests a pattern of life that was focused on settlements – and particularly houses. In Orkney, communities remained in the same places from one generation to the next, at a time when populations elsewhere were more mobile. I'm not suggesting that Neolithic farmers migrated around the country, but that farms could, and did, shift from one area to another as land grew wetter, or as soils became depleted. They could have returned to their original locations after a few years, but the basic settlement pattern was essentially flexible. This does not seem to have been the case in Orkney, where the house retained a strong hold on individual families for generations.

The importance of houses in third millennium BC Orkney has been revealed recently by some exciting new discoveries. The first of these was a settlement, now known as Barnhouse, which was discovered by the archaeologist Colin Richards a very short distance from the Stones of Stenness. One might expect a settlement that was placed alongside a contemporary stone circle to include houses alone, since any need for rituals or ceremony could readily be met by nearby Stenness, whose tall stones must have dominated life in the Barnhouse houses twenty-four hours a day. But when the site was excavated in the late 1980s, the dozen or so houses included two that were substantially larger. It would be reasonable to suppose that these might have been used by important people or families – priests or chieftains, perhaps – and there may well be something in this. But the layout of both buildings was rather strange: elongated, with side alcoves that resembled the cells found in chambered tombs, and with two or more hearths.[12] They seemed to have a lot in common with tombs, yet they were clearly buildings and located within the heart of the settlement.

It was believed that Barnhouse was a unique, one-off discovery until 2003, when local farmers reported some unusual stone slabs on a narrow spit of land that separated Lochs Harray and Stenness, a short distance to the north-east of Barnhouse. The site that was then revealed, the Ness of Brodgar, has proved to be one of the most remarkable discoveries in prehistoric Europe. I've had the great pleasure of visiting the excavations twice and on each occasion I found the experience strangely unsettling – but I'll return to that shortly.

In the past, students and archaeological enthusiasts had to rely on newsletters, newspapers and specialist journals if they wanted to follow the progress of an excavation. Of course, thanks to the internet, today things are very different and the Ness of Brodgar has an excellent website that publishes a daily diary.[13] But as with so much digital 'reality', the real thing is so much better. For a start, it's inhabited by real, living people with trowels, buckets, wheelbarrows and kneeling pads. First-time visitors to a dig can find the experience a bit strange and I can sympathize. I remember my first excavation as a student: I was a very, very small cog in a huge machine, but gradually I found my way around both the site and the organization running the dig and within a few weeks I was accepted as part of the team. During this process I learned how to view a series of post-holes, stubby walls and other small features in the ground as actual standing structures. That's the only way to reconstruct how the various posts and doorways fitted together into a coherent pattern. I remember once working out how a group of post-holes formed a possible house – until I realized I'd positioned the hearth directly below the main doorway. My imagined little house wouldn't have stood up long on a cold winter's day. But the ability – the knack – of reconstructing 3D buildings from a few marks or stones below the topsoil is made redundant at such a superbly preserved site as the Ness of Brodgar – or is it?

I've visited hundreds, maybe thousands, of prehistoric excavations, but I have never seen walls, doorways and stonework better preserved than at the Ness of Brodgar.[14] I can remember running my hand down the outside of a house wall in much the same way as I did in 1994 when we were building our own house. In our case, the bricklaying had been done by two professional craftsmen, who had done a superb job, and I couldn't avoid the conclusion that the ancient stonework had also been laid by people who knew exactly what they were doing – and how to do it. This wasn't even slightly amateur work. I remain in no doubt whatsoever about that.

Many of the large houses at the Ness of Brodgar were plainly more than domestic dwellings alone – just like the two larger structures at Barnhouse – but there is little evidence to suggest that this was a restricted settlement, either. It could perhaps be seen as a shrine to domestic life, as there was a lot of food and other debris. Some of the butchered animal bones suggest that these were the remains of huge feasts, involving large numbers of people. The site was occupied relatively late in the Neolithic period, reaching a peak around 3100 BC, before things quietened down, only to start again with renewed vigour when a truly massive communal house – one of the largest in Neolithic Europe – was constructed around 2900 BC.[15] After about 2500 BC it was partially demolished and a heap of stone, gravel and animal bones was carefully erected on top of it – in effect, this was a barrow or burial mound for the building and presumably, too, the souls of those who had used it.

A hundred years later, in 2400 BC, people returned to the house and surrounded it with a vast heap of animal bones. Subsequent analysis has shown this heap to have been carefully structured, with cattle skulls overlain by leg bones from no fewer than 400 individual beasts. Finally, red-deer carcasses were laid on top of the cattle bones. Radiocarbon dates indicate that the animals were all killed at the same time, perhaps in preparation for an enormous feast that would have drawn people to the site from all over Orkney, and probably beyond. The special house had been given a final ceremony that would surely have been fondly remembered for many generations.

The Ness of Brodgar excavations have thrown new light on the sophistication and complexity of life in a Neolithic settlement – and I don't think for one moment that somehow Orkney was a 'one-off'. The Orkney Islands played a major role in developing the concepts and ideas behind Neolithic religious beliefs, but they would have been but one of several major centres. Other centres we know about include Stonehenge and Avebury in Wiltshire and along the Thames valley; they are also found in parts of Yorkshire, Cumbria and south-western Scotland – all areas that have revealed large and complex ritual landscapes.[*] There is a tendency to view the prehistoric past as somehow inferior to the modern world – to believe that we have 'progressed' beyond such superstitious beliefs. I disagree profoundly with this rather patronizing view of our ancestors. When you study the intricacies of the seemingly endless reconstructions, rebuildings and reuses of Neolithic shrines, you can only come to the conclusion that they were based on a widely held world view that had remained remarkably stable for at least a millennium and a half – and maybe slightly longer.

---

[*] See Scene 4, page 59.

Scene 7

Axes and Identities: Bronze Age Individuality and Family Ties (2500–900 BC)

Holme-next-the-Sea – Stonehenge

Archaeology is about people in the past: how they lived, how they worked, how they relaxed and how they died. They have been the focus of all the research of my professional life and I have often felt humbled by the daunting task that faced me. Whatever else I might do, I cannot let them down. But it hasn't always been a simple process of revelation: my life has often interwoven with theirs – as if they have somehow become a part of my family. And just like real people in real families, they can appear to be obtuse, awkward and even irritating. I say 'appear' because of course it isn't *they* who irritate, but the nature of the evidence they have left behind them, which can often seem frustratingly inadequate. Being human, one tends to take these things personally – or at least I do.

Research rarely happens in a single, breakthrough moment. In archaeology, the basic research often takes the form of an excavation, which one then writes up and publishes, first in a series of short interim reports (today these often take the form of blogs), followed by a fully detailed final report. I've written my fair share of massive final reports and I have to confess that none of them have proved to be even slightly final. Many have triggered healthy academic debate, which I warmly welcome, and of course research in the area continues and new discoveries throw new – and often very unexpected – light on previous research.

This continuing process of debate, both in print and behind the scenes, means that I am constantly returning to old digs. I don't do this in a spirit of regret – did we miss something in that trench or that pit? – but because I'm still curious about the prehistoric people we were investigating; and the excavations I took part in remain my most vivid route into their lives. The strange timber circle on the Norfolk coast at Holme-next-the-Sea, which is widely known today as Seahenge, was just such a site.* Indeed, it has never been far from my thoughts.

Seahenge was an unusual site for me, because I was busy with other projects at the time and was only involved in the dig part-time. This gave me a chance to observe what was happening in a fairly objective way. If you're not on site every day, you can see progress much more clearly: rather like a speeded-up film. Seahenge consisted of a small circle of some fifty-five oak posts set around an upside-down oak tree, whose branch-like roots may well have been used to support a dead body, back in the Early Bronze Age, just before 2000 BC. As the dig unfolded, I began to realize just how much detail the extraordinarily fine preservation of the wood was going to reveal.

Shortly before the Seahenge excavations, Maisie and I had been building our house and farm. Now, when I say 'building', in actual fact most of the hard, skilled work was done by carpenters, bricklayers and other craftsmen. And there weren't many people involved in the work: one carpenter and his assistant did the timber framework. A few weeks later they

---

* It is briefly mentioned in the Introduction, page xxiv.

were joined by a bricklayer and his assistant and then, towards the completion of the project and long after the carpenters had gone, a joiner and his assistant started erecting interior features such as bookshelves, banisters and the main staircase. Rather to my surprise, these craftsmen didn't have a large repertory of tools: each woodworker had a favourite handsaw, and various mallets and hammers plus electric saws, planes, chisels, sanders and so forth. Yet when Maisie started to examine the tool marks on the Seahenge timbers, she eventually concluded that around fifty different axe-heads had been used – and possibly as many as fifty-nine. The uncertainty arose from the probability that the cutting edges of some axes had been altered during work through vigorous sharpening. Bronze, being much softer than iron, loses its edge quite rapidly and needs constant sharpening.

In the light of my own experience with house-building, I had rather expected her to reveal that Seahenge had been constructed by, say, six or maybe ten different axes. Bear in mind that around 2000 BC bronze was still a relatively new material and was by no means as common as it was to become during the next few centuries. In other words, bronze tools would still have been relatively costly and most people could not have afforded more than one axe. In modern terms, an axe would have cost the equivalent of, say, a car. They would have been well looked after.

The large number of axe cutting-edge profiles that Maisie was revealing on the surfaces and cut-ends of the Seahenge timbers could only be explained in two ways: either that bronze was cheaper and far more widely available than we used to think, or that many more people had been present at the construction of the monument than would have been strictly necessary had it just been a routine construction job. While I think that bronze may well turn out to have been slightly more common in Britain than we formerly believed, there is no evidence from any other sites that its introduction was dramatically sudden and in such high quantities. There is now considerable evidence to suggest that pure copper had been arriving in Britain for perhaps two to three centuries,[*] between 2500 and 2200 BC, before the first bronze appears on the scene.[1] Again, this would suggest that the introduction of bronze tools and weapons was a gradual process.

I'm in little doubt that the large number of marks made by different axes that were revealed on the various timbers of Seahenge provide direct evidence that many people were involved in the shrine's construction. They also support the suggestion that in prehistoric times, shrines and other sacred places were not built to be used in the way that modern and, to a lesser extent, medieval buildings were. Today, we erect a building, it passes various structural and health and safety examinations, and then it is deemed to be ready for use by the general public. Construction and use are two quite distinct and separate processes.

But there is now increasing evidence that this clear-cut distinction never applied in prehistory. In fact, the opposite was true and the construction or modification of a henge or some other similar shrine would actually have been an integral part *of* its use. This would suggest that the work was conducted in ways that were considered appropriate both for the shrine and for the ceremony being undertaken. And again, this shows that we must be careful about imposing our own ideas on people in the distant past. Today, for example, we Britons see death as something sad and sombre; there is nothing joyous or celebratory about it at all. Admittedly, we're not quite as gloomy as middle-class Victorians with their almost legally binding rules of mourning: newly bereaved widows, for example, were expected to wear full mourning dress for two years.[2]

But many societies have long taken an altogether different view. Instead, the emphasis is placed on the achievements in the

---

[*] This short period is sometimes called the Chalcolithic, or Copper Age.

life of the departed person and mourners at the funeral celebrate their passing into a new and better place. Frequently, such rites of passage are marked by dancing and feasting, although, of course, the nearest and dearest are given time and space to grieve – but this is often quite private. The origins of traditional jazz, for example, lie in the joyous return of New Orleans funeral processions from the cemetery. Songs like 'Didn't He Ramble' imagine that the dead man is now enjoying himself as much in death as he did in life.[3] Personally, I rather prefer this way of celebrating a person's life.

The different ways that the timbers at Seahenge were actually felled, transported and shaped provide us with hints that the large number of people involved in the construction of the monument did not work haphazardly. We must remember that shrines like this were part of a widespread pan-European tradition and that customs surrounding their erection and construction would have been quite well established. But again, I can see no reason to suppose that the work was carried out in gloomy, respectful silence; moving large timbers, such as the central oak tree, would have required huge efforts, and such tasks are far better performed by a group of people who are rejoicing, like the bands returning from the cemeteries in New Orleans. Much of the pottery buried in graves of this period consists of highly decorated drinking cups that may well have contained alcoholic beverages – versions of mead or ales. In many tribal societies the consumption of alcohol is, and was, confined to religious and ceremonial occasions, such as the interment of bodies, the construction of tombs and during feasts on special days.

The different axe marks at Seahenge suggest that the trees were felled, split and finished by different groups of people.[4] Eighteen different axe marks suggest that eighteen separate people worked on felling the trees used in the construction of the monument, which numbered between fifteen and twenty.[5]

7.1 The timbers of the Holme-next-the-Sea, Norfolk, timber circle during excavation. The site, dubbed 'Seahenge' by the press, featured a circle of fifty-five vertical oak timbers surrounding an upside-down oak tree, whose roots are cloaked with seaweed (in front of the bending figure).

The axe marks suggest that each tree was felled by two people chopping from opposite directions. Each pair of people felled one or, at most, two trees. The upper trunks of the trees were cut square by another twenty-three people. Lower branches were cut off and trimmed back to the trunks by a further group of ten people. This work almost certainly took place at some distance from the coastal plain, where Seahenge was eventually located, because the growth rings of the trees suggest they came from higher, well-drained land – maybe 5–8 kilometres (3–5 miles) from the foreshore. The massive central oak tree, which weighed about 2½ tons, had been dragged there, as one side showed clear signs of wear and a honeysuckle rope was found attached to two towing-holes. There was no evidence (in the form of surviving twigs and leaves) that the upper branches had been removed on the foreshore. So this work probably happened on the felling site, where the trees were reduced to bare trunks.

It is interesting that the felled tree stump was removed from the ground by cutting through the roots and toppling it over – probably helped by ropes and long levers. This is one of the techniques of prehistoric tree-felling that might help to explain how the woodlands of Orkney were removed without the growth of renewed coppice shoots.* It would also have been simpler to topple the stumps over, given the thinner topsoil and the hard, rocky subsoil.

Subsequent splitting and dressing of the timbers took place close by the monument. Taken together, the axe marks suggest that a minimum of fifty-one people worked on the preparation of the Seahenge timbers. In general, larger, wider-bladed axes were used for felling and smaller ones for trimming. But this wasn't a hard and fast rule: smaller axes were also used for felling. This is important, because it suggests that it wasn't so much the size of the axe that determined how it was used. Maybe fit young men owned the larger axes, the smaller ones belonging to older, more experienced woodworkers. But the overall pattern of axe use suggests with some clarity that each individual owned a single axe. This would also fit with what we know about the value of the earliest metal tools. Given such a clear pattern of use and possession, it would not be unreasonable to suggest that particular axes could become identified with individual people.[6] The complex patterns on the highly decorated so-called Beaker pots that accompanied the people who introduced metalworking to Britain from the continent are believed by many specialists to have represented and identified individuals and possibly their

---

* See Scene 6, and the introduction to the Orkney Islands, pages 113–14.

tribal or family ties, too. Clearly, identity mattered: everyone would have had names, although, of course, prehistory hasn't recorded them.

I am in little doubt that the experience of attending a funeral ceremony at Seahenge four thousand years ago would have been a very emotional one. Laying aside the fact that ideas surrounding death would have been subject to more vivid hopes, myths and fears than most modern people have ever experienced, the ceremonies involved were also quite prolonged. As we will shortly discover, travel – perhaps journeying would be a better word – also played an important role. These journeys are believed to have been physical expressions of the departed soul's voyage from this world to the next. It has recently been suggested that wood might have symbolized the world we live in and stone the permanent, everlasting realm of the ancestors. These notions aren't idle speculation, however: they are based on long-held beliefs that are still current in Madagascar – and while nobody is proposing any links between the southern Indian Ocean today and Britain in the Bronze Age, they suggest a form of symbolism that is known to have had enduring appeal for many people.[7] If one accepts this view of the soul's journey after death, then the Seahenge tree and timber circle marks the end of life and the start of the next stage, which would probably have been beneath an earth-covered barrow nearby – stone being rare in north Norfolk.

So let us take this idea, that the soul's journey or procession was framed in terms of the transition from wood to stone, a little further. At Stonehenge, for example, there is mounting evidence that ceremonial journeys were quite complex, starting at timber circles at the great henges of Durrington Walls and Woodhenge; then down a ceremonial avenue to the River Avon; from there onto a boat, which made the difficult journey downstream to the newly discovered Bluestonehenge and then, finally, by land along the great Avenue to Stonehenge itself. So the river and the boat represent death and the return to land at Bluestonehenge is the start of the afterlife. It was a journey that couldn't conceivably have been done in less than a full day – and would probably have taken longer.

We know that Seahenge was built in the spring of 2049 BC; archaeologists believe the site was probably used just once. The only problem with the single-use theory is that the sea could have removed evidence for subsequent reuse. However, even if that had happened, since the timbers were untreated and were positioned in such an exposed environment, they could not possibly have survived above ground for more than a few decades. In terms of Stonehenge's far longer chronology, Seahenge would fit comfortably within Stonehenge Stage 4 (c. 2100–1700 BC), which was a time when the stones within the main circle were being altered and added to. By this period, the concept of the ceremonial journey was already almost a millennium old and was well understood. It could have been adapted to suit individual circumstances – just as, very much later, the small and often restricted sites of nonconformist chapels meant that they often depart from the traditional strict east–west alignment of Christian churches.

I want now to dispel some of the impressions given by modern-day Druids and other neo-pagan groups at places like Stonehenge during the midsummer solstice. These modern rites either reflect (in the case of Druids) the Church of England rituals of the nineteenth century or (for the neo-pagans) a rather hippy, Woodstock-meets-Glastonbury view of the past.[8] For a start, there is increasing evidence that in common with the chamber tombs of Neolithic times, more than a millennium previously, greater emphasis at many ceremonial sites was placed on rituals associated with the mid*winter* solstice (21 December). This was when large numbers of pigs were slaughtered – presumably for lavish feasts. As we saw earlier in Scotland, the shorter days and deep darkness of midwinter have a 'magic' all of their own and doubtless help to explain why Christmas (the Christian version of the earlier solsticial celebrations) has survived for so long in western societies, where religion has otherwise been in steady decline.

I have often written about the extraordinary smell of tannin on the air when I first entered the completed reconstruction of the Seahenge timber enclosure, while we were filming a television documentary for *Time Team*. Oak bark is rich in tannic acid, which is formed by insects in the bark – traditionally, oak bark was used in the tanning of leather. But the smell I encountered when I entered the circle has stayed with me ever since. It was so strong: far, far stronger than the incense burned during a Roman Catholic church service. It actually made my eyes run and gave me the impression that the skin on my face was tightening or shrinking.

One must imagine such a strong smell during the ceremonies, compounded no doubt by darkness, fire and the sound of rhythmical drumming. Shamans,* who we know had been active in Britain since before 9000 BC, would have been present and many of the congregation would have been very tired and muddy after dragging the timbers to the dunes behind the foreshore, where the shrine was erected.[9] They may even have been rather tipsy, following the circulation of ceremonial beakers filled with beer or mead. There is little evidence that alcohol was consumed socially, or at meals, in the Neolithic or Bronze Age; instead, it was probably confined to religious or shamanistic ceremonies.

---

* The old term was 'witch doctor': essentially holy men and women who often performed extreme dances and were used to cure diseases or ease a soul's journey into the next world.

The reality of prehistoric religion is likely to have been often more about emotional catharsis and the celebration of family and community identities than the observation of rituals for their own sake. Past religions were complex and we can best understand them not just by reading books or watching filmed re-enactments but also by visiting the places where the ceremonies happened. This certainly applies to sites like Stonehenge or Avebury, but Seahenge had to be excavated before it was destroyed by the sea. Happily, it has now been preserved (a complex process that took a very long time) and the timbers, including the huge central oak, are now on display in King's Lynn Museum, where their original foreshore location has been accurately yet imaginatively recreated. You need to stand beneath the outstretched roots of that preserved central tree to appreciate its size and presence. It's a cliché, but in this case it's a valid one: Seahenge has to be seen to be believed. No book or picture can ever do it justice.

The concept of the body or soul's journey into the next world, as exemplified by the move from wood to stone at Stonehenge, would still have been capable of expression in places like the north Norfolk coast, where large rocks or stones are completely absent. It would have been the journey – and what it represented – that mattered.

The moving of the great central tree and the other smaller timbers would have been an essential part of the ceremony. The process of moving rocks from quarries to a distant ceremonial place or landscape has been closely studied and is now well understood; thanks to modern geology, and the fact that we have the ability to identify the origin of certain rocks with great precision, it can also be accurately mapped. Some of the best examples can be found in the stone circles of Orkney* and the

---

* See Scene 6, page 115.

western isles of Scotland.[10] The area of damp 'backswamp' behind the coastal dunes at Holme-next-the-Sea would have been seen as being at the sea-side edge of habitable ground: very much a case of 'liminality' and, as such, an appropriate location for a site like Seahenge.[*]

Once the circle of timbers and the inverted central oak tree had been set in place, the funeral rites could begin. The body would have been carried into the shrine through the single narrow entranceway. It was probably then ceremoniously placed on top of the inverted tree roots, which formed an outstretched, hand-like surface. Some of the pagan demonstrators who objected to us removing the site from destruction by the sea would sit, joke and sing on the precise spot within the oak tree's roots where the body would have rested in prehistory.[11] Although we were portrayed by the demonstrators as the insensitive ones, none of the archaeologists working on the dig thought this either funny or clever: that oak tree was the sacred centre of the shrine and we all instinctively respected it as such. It was as if somebody had sat on the altar of a Christian church.

Following the ceremony, the narrow entranceway of the timber circle was blocked off and the body was allowed to lie in peace, while scavenging birds such as kites and buzzards removed its flesh. The loose bones would probably then have been removed and interred within a hollowed-out oak coffin in the contemporary barrow (burial mound), known as Seahenge 2, alongside the timber circle. We know that there would have been a wooden coffin within the burial mound because we found one of the distinctive wooden coffin-bearers, which was still in place, near the centre of where the mound would originally have stood. We also know from tree-ring dates that the two

---

[*] I discussed liminality when referring to the 'Red Lady' of Paviland cave, in Scene 2, page 27.

sites were constructed at precisely the same time, in the spring of the year 2049 BC. Both the Seahenge sites – the timber circle and the barrow – are relatively small and are similar in many respects to hundreds – maybe even thousands – of other shrines and burial mounds known from Bronze Age Britain. Many of these have been ploughed flat and today only survive below the soil, where they can be spotted from the air as distinctive dark marks, labelled 'ring-ditches' by archaeologists, in growing cereal crops. Seahenge has revealed some extraordinarily vivid details that throw much light on the way people would have experienced the ceremonies that took place there. But do these insights have any relevance for major shrines such as Stonehenge? Can wood throw light on stone? Rather surprisingly, the answer is yes – and the other way round, too: stone can throw light on wood. It is time to head west, to Salisbury Plain.

My first visit to Stonehenge took place when I was a student at Cambridge. I think it was during my first year (1964/5) and I'm fairly sure it was a coach trip organized by the Department of Archaeology, but that's all I can recall about the day, because everything was eclipsed by the moment we walked up to and then entered the Stones. Maybe one of the lecturers was telling us about the various dates and phases of construction; if so, I'm afraid I must have wandered off – something I often found myself doing as a student. I remember standing outside the outer Sarsen Circle and being completely bowled over by the size and scale of everything. And those lintels: we had been told how they fitted onto the uprights with stone variants of a carpenter's mortise and tenon joint, but somehow their sheer weight and mass had escaped me. How on earth did they raise them so high? I moved closer, still staring intently upwards, and then I caught a glimpse of one of the sarsen Trilithons – those three-stone structures of two uprights and a lintel that were arranged in a horseshoe shape within the Sarsen Circle. I hadn't appreciated that they were significantly larger than the massive stones of the outer circle and I think it was then that I started to wonder at the motivation that drove people to create Stonehenge. And it's something I've been wondering about ever since.

Major ceremonies in national or family life can be made more memorable by personal involvement. Today, great events such as a coronation or a royal anniversary are shared either by attending the ceremony itself or by watching it on screen. The private celebration usually happens afterwards in a family gathering or street party. At a much smaller scale, something like a wedding, funeral or baptism will take place in church, followed by a family get-together with tea, drinks or whatever. Archaeological evidence for the form and structure of the ceremonies is provided by the churches and shrines where they took place – and in more recent times, memorials and gravestones record specific events. But in prehistory it is much harder to work out how often ceremonies took place and what they might have involved. So it is assumed that huge sites like Stonehenge and Avebury were host to major events attended by thousands of people from a large area of Britain. This may well have been the case, but was there another, perhaps more personal, side to these great monuments?

I remember first being struck by this rather different use of great structures when I attended a neighbouring farmer's wedding in the choir of Ely Cathedral. My friend's wife's family were also farmers in Ely and I recall the wonderfully welcoming and, yes, rural atmosphere of the church service and the reception afterwards. When I say rural, I don't mean there was anything even slightly crude or make-do about the event: there wasn't so much as a hint of baler twine or straw anywhere. But there is something about the way country people talk: their voices are slightly louder than you hear in towns and they carry further, too. While the congregation were waiting for the bride's arrival you could clearly hear what people were discussing, albeit in respectfully hushed voices, across the wide aisle and pews on the other side of the choir. Rural people also tend to be less reserved and more demonstrative, especially when they're among friends and relations. So there were frequent smiles of recognition, nods of greeting and the occasional restrained wave. I won't say the place had a pub atmosphere, because that would be a huge exaggeration, but there was a warmth and friendliness that you would not necessarily expect to encounter in such awe-inspiring, elevated surroundings as Ely Cathedral.

I have always enjoyed the lead-up to a formal church wedding: the ushers politely showing you to your seats: 'Are you with the bride or the groom?' From the outside, everything appears informal, but of course it isn't: it's highly structured and has been carefully planned for weeks in advance. As I sat in my pew listening to the organ, beautifully played, I need hardly add, I was thinking how little things actually change: my great-great-grandparents could have been sitting alongside us perfectly happily and we would all have known what to do at the bride and groom's arrival. Yet within their lifetimes, this part of Ely Cathedral had been rescued from severe dereliction, neglect and decay. Architectural historians can be quite snotty about 'the Victorians' and George Gilbert Scott often comes in for criticism, but his work (from 1850) in and around the choir at Ely is little short of inspired. It is restoration, but it is creation too.

That lovely wedding at Ely made me realize that the rites, rituals and ceremonies could be even more enduring than the stone structures built to hold them. I reflected further: did this just say something about the enduring power of religious belief, or was there more to it than that? I had gained a great deal from the service. I found it genuinely inspirational: it lifted my spirits at a time when I was having various medical problems that were – how can I put it? – lowering my morale. I was not looking forward to the next decade of my life and this wedding helped to point me in a new and better direction. So what gave the service in the great cathedral, and the celebrations that followed it, these restorative, life-enhancing qualities?

A few years later I was at the funeral of a close childhood friend and cousin. We had grown up together in rural north Hertfordshire. I would cycle out to his father's farm about five miles from our house and we would get up to all sorts of pranks together. I remember once blasting the lid off a milk churn using an explosive mixture of sodium chlorate weedkiller* and sugar. The vanishing lid (which we never discovered) left a neat round hole in the barn's loose slate roof.

The church service had finished and a small group of close friends and family were standing around Teddy's grave for the final blessing. When the vicar finished, I bid him farewell with a handful of earth from the heap left by the sexton on the graveside, which I sprinkled onto his coffin, deep in the grave. Instinctively, I found I was checking the soil and pebbles in my hand for flint tools. Immediately I reprimanded myself: how could I be so insensitive? Then I imagined Teddy's smile, six feet below me: 'You'll never change, Francis.' And the truth slowly dawned. Weddings and funerals are about people's lives, but not just the people who are the focus of attention: the bride, the groom or the dear departed. We are all part of such events. Rites of passage have an enduring appeal that transcends the mere passage of time. They epitomize what it means to be human. At a fundamental level, religion becomes irrelevant: I am a non-believer; Teddy was a vicar. And it feels like we are still as close as ever we were, when he was alive and well. Sleep well, old friend.

---

* Its use is now banned.

*

Every midsummer solstice, Stonehenge appears in the news and be-robed Druids worship and process up and down. That's the modern interpretation of the site's reason for existing. But what can serious archaeological research reveal? Is there any evidence that there would have been smaller-scale, family-based ceremonies, more akin to those two services, the wedding and the funeral, that made such a lasting impression on me?

The main revelation has undoubtedly been the long journey from wood to stone, along the River Avon, via Bluestonehenge to Stonehenge itself.[12] This could indeed have been a ceremonial route for grand occasions, but if that were the case I think people would have had problems navigating the River Avon in larger boats, simply because it is too fast-flowing and in places quite shallow. If large numbers were involved, any procession would probably have started at Bluestonehenge, headed along the Avenue and thence to Stonehenge. I can imagine family funerals taking the longer route, with the body being transported in a canoe-like boat. Most of these would probably have been smaller gatherings and, again, many people would have joined the corpse for the procession along the Avenue. This, at least, was what might have happened when Stonehenge had become a developed, major Bronze Age shrine, after about 2500 BC. Before that, things were rather different.

It isn't widely acknowledged, but Stonehenge is host to one of the largest cremation cemeteries in Neolithic Europe.[13] We know of sixty-three small pits containing cremations, and we suspect there may originally have been as many as 150 (later activity on the site would have disturbed or destroyed them). Radiocarbon dates show they were placed in the ground at various times between 3300 and 2300 BC – and almost certainly on numerous, separate occasions. So far, both the land within the circular ditch that surrounds the Stones and the landscape immediately outside has yet to produce good evidence for funeral pyres, which have to be large in order to cremate a human body.* This usually means that they char the ground red and permanently alter the geophysical properties of the soil, which can readily be detected from the surface. So it seems most likely that the bodies were cremated on pyres constructed near where they lived and their ashes were then taken to Stonehenge for burial. It's worth remembering, however, that the ditch surrounding the Stones is several centuries earlier. In other words, the big stones weren't there and the site would have resembled a simple circular ditched enclosure.

Circular ditched enclosures were quite widely used for the burial of cremated bones during the Neolithic.[14] Most of these occur in south-western England, although others are known in East Anglia, Yorkshire, the Scottish borders and north Wales. We know that the population of Britain was rising at the time and yet these enclosures rarely include more than fifty cremations – indeed, Stonehenge is by far the largest. This would suggest that most ordinary people were buried nearer to home and that only an elite would have been given final resting places within the special enclosures.

If we can assume that there were no breaks in the use of Stonehenge as a major ceremonial centre – and as research continues, this seems increasingly probable – then we can probably also assume that its role as a place for funerals continued too. Today, the archaeological map of prehistoric Britain is notable for the large numbers of round barrows that often occur along the tops of hills, where they can be clearly seen against the sky behind. They are also found in huge barrow cemeteries in river valleys and in the ritual landscapes, which grew up in landscapes that had long been regarded as sacred. The

---

* See Scene 5, page 92.

7.2 Three of the barrows on the King Barrow Ridge, overlooking Stonehenge from the north-east.

7.3 The view of Stonehenge from the King Barrow Ridge.

southern part of Salisbury Plain, around Stonehenge and Blick Mead, was just such a landscape and it soon accumulated the greatest concentration in Britain of Bronze Age round barrows.

Round barrows differed from the earlier traditions of long barrows and passage graves in being smaller, and there is also no evidence that bodies were removed once they had been buried. The tradition began sometime around 2300 BC and quite rapidly grew in popularity. In most instances, a new barrow was located alongside others – probably of family members – and would have been built to cover what is known as the primary burial, at the centre. Secondary burials, which sometimes included cremations, were often inserted into the original mound covering the primary burial, or else into enlargements of the mound. If the barrow has not been plough-damaged the secondary burials can be quite numerous, but they probably all belonged to members of the same clan or family.

The sheer number of barrows surrounding Stonehenge can best be appreciated by walking through the landscape on a spring or autumn day, when the air is clear and dry and before the crops become too high. Most of the hundreds of tourists will be trudging around Stonehenge and you can see them, and of course get some superb views of the Stones, from the groups of barrows in the surrounding landscape. When you have walked through them, you will be in absolutely no doubt whatsoever that they were carefully positioned both to see and be seen from the Stones. My personal favourites (which are readily accessible from the eastbound carriageway of the A303) are the large barrows arranged along the King Barrow Ridge.

This careful placing of the barrows around Stonehenge strongly suggests that there was a close ideological link between the two and I don't think it's stretching credulity even slightly to suggest that the link was Death. Bodies or cremated bones were transported to Stonehenge for a funeral service, before being

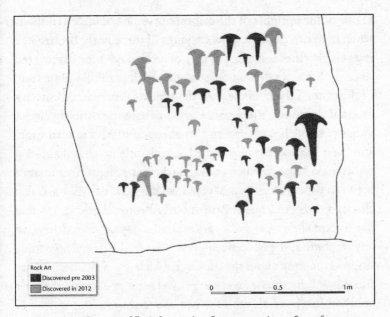

Rock Art
■ Discovered pre 2003
■ Discovered in 2012

0   0.5   1m

7.4 Carvings of Early Bronze Age flat axes on the surface of Stone 4 of the Sarsen Circle, at Stonehenge. More than half of the carvings were revealed in a laser scan carried out in 2012.

taken on another, much shorter ceremonial journey to their eventual place of permanent burial, within one of the barrows visible in the middle distance. I suspect that this final journey was also the most intimate and private one, attended by close members of the family alone.

Throughout most of the twentieth century, speculation about the ceremonies at Stonehenge centred around solar and other alignments and emphasis was placed on larger public gatherings, with huge congregations being confined to the area outside the encircling ditch and bank. The ground within the Stones was seen as a Holy-of-Holies where secret rituals took place that could only be glimpsed by the crowds standing outside. Then at about five o'clock on the afternoon of 10 July 1953, something very remarkable happened. Professor Richard Atkinson was looking at one of the uprights of the central horseshoe of huge Trilithons when he spotted the shallow carvings of three Early Bronze Age daggers. Further carvings, mostly of axes, have been discovered since, on Stone 53 and on other stones, both of the Trilithons and of the outer Sarsen Circle.[15] At the time of Professor Atkinson's original discovery, there was a great debate in scholarly circles about possible links between Stonehenge and Mycenaean Crete and these shallow carvings were triumphantly produced as being positive evidence for such contacts (there is a slight resemblance between the carvings and Mycenaean daggers, but they are also closely similar to known British Early Bronze Age daggers and flat axes). Then new radiocarbon dates demonstrated beyond any doubt that the Mycenaean link was a red herring. So people stopped thinking about the carvings, which was a shame, because subsequent discoveries were to prove far more exciting than yet another dubious link with the Mediterranean world.

Shallow carvings on the surface of rocks are an ideal subject for a laser scan and one was recently carried out at Stonehenge for English Heritage.[16] It was published in 2012 and revealed no fewer than seventy-five new axe-head carvings, which, added to what was already known, gives a grand total of 115 – plus, of course, the three dagger carvings originally discovered by Professor Atkinson. All the axe-heads belong to a distinctive type, known as flat axes, which can be closely matched with known examples from Early Bronze Age graves dating from about 1750 to 1500 BC, when Stonehenge seems quite rapidly to have gone out of use.

When I first read about the Stonehenge axe and dagger carvings, I simply assumed that they were Bronze Age graffiti – and thought no more about it. Somewhat later, I met somebody who had studied graffiti in medieval churches and this opened my eyes to their potential. There are two aspects of the carvings that are intriguing. The first is that none have ever been observed on the parts of the uprights that have always been below ground. This strongly suggests that the carvings were executed *after* the stones had been erected. The second is that no attempt seems to have been made to standardize any of them. Had they simply been used to record that a funeral or other ceremony had taken place, one might have expected the axes to have become simplified in some way. But that never happened. This would suggest that the precise shape of the individual axe-head was important. And why? Because in the eyes and minds of the people attending the ceremonies, that axe carving represented a particular person. Most probably the axe was a token of the person (being an axe or a dagger, this was probably a man*) whose body was carried to Stonehenge before being taken out to one of the barrows on the skyline for final burial.

So if particular axes could have been identified with certain individuals, could not a drawing, outline or carving of them not be seen as the equivalent, say, of a medieval coat of arms? Individual knights in the Middle Ages displayed their coats of arms prominently, often on their shields. It was as if they were displaying a poster with their name emblazoned across it. Most ordinary foot soldiers were illiterate, but they soon learned to remember the coats of arms of the leading generals, both friendly and foe. You didn't want to kill a friend. So could axes have been seen as something similar, back in the Bronze Age?

At this point we might recall what we observed at Seahenge. People would have been familiar with the minutiae of axes, because they played an important part in their lives. Think of cars in the modern world: James Bond is famous for his Aston Martin, but we all know the cars our friends drive, right down to the dents and bashes they can accumulate in supermarket car parks. Today, mobile phones are becoming symbols of personal

---

* In Bronze Age graves, axes and daggers tend to be buried with men.

identity; people choose unusual colours, or decorate them with sparkly covers. And of course the workings of the phone – the background 'wallpaper', the ringtone and alarms – are easily changed to suit individual preferences. If individual people in the Early Bronze Age became identified with a particular axe, as seems quite likely from the Seahenge axe marks, then it is not stretching credulity too far to suggest that they could also have become a symbol of an individual's identity – like those coats of arms in the Middle Ages, which, just like the carvings at Stonehenge, often included axes and daggers.[17]

And that leaves me with a final thought. The people who made the axe carving most probably knew the man who was being buried. And for many I suspect it would have been an intensely personal moment, rather like the sad time I sprinkled soil on my close friend's coffin. I also find it intriguing that all the axe-heads at Stonehenge are carved with their crescentic blades pointing skywards – in real life, they would mostly have been swung downwards; in archaeological reports they are always illustrated blade-down. Of course, I have absolutely no evidence to support me, but I sometimes find myself speculating that the upwards direction would have symbolized hope for the future: onwards and upwards; that the dead man had made the long journey and was now in a better place.

Scene 8

Getting About: On Land (4000–2000 BC)

The Amesbury Archer – The Sweet Track

Recent research in both British and European prehistory has clearly demonstrated that travel, and much of it long-distance, was a regular feature of life among early farming societies. There is also increasing evidence that, even earlier, people in hunter-gatherer communities moved around the landscape with far greater freedom than was once believed. Visions of vast tracts of impassable, impenetrably dense forests where nobody dared go are best reserved for fairy tales and fantasy fiction. The reality was very different: people needed to get about in order to stay in touch with relatives, to track game, seek markets for their farm produce or just to see the world.

The urge to travel, which I certainly felt in my twenties, was never just a modern phenomenon; indeed, in the seventeenth and eighteenth centuries, the Grand Tour through Europe became an integral part of being a young man from a well-off, cultured background. In the early days of antiquarianism and the development of archaeology, it was to play a significant part in raising people's awareness of the rich diversity of past civilizations.[1] There is a tendency to assume that in prehistory people didn't travel and consequently had restricted imaginations.

The truth is that thinkers and creators have always thought 'outside the box' – a process that in many, but not all, cases would have been greatly assisted by actual physical movement.

It is so difficult to remove modern prejudices, biases and assumptions from one's attempts to recreate life in the past, but it's essential that we make the effort to do this, because that is the way we will learn more about ourselves. Given this persistent modern perspective, prehistorians in the recent past have tended to view periods of major change in essentially nationalistic terms – visions that reflect the turbulent history of European states in the nineteenth and twentieth centuries. So we have waves of Celtic migrants sweeping across western Europe from the Alpine region and so-called Belgic invaders attacking southern Britain in the centuries prior to the Roman conquest. Sweeping mass migrations are also used to explain the arrival of farming and of metalworking – a process that is linked to the 'Beaker People'. Many prehistorians believed that at the same time that these migrations were happening, Europe was seeing the rise of more hierarchical societies with powerful 'Big Men' leaders. And it doesn't take a huge leap of imagination to link the migrations to the emerging Big Men and suddenly you have a vision of the past that quite neatly mirrors recent history – and therefore finds wide public acceptance.

The principal problem with many of these explanations is that they imply wholesale population displacement. My experience, however, and I write as somebody who has devoted his professional life to quite localized landscape archaeology, is that the actual evidence in the ground suggests continuity. Farms, fields, settlements and boundaries remain remarkably persistent across the centuries, and even the millennia. So does this mean that these changes never happened? No, it doesn't. They certainly happened: farming began and metal came into use, but the actual mechanisms whereby the transformations took place were complex, often differed regionally, and will take a long time to be fully revealed. There are also lessons this can teach us about our own times. We should try to look beyond the headline event and think instead about its underlying social and economic processes.

Archaeological science has provided us with important new evidence on the subject of human movement and genetic links between different populations in Europe and further afield. The movement of people, for example, can be detected by analysing the molecular composition of tooth enamel. The famous burial of a man known as the Amesbury Archer, not far from Stonehenge, is a case in point.[2] His grave, which has been radiocarbon dated to between 2470 and 2280 BC, was carefully arranged with five complete Beaker pots, a large collection of fine flint and polished stone objects, and no fewer than three copper daggers, plus a pair of gold earrings. A sort of anvil, known as a cushion stone, suggests he was most probably a craftsman in metalworking. Who knows, he may well have made some of the axes that were portrayed in the carvings at Stonehenge. He was clearly a man of great local influence and highly regarded, yet he wasn't from the area at all. The enamel of his teeth shows that he was in fact raised in central Europe, around Bavaria or the Swiss Alps.

The Amesbury Archer suggests that the process of metalworking was introduced by very skilled individuals who were highly regarded by the local communities they visited – and probably on a regular basis. The diverse and complex reality involved in the spread of new ideas, technologies and materials can be demonstrated by archaeology, but this varied picture only makes sense if people at the time had access to good communication systems.[3] Travel would have been essential, as would regular links to our neighbours on the European mainland. This suggests that roads, paths and trackways were well established and had probably been in place for a long time. They would also have formed the boundaries between different communities. As the population grew and neighbouring tribes merged into larger chiefdoms, and by the first and second centuries BC into the first Iron Age kingdoms, many of these routes would have become important political boundaries, too. Doubtless they would have witnessed quite frequent diplomatic journeys, which brings me briefly to a topic that is often ignored when discussing prehistoric roads and tracks: the traffic they carried.

I have always tried to take a long view of history and archaeology and I can remember being fascinated when, as a student, I read about the emergence of the first turnpikes in the seventeenth and eighteenth centuries (AD) in W. G. Hoskins's pioneering masterpiece of landscape history, *The Making of the English Landscape*.[4] This was published in 1955 and I first encountered it as a student, some ten years later. At that time, the relatively new subject of Industrial Archaeology was starting to make a big impact in academic circles: places like Ironbridge were very much in the news and I can remember my fascination as I discovered just how long it took for the Industrial Revolution to happen – in fact, it wasn't a 'revolution' at all. New forms of transport – first navigable rivers, then canals, then railways – were to play a key role in the movement of heavy goods between the seventeenth and nineteenth centuries. These were exciting, indeed enormous engineering challenges, but I found my attention was being gripped by what happened somewhat earlier, in the sixteenth and seventeenth centuries, when Britain pioneered some rather different systems, which have received less attention.

In the early post-medieval period (i.e. after about 1550), the upkeep of roads was the responsibility of the cities, towns and parishes they passed through. So inevitably they would have carried out repairs and maintenance work on those stretches of road that were most used by local people going about their daily work. But as long-distance travel grew in importance, as workshops expanded and goods had to be moved from one part of the country to another, the old system was found wanting. Many of the new road-users were associated with the rising number of workshops and new industries. As a consequence, the poor state of the roads became a hot topic, but not just at a local level. A solution to the problem was proposed in the mid-seventeenth century, when the first Turnpike Trusts were established along the Great North Road (now the A1) in Hertfordshire.[5] Parliament approved the setting up of these trusts, which in essence were small companies with the power to charge tolls to use the road. The money raised was used for the roads' maintenance and improvement.

The turnpikes provided a system of well-maintained roads that ran between Britain's towns and cities. Soon, fast stagecoaches made these journeys shorter. The Royal Mail[*] was quick to take advantage of the new network, which was as much about the spread of information and ideas as the movement of actual physical objects. In this respect you could see it as a precursor of telephones, or indeed the internet. But the turnpike tolls cost money and the transport of heavy goods in bulk was expensive. So these larger items, together with flocks of sheep and herds of cattle, continued to be moved on a less formal network of so-called drovers' roads, which also acquired its own infrastructure of bridges and drovers' inns.[6] From the eighteenth century the drovers' roads were slowly replaced by canals and then, in the mid-nineteenth century, by railways.

I have taken this brief diversion into recent history because I want to avoid the trap of placing all prehistoric routes in the catch-all category of 'trackways'. Just as with modern roads, we need to think about the people who used them and what

---

[*] Whose roots go back to 1516.

they were moving. Sometimes the journeys were about the movement of goods; at other times they were used for less tangible purposes – for diplomacy, family connections and the spread of information. And on certain special occasions, they were used for both at the same time. But do we have any actual evidence that prehistoric roads *were* used for these less tangible purposes, for reasons other than the simple transport of goods? And if so, how do we prove it, given that writing was not to reach Britain for almost four millennia? One might suspect that hard evidence for the less tangible uses of an ancient road or trackway might be better preserved on a route that was built and used quite late in prehistory. But you would be wrong. In fact, you couldn't be more wrong: it is time to visit Britain's earliest trackway, deep in the peatlands of the Somerset Levels.

I have long been a keen gardener and I frequently find myself having to buy compost for potting up my tomatoes and house plants – and for at least twenty-five years I have studiously avoided all that were peat-based. The substitutes aren't always very good, but they're getting better; even so, nothing will persuade me to return to peat. The reason for my horror at using peat isn't simply the environmental damage that its extraction causes – although that is serious and usually irreversible – but I have also witnessed the archaeological harm caused by peat-digging. If anything, that is even worse and it is *certainly* irreversible. Given time and sufficient water, peat will eventually regrow, but it's a process that is very slow – think more in terms of centuries and millennia than the mere years or decades it takes to remove entire peat bogs.

Archaeological sites, however, are irreplaceable. Once they have been destroyed they have gone for ever. Sadly, peat extraction has removed thousands of important prehistoric sites, for the simple reason they occur relatively high in the bogs. Most peat bogs in Britain and Ireland originated in the final centuries of the Ice Age, around 12,000 years ago.[7] This was a time when Britain had still not been re-inhabited following the end of the last Ice Age. And when people did return, it was a slow, gradual process.* So archaeological remains are relatively infrequent in peat bogs until about the fifth millennium BC, during the later Mesolithic and Neolithic periods – and with the start of farming, the evidence for settlement increases rapidly. These later remains tend to be found in the higher layers of peat, which of course are – or in most cases, sadly, *were* – the first to be removed during the process of extraction.

Certain peats are better than others for making into composts and growbags. Some of the best are found in Ireland and in the Somerset Levels and this is where many spectacular archaeological discoveries have been made. Happily, extraction has been massively reduced in the Levels, but it continues in Scotland and in England it still takes place in the lower reaches of the River Trent, between Doncaster and Scunthorpe. This low-lying land in north Lincolnshire is known as the Isle of Axholme. Peats from the Fens tended not to be used in composts, largely, I suspect, because they were very fertile if left in place. I suppose you could see the Fens as a vast growbag – but one quite rapidly approaching the end of its useful life.[8]

Peatlands are archaeologically important because of the process of peat formation, in which the natural rotting of soft, and once-living, material is halted through a mixture of acidity, waterlogging and a shortage of oxygen. This occurs in situations where water flow is slow or absent and where drying out never happens. This process can lead to the near-perfect preservation of organic materials including plant matter, fabrics and even flesh, skin and hair. When ancient peat bogs and fens are drained,

---

* As we saw at Star Carr and the Vale of Pickering (see Scene 3, page 43).

the airless water soon acquires oxygen, which allows fungi and other natural agents to resume the natural processes of rotting and degradation that had been halted centuries, even millennia, previously. This process releases huge quantities of CO_2 into the atmosphere.

Close examination of peats under a microscope will reveal preserved insects, minute mosses, seeds – even pollen grains. These accumulated gradually and formed distinct layers. The pollen grains ultimately derived from the 'pollen rain' that is everywhere in the atmosphere and causes so many people distress in springtime, thanks to hay fever. This 'rain' reflects the pollen growing not just in the immediate vicinity, but in a very wide area round about. So when the pollen grains are identified and counted, the information can be used to reconstruct, for example, the extent of woodland coverage at a particular time in prehistory. Pollen analysis, as it is known, has played an important role in mapping the spread of woodland clearance in the early stages of agriculture.

Archaeologists had known about the extraordinary potential of wetlands long before the Second World War, but the realization of the growing extent of peat extraction, and the archaeological damage it was doing, only started to make an impact in the 1960s. One of the pioneers of what would soon become a very rapidly growing subject in its own right – Wetland Archaeology – was Dr John Coles, of Cambridge University. John was Canadian and I had the great good fortune to have him as a supervisor for my last two years at college.[*] I enjoyed his easy-going appeal and relaxed attitude; I also hugely admired his academic discipline and breadth of knowledge. But there was another side to John that was to have a lasting effect on the subject he loved so much – and that was his practical ability, his love of rolling his sleeves

---

[*] Sadly, John Coles died in October 2020.

up. I know it's an old cliché, but archaeologists really do like to get their hands dirty. And I'm no exception: hardly a day goes by when I don't find myself trying to extract a rose thorn from my thumb or prising stiff clay from behind my fingernails.

John Coles and his Somerset Levels Project team pioneered most of the specialized techniques you need to employ when excavating something as soft as waterlogged wood. Steel trowels – the normal hand tool of all archaeologists – can do terrible damage to an ancient timber. The chemical composition of the wood itself is altered by centuries of waterlogging and a timber as hard as the heartwood of oak can be quite badly damaged even by a plastic knife, let alone a sharp-edged trowel. So the Somerset team developed new techniques involving wooden spatulae and even lollipop sticks. This care was essential if they were to reveal the delicate axe and chisel marks that can tell us so much about prehistoric woodwork. They even worked out how to kneel in soft peat without leaving deep knee- and toe-impressions. These tricks of the trade were to prove vital when we began our own researches in the Fens, a decade later. We copied them shamelessly.[9]

John Coles took his love of practical things a stage further. He realized that by trying to replicate the way people performed certain everyday prehistoric tasks, you would gain remarkable insights into their lives. In the late nineteenth and early twentieth centuries, pioneering prehistorians discovered that flint-knapping took great skill and that it involved far more than merely bashing two stones together. It was an extraordinarily difficult process and it took hundreds of thousands of years to perfect. For many decades, archaeologists mostly confined their attempts to replicate prehistoric techniques to flint-working. After the war, however, academic horizons widened. John Coles and other colleagues believed that a practical approach could be applied to the replication of other ancient skills, ranging from woodwork to quarrying, house-building and metalworking. Experimental Archaeology had been born, and John wrote one of the first and best guides to it.[10]

Much of John Coles's pioneering work in the new sub-discipline of Experimental Archaeology was carried out as part of his researches into the Somerset wetlands, where I saw what he was doing – and I have to say I found it inspiring. I know that the felled trees and the replica tools were modern, but they seemed entirely authentic and, yes: real. Their authenticity wasn't just the result of discipline and strict adherence to the tools and techniques that would have been available at the time, it was about more than that. I felt that the archaeologists who did the work loved their subject and took it very seriously, but they also wanted to learn. When you looked at their reconstructions, it was like you were witnessing an historic explorer returning from a distant land. There was something inspirational in what they were doing and it certainly inspired my own work in the 1980s, when I was able to reconstruct Bronze Age fields, droveways, a farm and houses in the flat, open landscapes of Fengate and Flag Fen. Today, that reconstructed Bronze Age landscape is still open to the public.[11]

In the early spring of 1970, John Coles was working in the Department of Archaeology at Cambridge when he received a package in the mail from the Eclipse Peat Works of Shapwick and Meare Heaths, two of the large peatlands of the Somerset Levels. Opening the package, he found a fragment broken from a waterlogged ash plank. The plank had clearly been split from out of a large ash tree. Once you've seen a few split wooden planks you can immediately differentiate the ones that had been split deliberately – to make planks – from those that happened by accident, when, for example, a large branch is blown down during severe gales.

John headed straight down to Somerset to meet the man who had discovered the wood. His name was Raymond Sweet.[12] They both went to the place where the wood had been found and John organized a rapid exploratory excavation, which soon revealed more of the plank plus some wooden pegs that had been driven into the ground. It was clearly part of a prehistoric trackway, but of what date? Earlier, Raymond Sweet had found a very finely made leaf-shaped flint arrowhead, which could only have been Neolithic; the date was confirmed by the discovery of a hoard of Neolithic flint flakes. Later, tree-ring studies of the oak and ash timbers from what was soon to be called the Sweet Track showed it to have been constructed during the winter of 3807 to 3806 BC. Further tree-ring research was able to demonstrate that repairs continued for another ten years – which suggests that it was relatively short-lived.

The Sweet Track was constructed from the dry ridge formed by the Polden Hills, out across the peatlands to the higher ground of the 'island' today occupied by the villages of Westhay and Meare. Meare and Glastonbury (about 5 kilometres/3 miles to the south-east) were to become important 'lake village' settlements in the Iron Age, some three millennia later.* You might suppose that such a short-lived wooden footpath was built without a great deal of care and preparation, but nothing could be further from the truth. It follows a very straight path and can be traced for about 1,800 metres (1 mile). Far from being cobbled together using different methods in various places, the way it was built was uniform, but simple; it was also highly effective. It was adjustable so that the builders could achieve a level walkway and repair any subsidence or tilting. The aim of the structure was to raise a wooden path well above the flooded ground, in order to keep it relatively dry. As anyone knows who has tried to walk across one of those decking

---

* See Scene 12, pages 236–7.

patios that were so trendy in the 1990s, the surface of wet wood soon becomes lethally slippery – especially when it acquires a light coating of green algae.

John Coles set about building an accurate replica of the track, using appropriate tools and techniques, all of which were based on what they had observed during their excavations.[13] First a long log (say 4 metres/13 ft), about the size of a large fence post, was placed on the ground. This was carefully lined up on the trackway's alignment. Then two sharpened pegs, each a bit longer than a person's arm, were driven into the ground, forming an X-shape, with the log immediately below the cross. Next, a wide plank was propped between the pegs, along and above the log. Then further crossed pegs were driven into the ground at the other end of the log and the plank was lifted onto them. It now lay above and parallel to the log lying on the wet surface. Finally, additional crossed pegs were added along its length, to better support the weight of the plank – and of anyone walking along it. Rather to their surprise, John and his collaborators found that adjusting the crossed pegs to support the plank and keep it level was remarkably easy. Erecting the trackway was to prove a rapid and straightforward process, providing, of course, that the various components had been prepared in advance. The team found that about 10 metres (11 yd) of trackway could be laid, erected and adjusted in about half an hour, and with practice they were able to reduce this to just fifteen minutes.[14] So although over six thousand years old, the Sweet Track had been planned and constructed with extraordinary efficiency by people who clearly understood what they were doing.

The other aspect of prehistoric trackway construction that the Sweet Track experiments illustrated was the need to plan in advance. Distances had to be measured and the correct number of components – logs, pegs and planks – had to be prepared. This was something we also found at Flag Fen, near Peterborough (a much later site of about 1000 BC),* where there was also good evidence for sophisticated woodwork and a controlling authority who assigned materials, such as pre-split oak posts, for separate repair projects along the post alignment – the term we used to describe a large ceremonial trackway and boundary.

In addition to precise dates, the tree-ring research showed that the oak trees that were felled and then split to provide the Sweet Track's walkway planks came from mature trees in the trackway's northern half and from younger ones closer to its southern section. Again, this suggests prior organization and it also indicates that different communities were co-operating in what today we would refer to as the 'supply chain'. As a general rule, prehistoric construction projects were often organized through community, tribal and family groups and it is likely that the Sweet Track, like Flag Fen, very much later, was a trackway that was rather more than just a means of getting from A to B. There was another dimension to it.

Wet areas have long been regarded as special. In part this reflects their liminality, but there is also something supernatural about water itself: a mirror on life, but a cause of death.† These ideas probably help to explain why so many dry 'islands', such as the Isle of Ely, were seen in the past as sacred places. Glastonbury is and was the equivalent of Ely in the Somerset Levels – but it wasn't just the larger 'islands' that were treated with respect, and it seems quite likely that smaller 'islands', such as the one that today includes the villages of Westhay and Meare, were also venerated. When the Sweet Track was first revealed, we all thought it was just that: a track, albeit the earliest trackway so far discovered in Britain (which it remains to this day). It was a track (a raised footpath would be a more

---

* See Scene 13, pages 256–64.

† For the sacred significance of water, see Blick Mead, Scene 4, pages 67–8.

accurate description) from one area of dry land to another. But then, and to everyone's surprise at the time, clear, unambiguous evidence was revealed that it *wasn't* that straightforward: there were other, more intangible, aspects to it as well. I love it when this sort of thing happens, when a little magic is bestowed on an apparently uncomplicated discovery: somehow it becomes more human – and alive.

The Sweet Track was intensively investigated for more than ten years in the 1970s and 1980s and work has continued there ever since.[15] This research has revealed a great deal not just about the trackway itself, but about its immediate surroundings. Finds alongside and directly beneath the walkway's timbers have included flint arrowheads – some still attached to partially preserved shafts – and caches of broken pottery. The pottery was all of very good quality, thin-walled and well made; the people using the walkway didn't carry any of the coarser so-called domestic wares. One vessel still contained hazelnuts, and a stirring stick (or spurtle – the best thing for stirring proper Scottish porridge!) lay alongside it. At least three wooden bows were found near the southern end of the trackway in an area that pollen analysis shows would have been wooded in earlier Neolithic times. Some of these finds could simply be explained in terms of accidental loss, although I find it hard to believe that the fine pottery was simply discarded – like an old lunch box. This was top-quality tableware and I suspect there was more to it than that.

A hint at what might have been going on along the Sweet Track is provided by the three flint axe-heads found beside the trackway. One was unused and all were unhafted – just like the axe-heads found in graves, such as that of the Amesbury Archer. Strange as it may seem, in my experience prehistoric flint, stone or bronze axes are rarely found on sites where woodwork has been taking place. Sometimes you might find their broken wooden hafts, as we did at Etton.* But for reasons that remain entirely relevant to this day, craftsmen have always cherished their tools: they clean them, sharpen them and keep them in good condition. It's all part of taking pride in your work: you won't find blunt chisels on building sites. In fact, you won't find chisels at all, because good craftsmen clear up behind them. So why did John Coles and his team find three unhafted flint axes alongside the Sweet Track? The rather surprising answer to that question lay in yet another stone axe.

Perhaps the most remarkable find from the Sweet Track was revealed beneath a piece of wooden board, just a couple of feet to one side of the plank walkway. It was a polished stone axe, clearly of Neolithic style and shape, but not fashioned in one of the known British axe quarries, such as Langdale.† Like the Langdale axes, this axe was green, but a somewhat mottled green. On closer examination the material turned out to be jadeite, a very attractive mineral that polishes up well and is often used today in jewellery. Microscopic examination revealed that the source for the Sweet Track jadeite was the Alpine region of central Europe.

The discovery of the jadeite axe from central Europe alongside a timber trackway in rural Somerset caused huge excitement. It was plainly a very special and valuable item, which was never intended to be used. Rather like the humbler British polished stone axes, which were sometimes never used, or those carved bronze axes on the uprights at Stonehenge,‡ this axe would probably have symbolized either an individual, a family or a clan/tribe. Maybe its careful deposition so close to such an obvious pathway through a bog was a protective measure of

---

* See Scene 5, pages 77–81.
† See Scene 6, pages 101–110.
‡ See Scenes 6 and 7.

SCENES FROM PREHISTORIC LIFE

8.1 A close-up of the Sweet Track, Somerset (built 3807–3806 BC). The main oak plank of the walkway is clearly visible, as are some of the smaller roundwood pegs used to support it (although these are somewhat disturbed). To the right of the walkway is a polished jadeite axe-head, which had originally been concealed – perhaps deliberately – beneath a piece of board.

some sort: perhaps to ward off unwanted people or spirits from approaching the special island of Westhay and Meare. It could have been placed in water alongside the track as a symbol that somebody's soul had joined the realm of the ancestors – most probably on the island. This again suggests that the island would have been seen as special or sacred. These explanations could also apply equally well to the three other known complete axe-heads found near the trackway.

There is, however, a problem here: the careful deposition of axes – especially such a valuable one as the jadeite axe – is not likely to have been part of a process that started and finished in just ten years – the known use-life of the Sweet Track. Such religious observances take time to develop and evolve. Indeed, I firmly believe that many of the rituals and rites associated with Neolithic monuments have origins that probably lie thousands of years earlier, in the Mesolithic. We can certainly see good evidence for continued respect for the Stonehenge landscape some four millennia before the great stones were erected. So was the Sweet Track a one-off? I think not – and I do have some evidence to support my doubts.

I have to confess that I deliberately slightly misled you when I said that the Sweet Track was the earliest timber trackway in Britain. But I can be forgiven because the earlier one was only revealed when the Sweet Track was excavated, and besides, it wasn't *that* much earlier: it dates from 3838 BC. The Post Track was originally thought to have been a temporary track that was built as part of the construction process for the later, straighter, Sweet Track. The trouble with that argument, however, is that it was significantly earlier (some thirty years) and was built in a slightly different way and used ash and lime wood for the walkway planks, rather than oak.[16] A more likely explanation is that the Post Track was a forerunner of the Sweet Track and showed that the route taken by both tracks (and quite possibly by others also?) had been important for more than a mere decade. This would accord better with the known situation elsewhere in the Somerset Levels, where Bronze and Iron Age tracks abound, somewhat later in prehistory. It would also support the idea that the Sweet Track was providing access to a place that had been widely regarded as spiritually important for a very long time.[17]

I can still recall my own first visit to the Sweet Track, sometime in the late 1970s. At that time, the general climate of opinion still favoured the more straightforward, functional explanation and I won't say for one moment that I thought differently. But I *did* find the experience strangely moving: the straightness of the track and the precision of its construction were one thing, but something about the superbly preserved timbers set me thinking.

Before that visit to the Sweet Track, my only insights into the vanished world of prehistory had been provided by more indirect archaeological evidence: the holes dug to receive posts, filled-in ditches and ploughed-out, flattened barrows. But here I was looking at something that Neolithic eyes would instantly have recognized. It was rather like being allowed a glimpse into somebody's bedroom: it was both personal and intimate. And of course it made me wonder about what those Neolithic men, women and children would have been thinking about as they walked towards Westhay 'island'. Their world was complex and very varied, just like ours is today, and their thoughts and motivations would have been similarly rich, varied, amusing, happy and sad. Half a century later, I am still thinking about them and their world – and my ideas continue to evolve. Will I ever arrive at 'the truth'? I once believed such a thing might be possible, but now I'm glad it isn't. The more I research the past, the more I respect the people who created it. It has been a privilege to have been given the chance to speculate. It has taught me so much about myself and the times in which we live. I am constantly reminded that there is more to history than just the past.

But now I want to take the story forward. The actual timbers of the Sweet Track may have been quite short-lived, but they followed a well-established route, from the dry land to the south, out towards Westhay 'island'. Were there other such routes in the Somerset Levels – or indeed elsewhere? I won't go so far as to say that wherever there are wetlands there are prehistoric trackways, but they do occur widely in the Fens, the Thames valley and elsewhere. In the Somerset Levels, people continued to build trackways throughout the Neolithic and into the Early Bronze Age. The elaborate raised construction of the Sweet Track wasn't replicated in the dozen or so examples that have been discovered to date: most were either based on logs laid side by side (rather like the squashed-up sleepers of a railway line – a pattern of construction sometimes described as 'corduroy'). After about 2000 BC, we see the appearance of lighter-weight footpaths based on woven wattle* hurdles.

Construction of corduroy trackways continued throughout the Bronze Age and into the Iron Age. But the Sweet Track wasn't the only one to have been very carefully made: several of the hurdle and corduroy tracks were very well built and the one that crossed the deep, soft peats of Meare Heath was particularly fine. The Meare Heath track was made from heavier oak timbers than the Sweet Track, but was much later (c. 900 BC).[18] It was laid out rather like a railway with close, sleeper-like, heavy-duty split oak bearers, some of which had been fixed into position by long sharpened pegs that passed through mortice-like holes in the bearers. Two substantial oak planks were then laid next to each other, and resting on the bearers. Many of the Bronze and Iron Age trackways could have been crossed by cattle, horses and even light vehicles. Certain traditions persisted, however, and many of the later routes also appear to have included a religious or ritual element, with offerings being placed alongside or below them.

When one steps back and looks at the prehistoric trackways across the Somerset Levels, you have to conclude that these were structures built by people who not only knew what they were doing, but who had learned from the experiences of their friends, relations and neighbours living around them. Too often, people have imagined that wetlands such as the Somerset Levels and the Fens were inhabited by communities who lived isolated lives out there in the watery wilderness. But those trackways tell a very different story: that people valued the fact that they could stay in touch with one another and went to great lengths to ensure that

---

* 'Wattles' are pliable rods, usually of hazel or willow, which were woven through uprights to make hurdles or walls for houses and barns.

it happened. Certainly the trackways of the Levels did help to cement communal ties, but they also provided imaginative people with insights into realms far beyond the physical constraints of daily life. Earlier, I noted that there is more to history than the past; I should perhaps have added that there has always been more to a road, track or path, than travel.

Scene 9

Getting About: On Coastal Waters
(2000–70 BC)

The Dover Boat – Folkestone and Flag Fen

The first half of the second millennium BC (from 2000 to 1500 BC) was a fascinating period of change and innovation and if I could somehow be transported back in time, this is where I would like to end up. In previous books I have described the major social changes that were taking place around 1500 BC as a 'Domestic Revolution' (see Table in the Introduction, pages xxvi–xxvii).[1] Revolutions are supposed to happen quite quickly. The blood-soaked French Revolution of 1789–99 is a good example: it took just over ten years. Many, however, were very much slower. Britain's Industrial 'Revolution', for example, took a minimum of four centuries to happen. If anything, I reckon the changes of the Domestic Revolution took about half that time – again, hardly swift and dramatic by French standards, but not protracted either.

The underlying causes of the Industrial Revolution are fairly clear: greater social mobility at the close of the Middle Ages, following the decline of the more feudal manorial system; and the rise of a new class of independent 'yeoman' farmers and with them the appearance of small workshops producing textiles and fabrics – both of which had to be serviced and supplied.

In time this led to the first turnpikes, canals and latterly, of course, railways. You can plot the growth and progress of industrialization in the layout of major centres of industry, such as the Ironbridge Gorge or the large, sprawling city of Birmingham with its still magnificent network of canals.[2] But what were the causes of the major changes that happened two millennia earlier, around 1500 BC?

It has long been recognized that the middle of the Bronze Age was a time of considerable change. The great henge monuments were abandoned (those axe carvings at Stonehenge, for example, include no outlines that could belong within the Middle Bronze Age). Barrow burial rapidly declined in importance and very few new barrows were erected. Burials and cremations within barrows after about 1500 BC tend to be 'inserted' into pre-existing mounds. Right across Britain, the specialized Ritual Landscapes that had grown up over the previous 2,200 or so years cease to be maintained. Indeed, by 1300 BC large areas of what was once the Stonehenge Ritual Landscape were now occupied by farms, settlements and a network of small rectangular fields.[3]

There were probably many reasons underlying these moment-ous changes. The available evidence suggests that the population in Britain's various regions had been steadily growing since the arrival of farming around 4000 BC. You can see this in the progressive stages in which the landscape evolved. Woodland and scrub were steadily cleared to make way for smaller arable fields and large areas of pasture. Existing farms and settlements grew in size and many new ones were founded in areas that had been previously uninhabited. Slowly, a network of roads and tracks was established and by the mid-second millennium BC, if not earlier, many lowland rivers would have supported communities who existed by fishing, trapping eels and hunting wildfowl. We used to think that freshwater craft were quite rare, but recent discoveries at Must Farm, on the western edge of the

Cambridgeshire Fens, near Peterborough, have shown that large numbers of small craft could have been seen on any suitably sized stream or lake at any one time. All of these developments point towards an increasing population.

By the centuries leading up to 2000 BC, the landscape of lowland Britain had been transformed by human action. Rivers, for example, were being increasingly exploited. They probably also formed boundaries and, of course, routes of communication; roads and trackways were now well established and would have been respected by all the communities they passed through, or around. Field systems would shortly start to be constructed and by 1500 BC they would cover substantial parts of both uplands and lowlands;[4] even larger areas of what today we would call common land and open pasture were controlled by grazing agreements and other arrangements between the farmers and villagers around them. These local agreements would have been negotiated and updated by the representatives, the elders and the chiefs of the tribes who inhabited and controlled the settlements. This tribal, or family-based, organizational system would have provided the basic structure of all important aspects of communal life.

It was more than a millennium later (around 900–1000 BC) that we start to see the emergence of the first Iron Age kingdoms (the Iceni etc.), which were all based on earlier tribal systems. I would suggest that these earlier systems first began to appear in the centuries around 1500 BC. This was when local communities became more powerful and influential, perhaps superseding an even earlier tradition where cult or religious leaders played a more prominent part in keeping more widely separated, even far-flung, communities together. One reason why the older way of doing things was replaced by more locally based, tribal and communal systems was that the landscape was now far more fully developed. Communication was now much simpler. There was no need to travel vast distances for major gatherings. Cohesion between different communities could be maintained more simply and more flexibly. I believe the mid-second millennium BC (i.e. from 1500 BC) was when prehistoric people developed their own systems of local governance. They would have been exciting times to have lived through.

We see the effectiveness of these more locally based arrangements in the rapid development of field systems in the centuries after 2000 BC. Speaking as a sheep farmer myself, I know that fields only make sense if everyone in the region acknowledges your rights to own or lease them. Making good use of land requires agreements and permissions. So locally binding laws or rules (unwritten, of course) would have been essential for the system to work at all. In farming, no two seasons are ever the same, and grazing requirements can change quite rapidly. So again, the rules surrounding communal grazing must be flexible and easily modified, if needs be. To achieve this, you must have a well-established system of local land management. In the Middle Ages this was provided by the courts, committees and officers of the local lord of the manor and there must have been equivalents of the manorial system, doubtless tribally based, in earlier times.

We see the shift towards more local control in the new religious rites that start to appear in the centuries prior to 1500 BC. These do not centre on massive shrines or large Ritual Landscapes; instead, people chose to convene more locally at rivers or wet places, where they made offerings to the waters. We can tell by the objects that were placed in the water that these offerings were about people's rites of passage,* the big events of their lives: births, marriages and deaths – even successful apprenticeships. These water-based shrines and holy places are probably best thought of as the prehistoric equivalents of parish churches: they

---

* For more on rites of passage, see Scene 4, page 72.

were places where local people solemnized and then celebrated the important events in their lives. Sometimes the wetland shrines actually incorporated existing roads or trackways, as at Flag Fen, in Peterborough (1300–900 BC), where hundreds of offerings of bronze, pottery and other valuables were placed in the waters both beside and within the structure of a massive timber trackway that ran from the Peterborough fen-edge for over a kilometre, across the seasonally flooded Flag Fen, towards the higher ground of Whittlesey 'island' to the south-east. We will return to Flag Fen later in this Scene.

The profound social changes that were taking place between 1500 and 1000 BC need to be understood if we are to make sense of the huge increase in evidence for travel that now becomes apparent. Sites like Flag Fen are by no means unique: we know of similar examples in Sussex, the Thames valley, the Witham valley and of course in the Somerset Levels, where Bronze and Iron Age trackways proliferated.*

We used to believe that the steady increase in the size and number of settlements throughout the last fifteen centuries BC was essentially a self-contained process: that the different communities of the British Isles maintained close contacts with each other, but rarely looked further afield. More recently, however, scientific analysis of bones and teeth, together with an increased appreciation of pottery and metalwork, have led us to conclude that this self-contained, essentially insular picture of life in pre-Roman Britain was most misleading. The fact that there were regular overseas contacts has now been established beyond any doubt. Britain, of course, is an island; so that must mean there were seagoing craft. It is time to head towards the south coast and to Dover, in Kent, where on a clear day you can still glimpse the French coast, just 33 kilometres (20 miles) away.

---

* See Scene 8, pages 163–4.

*

Sadly, I never managed to visit the Dover Boat excavations, but that was because they happened under difficult and sometimes dangerous circumstances, deep below the surface. In the early 1990s Britain was going through quite a rapid phase of infrastructural development: roads and houses seemed to be being built everywhere. Fortunately for archaeology, in 1989 the government modified planning legislation, making it a legal duty for developers to pay for any excavation or other archaeological work needed to repair the damage caused by their various schemes. 'Rescue' archaeology,* as it was then known (we now refer to it as 'contract archaeology'), had been formalized in law. It had actually come into existence, as a way of doing archaeology, in the later 1960s and 1970s.†

Today, most archaeological digs take place either as a response to an unexpected discovery made during other work – such as a civil engineering project – or else they are scheduled and executed in advance of development. These pre-planned excavations can be very large indeed and they usually precede housing developments, road-building or gravel extraction. Sometimes they are opened to the public on specific days, but often these events are quite restricted due to time pressures – and the cost of public liability insurance etc.

The Dover Boat was discovered in September 1992 as part of the building of the A20 Dover bypass.[5] It's probably no exaggeration to say that she's one of the best, earliest and most completely preserved of prehistoric seagoing vessels. Radiocarbon dates carried out on the outer growth rings of the timbers suggest that she was built sometime between 1575 and

---

* See Scene 4, page 60.

† A few important rescue excavations had taken place even earlier, in the 1930s, 1940s and 1950s ahead of specific developments, such as the digging of new gravel pits or the expansion of Heathrow Airport.

1520 BC, which would place her at the very beginning of the British Middle Bronze Age.[6]

When the remains of boats are discovered, they are usually described in the press as 'wrecks' – the most familiar one being the *Titanic*. The Dover Boat, however, never hit a glacier, nor even a floating log. So far as we can tell, she was in good order when she was pulled ashore onto tidal muds and silts in the mouth of the River Dour, at Dover. The River Dour may not be widely known outside south Kent, but it has a long history. The river gave its name to the town: 'Dover' comes from the Latin *dubris*, which in turn derives from the river's pre-Roman Celtic name: *dubras*, meaning 'the waters'.[7] The River Dour is one of the very few streams of any consequence that has eroded a steep valley through the chalk mass of the famous white cliffs of Dover. When you visit Dover you are very aware of the high hills that surround the port and town, but despite its proximity to France, it has never been a major landing place for military forces: Caesar's two expeditions (of 55 and 54 BC) didn't land there; nor did the Roman invasion of AD 43, or the Normans in 1066. They would never have fought their way out of the natural harbour, and up the narrow Dour valley.

The boat was found near the mouth of the river under about 5 metres (16 ft) of tidal silts that had accumulated over it. These silts hid it, but they also kept it wet and protected it. When it was revealed, the excavators discovered that the pointed board at the bow had been removed, as had the upper planks along the boat's sides. It's not easy to explain why this was done other than to suggest that the removal of these important parts of the boat's structure was a deliberate act to render the vessel incapable of putting to sea. It has been suggested that the timbers were taken off to be used as spares in another vessel. The trouble with that explanation is that seasoned oak is almost unbelievably hard. I've tried to cut it with a bronze axe and it simply bounces off, or makes a rather bruised, shallow cut. It's hard enough to work with a sharp steel blade. This means that it would be extremely difficult to fit the pieces that were removed into another vessel. When Bronze Age boats are made, the boatbuilders use freshly felled, unseasoned oak, which splits readily and can easily be cut by a bronze axe or chisel. It's also quite pliable and can be steam-treated to bend it to fit curved shapes; again, this can't be done with old, hardened, seasoned oak. So why was she treated in this way? We will probably never know for certain, but for now I think there is no other explanation than that it was a deliberate act. Her owners believed that the time had come to cease sailing, despite the fact that she had many miles, indeed years of sailing in her. One could think of her as a sort of sacrificial offering for reasons we will never understand: maybe somebody had drowned when out at sea? We just don't know, but I feel quite certain that the reasons for her abandonment lie in the realms of ritual and religion.[8]

Bronze Age boats come in a wide variety of shapes and sizes. Most of the examples we know about resemble the dug-out canoes featured in *The Flintstones*. They are described by archaeologists as log-boats. In essence, these are hollowed-out tree trunks. I always feel that the name lets them down: log-boats somehow sound rather crude and unexciting, but when you actually get to see one you will be amazed by the craftsmanship. They are astonishingly thin-walled and carefully made.

Other boats would have resembled coracles – hides fixed to a stout wooden frame, which are mostly known from rock carvings in Scandinavia. Log-boats were quite rigid vessels and were best suited to the calmer freshwaters of rivers and lakes, than out at sea. Some hide-covered boats could have been used at sea, but robust and more flexible seagoing vessels were often made from carefully split planks, usually sewn together.[9] The Dover Boat was plank-built.

We don't know the actual length of the Dover Boat, because her stern still lies underground, deep beneath the A20, but we do know her width (her beam), which was about 2.25 metres (7 ft 6 in); she had a minimum length of 14 metres (46 ft). She was constructed around two large planks that formed the floor of the vessel; these were joined together by a series of wedges, which passed through ridges in the planks at the centre of the boat. In addition, there were four substantial transverse timbers, which passed through matching upright cleats in each plank. The two side planks, or iles, were fixed to the base planks using rope-like fastenings of twisted yew. All the planks of the boat had edges that fitted into each other; these were made more waterproof using pads of moss. Stitch holes were made watertight with a mix of wax, fats and resin. We know for a fact that the boat had at least one more pair of side planks that fitted onto the shaped upper edge of the side iles. They had been removed shortly before the boat's abandonment because the freshly cut yew ropes that once sewed them together were found still dangling in situ when the boat was excavated. With just two side planks, the Dover Boat could have weathered fairly rough seas, but with three (i.e. with two planks above the side iles) she might even have coped with moderate gales (Force 8) for short periods.

There is no evidence for a mast, or for sails, so we must assume that the Dover Boat was propelled by paddling. Single-piece wooden paddles are by no means rare in prehistoric north-western Europe. The boat was wide enough to allow two people to paddle, canoe-fashion, next to each other, and long enough to accommodate about ten people along each side. With a crew of that size, quite reasonable speeds could have been maintained; although a smaller crew would have allowed more space for passengers, or cargo.

Sadly, museum displays rarely excite me. Even modern ones with all their subtle lighting, digital enhancements and clever

9.1 Half-scale replica of the Dover Boat during construction. Note the thick carpet of oak chips covering the floor of the workshop.

9.2 The Dover Boat reconstruction: a worktop showing yew rope bindings in preparation and two hafts for Middle Bronze Age axes (right). The top of an axe blade would fit between the two 'fingers' of the haft and then be bound securely in place.

technology are usually sterile reflections of the mud-soaked reality of an active excavation, but the display devoted to the Dover Boat in Dover Museum is a memorable exception: it focuses entirely on the vessel and the superb craftsmanship that created it. It also makes much use of experimental archaeology, which is why I have visited it several times. In February 2012, I received a phone call from one of the producers of Channel 4's very popular archaeological series *Time Team*, of which I was then an active member.[10] They were planning to make a documentary about the Dover Boat – and was I interested? For some reason, he sounded a little doubtful. Before I could reply, he asked if I suffered from seasickness, because apparently I'd have to sail in a replica. While he was talking I could feel the excitement rise, and when I did eventually reply, I almost bit his hand off. He was offering me a fee to do something I would have paid a small fortune for! During the next few weeks I could think of nothing else.

A month later, in March, I found myself in a tent-like structure near the south coast. I was lined up to do various interviews, but first I was given a detailed tour of the workshop where the half-scale replica was being built, using casts of Bronze Age tools and authentic materials (such as moss and wax, rather than modern waterproof fillers). The skilled boatbuilders were all archaeologists and friends of mine from our years of research into ancient woodwork in the Fens. So the atmosphere was very genial and I was looking forward to a good session in the pub when we wrapped things up. Meanwhile, I could feel that slight prickle around the eyes that I'd experienced when we made the Seahenge reconstruction: there was a lot of tannin in the air.* Then I looked down at my feet, where the ground was covered by a thick carpet of oak woodchips. There must have been literally

---

* See Scene 7, page 130.

millions of them. If nothing else, that told me about the immense amount of work that was needed to make something like the Dover Boat. But the required levels of skill took my breath away: this wasn't any old carpentry. I'm quite good at knocking up bookshelves and doing building work around the farm and I have worked with professional carpenters, but even they would have taken a long time to have acquired the additional skills of a Bronze Age shipwright. These men were not only highly skilled, but they plainly took enormous pride in their work: everything fitted together snugly; nothing was botched.

I think it was a year later, in 2013, that I got to sail in the replica boat and I have to admit it was something of an anticlimax. I was expecting something a bit scary: waves over the sides and unsteadiness in choppy waters, but it was nothing like that. In fact, it felt like we were sailing in a modern vessel. Sure, this was only a half-sized replica and I'd certainly have hesitated to cross the Channel in her; but I knew I wouldn't have been even slightly doubtful about sailing to France in the full-sized Dover Boat. You can read about these things and make decisions on a sober assessment of the observed facts, but nothing beats sitting in a real boat with damp trousers and salt water in your socks. It's only then that you know what a boat would actually be capable of achieving.

The Dover Boat was beautifully constructed, but she certainly wasn't a high status or special craft; no great care had been taken over her finish. Chisel cuts, axe and adze marks hadn't been smoothed off. She was plainly a working vessel. So now I want to consider how she might have been used and what it would have been like to travel in her. But first I must break off to describe a remarkable revelation that was directly relevant to our story – although I didn't realize it at the time.

During the mid-1990s, the team that had excavated Flag Fen since its discovery in 1982 were busy finishing the first campaign of fieldwork. While fieldwork was winding down, we were also starting to analyse artefacts and hundreds of samples for the production of the final report. I had read about the finding of the Dover Boat when it was announced, in 1992, and there was a good deal of television and press coverage as well. Meanwhile, Flag Fen was still regularly in the news as one of the best-preserved Bronze Age sites found to date in northern Europe. And yet I had no idea that there could well have been a direct link between the two. It was a link that would provide some fascinating insights into how the Dover Boat might have been used and the likely reaction of its passengers to their journey.

As most working archaeologists will tell you, the writing of excavation reports can at times be a rather tedious process. There can be exciting moments when things come together and new explanations emerge – often quite rapidly. But there is so much data to sift through and analyse. Specialists' reports are constantly coming in and these must be carefully read and filed in the right place (i.e. where you can find them when needed – and not in a box at the back of the shed).

Flag Fen is best known for its tens of thousands of superbly preserved timbers, along with hundreds of Bronze Age weapons and tools that were placed in and around them in the ground, as offerings. But other items were also carefully placed in the waters near the wooden posts. These included pottery vessels, the bones of dogs, shale bracelets and other ornaments, plus four large querns or corn-grinding stones, which appeared to be unused or very slightly used.[11] They were probably deposited at Flag Fen during ceremonies to do with establishing a new house in one of the many settlements nearby, sometime between about 1300 and 1100 BC.

Quernstones, which are quite frequently found in special

ceremonial deposits, probably symbolized hearth and home. We know that querns were kept in the house and were used by the central hearth in the preparation of flour – to make dough for bread. So it does not take a huge leap of imagination to see how and why they could have come to symbolize home life and the family. The fact that we found four complete querns in our tiny excavated sample at Flag Fen suggests that rites involving the ceremonial deposition of querns probably took place regularly. There must be dozens more – maybe even hundreds – waiting to be discovered. When we excavated it, Stone 27 looked much like any of the others: it was certainly very heavy. One man could carry it, but not for any distance. Three of the querns were made of sandstone and one was of gabbro – an igneous (volcanic) rock, probably from Wales. The sources of all these rocks were far away from Flag Fen, where there are no rocky outcrops of any sort. On closer microscopic examination, however, Stone 27 (one of the sandstone querns) was very distinctive. It could only have been quarried from the Lower Cretaceous Folkestone Beds, on the coast of Kent, just a short distance west of Dover. And it's certainly not coincidental that these quarries were an important source of quernstones in Roman times.

Folkestone is a seaside town and this coastal location surely helps explain why its querns were so widely traded in Roman times. But the Flag Fen quernstone is almost 1,500 years earlier. We can only speculate, but its journey from the south coast of Kent up to Flag Fen would probably have been made by boat, across the Thames estuary, around the coast of East Anglia, into the Wash and thence up one of the courses of the River Nene to Flag Fen. A seagoing vessel like the Dover Boat would have been perfectly capable of making such a voyage.

There is evidence that voyages in Bronze Age Atlantic Europe tended to be over relatively short distances. The heroic voyages of the post-Roman Vikings would not have been possible two thousand years previously. Even the largest Bronze Age vessels would not have been able to sail through a severe gale or storm, so mariners preferred to undertake shorter journeys, where land was in sight for most of the time. There is growing evidence that these coastal vessels made use of small, informal landing places, often in protected bays where they could take refuge from passing storms. When I think of such places, I always imagine the tiny sandy beach beneath the towering heights of Tintagel Castle in Cornwall.[12]

Every mariner would have had a detailed mental map that would have included all the small bays and inlets along the route of their voyage. The journey itself would have been carried out as a series of shorter loops from one stopover point to another. In fair weather the loops were larger than in wintertime. So far, none of the Bronze Age seagoing vessels found in Britain have deep keels or protruding rudders. This means they were probably run up onto beaches, so docks and landing stages would usually have been minimal. Some substantial pieces of rock were found near the hull of the Dover Boat and these may well have formed a drier walkway or step-path to the craft after her final journey.

So what can we deduce about the journey that carried the newly quarried quernstone from an inlet near Folkestone around the coast to the Wash? We can only guess about the stopping-off points en route, but there would have been no shortage of these: the long Essex coastline has numerous backwaters and marshy river outfalls and Kent, too, has many possible Bronze Age landing places.[13] Sometimes, however, skippers could be too ambitious and get caught by nasty storms.

Bronze Age wreck sites – usually consisting of dumps or spreads of bronzes on the seabed – have been found all along the south coast. Some 400 bronzes have been found on the seabed near the Eastern Arm of Dover Harbour, by Dover Sub Aqua Club.[14] This material dates to 1100–1000 BC; it was probably scrap that originated in France and was on its way to Britain, presumably to be melted down and recast. Another presumed wreck site, dating to about 1200–900 BC, was found just outside Salcombe Bay on the southern tip of Devon.[15] Its position suggests the vessel was heading for the shelter of the bay, but sadly failed to make it. The cargo included 295 bronze objects, again mostly scrap but originating even further afield in Europe – as far away as Switzerland and the Alps. Taken together, the Salcombe bronzes weigh a hefty 84 kilos (185 lb).

Finds of scrap metal can be explained as business transactions – although in this era of prehistory there was almost certainly a degree of religion or ritual involved as well. But what about Stone 27 at Flag Fen: how does one explain that? Earlier, I stated that quernstones like Stone 27 were sometimes placed in the ground to represent domestic life – hearth and home – and there is good evidence that this practice goes back as far as 3700 BC, in the earlier Neolithic period. When we were excavating the Neolithic causewayed enclosure at Etton,* we found several places where offerings had been made that involved querns. In one instance, broken pieces of quern had been carefully incorporated into a series of deposits in a special segment of ditch. I now suspect that the quern had been broken on the death of an important person and that the position of the fragments in the ditch symbolized his (or more probably her) status within the family – although now as a revered ancestor, rather than a living person.

If broken querns were used to symbolize the demise of an individual and perhaps the abandonment or demolition of their family home, complete, even new querns might also have been important when a new home was being established, or when a new family was begun. Bronze Age houses could have been maintained in use for several generations, but signs of frequent

---

* See Scene 5, pages 77–81.

post replacement and new porches or doorways are not very common, which might suggest that major repairs were not often needed, because individual homes were generally used to house just one nuclear family.* There is some evidence – for instance, on Bodmin Moor and Dartmoor – that houses abandoned in this way were ceremonially sealed off – ruled out of bounds – by placing a symbolic burial mound (without a body) within them.[16]

Viewed in this way, the complete quernstones found at Flag Fen take on a new significance. Had they been broken or well-worn I would suggest they might have symbolized the end of a life, but the fact that they were either new or very fresh suggests something less gloomy: maybe the start of a new relationship – engagement, marriage or the birth of children. But given the quern's central role as an object within the home, I like to think that our stone, Stone 27, was taken to Flag Fen as an offering to thank the ancestors for the successful construction of a new home, for a young family.

There has been much stress in academic circles on the competitive nature of later prehistoric society in Britain. The rise of powerful leaders, the importance of impressive hillforts and the growing luxury of fine objects, including massive gold neck-rings (known as torcs) and even the importation of wine from the Mediterranean.† Powerful people usually meant powerful men, but women also played a very important role. I don't say this just to be politically correct, but because there is a great deal of archaeological evidence for it – and not just in some rich burials, but in the very fabric of society.[17] Bronze and Iron Age communities were organized around the clan and family, of which the principal building blocks were the individual nuclear families, where women played, then, as now, a central role.[18]

---

* By 'nuclear family', I mean parents and their children.
† See Scene 15, page 289.

So if we assume (and this is quite a big assumption) that in the Bronze Age, as today, women went to live with their partners, rather than vice versa, then we can imagine that our quernstone, Stone 27, might have been a gift from a young wife's family for her, in her new home. If that were the case, then it is quite likely that it was a member of her family that went to the quarries at Folkestone. Where this person and their family originated is anyone's guess, but I would be prepared to bet it was somewhere in the region we know today as Kent. Certainly, communications would have been good enough for families to have maintained long-established connections with communities some distance away. So let us suppose that the young wife's brother accompanied Stone 27 on the loops of its long coastal voyage towards the Wash. He would have helped lift it out of the boat whenever they beached for an overnight stay. Maybe friends and relatives of the two families came down to the shore to see the stone and give it their blessing. These would have been the sort of short ceremonies that might have been accompanied by a few mugs of ale or mead.

So what was the young man feeling as he rounded North Foreland and headed up into the North Sea? Was it hope? Fear? Or trepidation, perhaps? We can only guess, but I very much doubt that this journey would have been a joyride for him. If he had failed to deliver the quern he would have let down his much-loved older sister, but at the same time he would also have tarnished the honour of his entire family. At first glance, this was a simple enough task: take a large piece of rock from A to B. But the reality was very different. The movement of Stone 27 would have had long-lasting consequences for maybe hundreds of people in at least two families. For everyone concerned, it would have been an anxious time – and we can only hope it all turned out well. To reiterate an earlier theme: journeys were about much more than mere movement.

Scene 10

Food and Round-houses (1500 BC–AD 43)

Cornish Samphire – Fengate Turf Roof –
Little Butser

Archaeologists love to classify things – and sometimes in vast detail. There are hundreds of different types of flint tools and literally thousands of styles of pottery and metalwork. And all of these can be dated with greater or lesser precision. In our digital world there are countless easily accessed images of sites and landscapes and, of course, thanks to DNA, science can now trace human ancestry and movement with extraordinary accuracy. Nothing, one could be forgiven for believing, lies beyond the reach of modern research. The trouble is, this view assumes that we all want to ask factual questions with readily defined answers. But life has never been as simple as that. Being human, we also want to ask those questions that might throw light on what prehistoric people felt at various – often quite specific – moments in their lives. I was contemplating this the other day, as I drove home after a late evening book-signing. I was tired and hungry. All I could think about was what I was going to eat before going to bed: an egg? Perhaps toast and a tin of soup? Maybe just some cereal? And then I found myself wondering what a Bronze or Iron Age man would be thinking about in the same circumstances, after a long evening away from home and feeling very peckish.

Having spent most of my professional life excavating sites where people had built their houses and lived out their lives, I was familiar with what you might call 'the basics': we had dug countless rubbish pits and ditches where people had discarded their household waste. So we had a fair understanding of what they ate: beef, mutton, lamb and pork. The bones we recovered were in good condition, because the soils of eastern England are generally low in acid and, as a result, their surfaces were still intact and carried clear traces left from butchery. Direct evidence for the consumption of vegetables is harder to come by, largely because the presence of a leaf in a waterlogged deposit in a settlement does not indicate that it was necessarily brought there to be eaten. But we know that in prehistoric times the fibrous stems of stinging nettles were used to make twine, so it seems reasonable to suppose that its leaves (which cease to sting when boiled) could have been cooked. They are rich in iron. Today, nettle leaves are used to wrap Cornish yarg,* a cheese whose origins can be traced back to the seventeenth century – and quite possibly even earlier.[1]

Onions provide the basis for many modern dishes, but the large cultivated varieties originated in the Middle East and Asia and probably only reached Britain in Roman times.[2] The native British onion, sometimes called ramsons, or hedge garlic, has a strong oniony taste when raw, but quickly loses it when cooked. It is best chopped up and added to salads or stirred into stews; in our house we eat it a lot, but only for a few weeks in the year, when the leaves are still fresh, crisp and young. In the mid-1990s

---

* 'Yarg' is simply 'Gray' spelled backwards, the cheese being named after the artisan cheesemakers Alan and Jenny Gray, who found a 1615 recipe for a nettle-wrapped semi-hard cheese in a book in their attic. The original recipe is thought to date back to the thirteenth century. www.independent.co.uk/life-style/food-and-drink/features/yarg-cornish-cheese-s-conquered-america-9647985.html

we planted a large wood to protect our farm from north-easterly gales blowing off the Wash, and it's now rapidly approaching maturity. Sadly, the ash trees are suffering from ash die-back disease, but every spring the grim sight of so many collapsing trees is enlivened by a strong odour of garlic from the many thousands of ramsons that have spread rapidly through it, since we introduced them to the wood about fifteen years ago. I know of a local wood where they have formed an almost impenetrable ground cover.

My views on prehistoric cooking were fairly typical of most archaeologists: I knew what they ate and I imagined it wasn't particularly pleasant. Although I would never have said it, I imagine I assumed that in prehistory people were so worried about eating enough to stay alive that the actual quality of their food didn't really matter. It was a case of eat till stuffed, then lie back and digest. I rather assumed that the night-time peace of a Bronze Age settlement would have been frequently disturbed by intermittent belches, rumbling stomachs and echoing farts. Then things changed for me. We were filming an episode of *Time Team* somewhere on the Cornish coast.

The filming in Cornwall was rather different from normal. Usually when we were making an episode of *Time Team* we had to follow quite a rigid timetable. Fifty minutes of completed, edited footage is quite a big ask in just three days of filming. So we had to be disciplined about our meal breaks. The midday meal was supplied by professional location caterers and it was always delicious. But on this particular occasion the food was provided by Jacqui Wood, who was in charge of the prehistoric cooking for Phil Harding's experimental sequence. And today the menu included rock samphire. I'm more used to marsh samphire, which I buy every Friday in summer, at Long Sutton market. But the sort of samphire they ate in ancient Cornwall is known as rock samphire and is very different. It's actually a distant relative of carrots and, as its name suggests, it grows on coastal outcrops of rock, as distinct from marsh samphire, which prefers intertidal mudflats, like those around the Wash – a few miles from Long Sutton. I had heard rock samphire described as the poor relation of marsh, so I had never been in a rush to try it. But then I tried Jacqui's dish and I almost floated away. It was delicious and made with a traditional Cornish recipe.

That dish (and others that followed it) alerted me to the potential of prehistoric cooking. The ability to taste subtle flavours may originally have evolved as a means of survival: we all know, for example, that putrid meat and decayed plants smell and taste vile. But the passage of time allowed more sophisticated culinary understanding to develop; long before the arrival of the Bronze Age, our ancestors had learned to create some very appealing forms of food and drink by encouraging ingredients towards safer forms of decay. Fungi are the most important agents of the process and of course yeast is a tiny, single-celled fungus. Bread and beer are the end products of using selected strains of yeast in carefully controlled circumstances. Having worked in a commercial brewery, I have seen what can happen when the wrong strains of yeast are blown into the brewhouse from outside. Raw beer can acidify very rapidly – and is truly disgusting.

So I am in no doubt that the ability to cook good, tasty meals has long been appreciated and that the rock samphire that Jacqui Wood prepared for us was a very important moment for me. She had recreated a dish from the past, but in the process she had brought it back to the present, in a very personal and vivid way.[3] I think I found it particularly moving because over the previous few years I had been busily involved in the reconstruction of a Bronze Age farming settlement in the park at Flag Fen. We had acquired a small flock of Bronze Age sheep (of the prehistoric Soay breed) and had reconstructed a Bronze Age round-house in

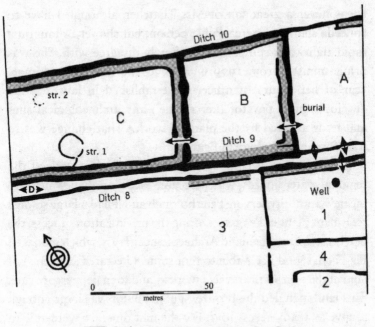

Bank ◄──► **Entrance way** ◄D► **Drove**

10.1 Part of a Bronze Age field system revealed at Fengate, on the Fen margins in eastern Peterborough. These fields were laid out between 1900 and 1400 BC and probably went out of use around 900 BC. The droveway for taking livestock to and from the open pastures of Flag Fen, some 500 m (550 yd) to the south-east, is formed by Ditches 8 and 9. The other paired parallel ditches marked out banks (shaded) on which hedges were planted. Note the round-house (str. 1) in field C (see Illus. 10.2).

its original setting, near a hedged and ditched droveway. It was when I was closely involved with the rebuilding of the house and its surroundings that I began to appreciate that the past is like a great country house: it is better appreciated if you can approach it from several directions. It is a lesson I have never forgotten.

I was never a great fan of Mrs Thatcher, although I have to concede she was a remarkable person; but she set Britain on a rapid rightward course that I strongly disagree with. She was prime minister from 1979 until 1990 and in the penultimate year of her tenure of office, she established in law that the developer must pay for (i.e. 'rescue') any archaeological sites and finds affected by the planned work.[4] That change was to transform archaeology in Britain.[*]

Earlier in her premiership (1979) she had privatized the regional water boards, which became PLCs. Anglian Water was the new authority serving Peterborough and it had a large sewage treatment plant in Fengate. During the privatization process, the newly established Fenland Archaeological Trust, which managed Flag Fen, found itself able to rent some 8 hectares (20 acres) of land at the edge of the sewage works – and for a peppercorn rate. This land included the Bronze Age site, but it was large enough to give us ready access to it. For the first time, we were able to drive to the site rather than having to trudge beside a huge dyke carrying everything we needed for the day's excavation: spades, shovels, cameras, surveying equipment and of course seed trays for finds and polythene bags for waterlogged wood.

The new management team at Anglian Water included many people who lived locally and who valued Flag Fen highly: the site had put Peterborough on the archaeological and historical map. In 1987 we opened a temporary visitor centre at Flag Fen and it soon started to attract appreciable numbers of tourists to the area – which was also good for the local economy. When I mentioned that I wanted to use the proposed new land to reconstruct a Bronze Age farm in its landscape, local Anglian Water managers greeted the idea enthusiastically. Now, in theory it would have been great if we could have dug the field and

---

[*] See Scene 4, page 71.

droveway ditches by hand, using authentic Bronze Age tools. But there were two problems. First, even today we still don't know how they would have done the digging. Digging-sticks have been discovered, but these would have been used to lift roots or set cuttings: they'd make useless spades. Hand shovels were made from ox shoulder blades, and these have been found from time to time in ancient ditches, but I cannot imagine them as heavy-duty tools for breaking through turf or digging into tightly packed gravels.

The other problem was more immediate: time and money – or rather the lack of both. I mentioned the second problem to my friends at Anglia Water and a week or so later a Hy-Mac tracked excavator appeared on site, with a full tank of diesel. I had 'casually' mentioned that I had a digger-driver's licence and to my delight they had taken the hint.

I spent the next few weeks driving the Hy-Mac while a couple of archaeologists rushed about with tapes and levels. They were surveying in the precise outline of the Bronze Age fields that we'd excavated half a mile to the west, on the dry land at Fengate, immediately next to Flag Fen. I still have the copy of the Third Fengate Report that they used as a source for the layout of those fields – it's much thumbed and still covered with mud.[5] As I dug out the ditches surrounding our recreated Bronze Age fields, I was constantly reminded of the back-breaking work this would originally have involved. Now, admittedly, I don't think they were initially dug to the depths we revealed when we excavated them: that would have been the result of many hundreds of regular maintenance and cleaning-out operations, which I presume were carried out during the quieter times of the farming year, but only when it was dry. I'm writing this during the record-breaking wet winter of 2019–20, when nobody in their right mind would be thinking of digging out ditches. Having said that, I don't think Bronze Age Fen farmers would have been impressed by the sodden state of the fenland fields I saw when I made a much dreaded trip to the dentist yesterday. Bronze Age farmers had many problems to contend with, but man-made climate change wasn't one of them.

I would never have made a good academic because I have always believed in following my instincts. The sort of imagination-restricting discipline you require for certain types of analytical research is not for me, because occasionally I have to change my mind and head off in new directions. However, now that I have reached a period in my life when I can look back reasonably dispassionately, I can appreciate that my digressions were all heading in a particular direction. They weren't as random as I once thought. We had completed the Fengate project and were starting to think about the Flag Fen reconstructions when Maisie and I together decided that it would be fun to run a few sheep in the paddock alongside the old Fen farmhouse where we lived. Maisie's father's family had kept cattle in the Scottish Highlands and my family are still active farmers in north Hertfordshire. You could say that farming was in our blood. I also felt a degree of frustration, because I knew that I didn't fully understand how the field systems we had revealed at Fengate actually 'worked'. In other words, how would they have been used and why were they laid out in what was clearly a very carefully thought-out fashion. Those people clearly knew what they were doing. Slowly it dawned on me that I could share their knowledge and expertise if I learned a bit about livestock farming myself. So we became sheep farmers. At first our flock was very small, but from 1995 it rapidly expanded and for the next twenty-five years it consisted of about a hundred breeding ewes.[6]

Certain aspects of animal behaviour have remained consistent for a very long time. Sheep, for example, often panic when isolated from the rest of the flock, so animals tend to bunch together when threatened. And yet all the textbooks on prehistoric farming maintained that primitive breeds of sheep couldn't be managed with the help of sheepdogs. It didn't take my well-trained Border collie long to show that was a myth.[7] I concede that modern sheepdogs are not precisely like their Neolithic equivalents, but sheep behaviour was very similar and I am sure that prehistoric farmers could have managed their flocks far more effectively than we believed until quite recently. Indeed, the sophisticated layout of their fields and stock-management systems proves this.

If we were to reconstruct a Bronze Age round-house, it would have to be set in an accurate recreation of the fields and yards around it. One feature of the fields and yards we had revealed in our excavations was the number of closely set parallel ditches. We knew from their arrangement that some undoubtedly formed the sides of droveways, but many of the narrower settings simply didn't make sense as droves, which have to lead to and from somewhere – but these narrower settings seemed to closely follow the edges of fields. We now realize that they were dug to provide earth for the low banks on which hedges were planted. And that was how we recreated them when we laid out our own Bronze Age-style fields at Flag Fen.

The house we chose to rebuild had originally been located alongside the droveway defined by Ditches 8 and 9 (Illus. 10.1: str. 1). I won't pretend for one moment that we reconstructed the Bronze Age round-house using entirely authentic tools and equipment. Frankly, that was a luxury we couldn't afford, as we were doing most of the building after work and lacked the time and certainly the money to be 100 per cent authentic. But I was at pains to finish all visible timbers using axes and adzes because it irritates me to see chainsaw cuts and suchlike in a supposedly 'authentic' reconstruction (and I have seen more than a few!).

Before we started the project, we closely studied the plan of a house we had excavated back in 1976. One thing puzzled us. There was quite clearly a ring of post-holes for posts that would have supported the roof. By the Iron Age, the conical roofs of round-houses were nearly always thatched and were pitched at an angle of forty-five degrees. That angle is important, because it makes the roof timbers form a very strong equilateral triangle, which for most single-family houses does not require internal supports. It's also the pitch that allows a thatched roof to shed water most effectively: any flatter and water will start to seep into the roof – especially if the rain is prolonged. The thatching of steep-pitched roofs demands secure fixing and most of the complex skills of a modern thatcher. But for some reason, thatched roofs seem to have had flatter pitches in the Bronze Age.

A roof pitch flatter than forty-five degrees is less integrally strong and cannot be secured as well with tie beams; so supporting posts are needed – like those we discovered in 1976. But twelve or so years later I was beginning to understand more about livestock management and I couldn't help wondering about the thickly thatched roofs you see in rural villages today and which invariably crown all reconstructed round-houses. I found it hard, and still find it hard, to look at a picture postcard Cotswold roof and not think that it represents half a winter's fodder for a medium-sized flock. There are tons of top-quality straw up there!

Shortly after we began work on the reconstruction, I found myself showing a group of Scandinavian archaeologists around the site. We began discussing the roof. I said I was very unhappy about using thick layers of thatch. One of them was smiling at me, but in a puzzled way. I started to re-explain my problem, but he interrupted me. I can't remember his precise words, but the gist of what he said was: 'No, they didn't use thick thatch. With a flatter roof pitch they would have used turf.' And then I thought of those many 'green roofs' in Norway and Sweden and the turf-roofed blackhouses on Lewis and elsewhere in the Highlands.[8] He was right! All I had to do now was prove it.

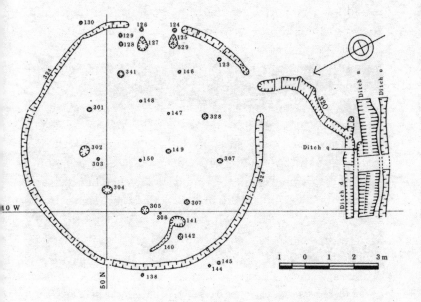

10.2 *Ground plan of the Middle Bronze Age (c. 1500 BC) round-house excavated at Fengate, Peterborough, in 1976. The shallow circular gully was to take water running off the roof. This was taken into the field boundary ditch system, to the right. The doorway, framed by four posts, is at the top of the plan and faces south-east. The pair of larger posts provides the door frame; the outer, smaller posts are for the porch. The circular walls (not visible on the ground) would have lined up with the larger doorposts. There are nine roof-support posts. The three smaller stake holes at the centre may be something to do with a spit or frame for the hearth.*

We spent quite a long time cutting turf and laying it carefully on the roof, which we had pre-prepared using hazel brushwood. We laid it in two layers: the first with the grass face down, the second with it up. I gather this was what was traditionally done in Scotland and it allowed the roots of the upper layer to grow into, and bind with, the one beneath. We watered the new green roof regularly and it looked magnificent – a sort of conical Wimbledon Centre Court. And then at last it rained. We'd been waiting for days for the chance to test our new creation.

10.3 The reconstructed turf-roofed Bronze Age (c. 1500 BC) house at Flag Fen, Peterborough, during maintenance in late summer. The sedge cone crowning the roof is being removed before replacement. Behind the house is the young hedge growing along a low bank beside the main droveway. The sheep are Soays.

It started quite slowly and I looked up at the sky. I hoped the clouds would get darker and more threatening, as this rain was only a little worse than drizzle. But if anything it was starting to clear up. It was very disappointing.

I nipped back through the smart new front doorway to tell the team inside the bad news. As I stepped across the threshold I felt something cold down the back of my neck. Had an earthworm dropped off the turf? I shuddered, and as I did so I noticed that I wasn't alone. Several people were fending off drips. The smart green roof leaked like a sieve. It was a very disappointing moment.

I spent the next few days on the phone to friends and colleagues in Scotland and Scandinavia and I learned that traditionally the turves are laid on quite a thick layer of carefully laid bracken, reeds or straw.* The idea of this is to guide water to the ground slowly, without dripping through. Then the weight of the turf will hold all the roof-covering in place. We removed the turf and added a layer of reeds and straw, which we were given by the local Internal Drainage Board. Then a few weeks later it was autumn and the skies grew darker again. This time it looked like real rain. And it was: good, no messing, thundery English rain. And the roof held it back superbly. After about half an hour of consistent downpour, we noticed some drops had come through, but these mostly ran along the underside of the reed/straw layer. Only a very few actually dripped onto the floor – and it really was chucking it down outside. I can remember mentally thanking those kind people in Scotland who had so generously shared their expertise with archaeologists and historians.

Post-war experimental archaeologists, such as Peter Reynolds and John Coles, realized that if a hole was left at the centre of a conical or pitched roof for the smoke to escape through, it would encourage a draught to develop, which would eventually dry the thatch and upper roof timbers. However, it would also take only a few rising sparks from the hearth below to set it alight, and that was precisely what happened, in 1958, to an experimental thatched prehistoric house at Allerslev, in Denmark.[9]

The traditional turf-roofed blackhouses of Lewis were rectangular and were provided with a double-thickness stone wall and a pitched turf roof, without gable ends.[10] The ridges were rounded and gentle, to accommodate the turves. No provision was made for chimneys and the hearth was at the centre of the building. Smoke simply filtered out through the roof, thereby

---

* In Scandinavia, birch bark is used.

staining it with carbon – hence their name. Blackhouses built more recently (they are increasingly popular as holiday cottages) have stone gable ends, with fires and chimneys.

I just mentioned that the roof ridges of some turf houses were rounded, which is fine if the roof is fairly long and narrow, but if it is conical, it doesn't work – or at least that's what we experienced. Yes, you could tie and pin turves in place for a few weeks, but they soon either crumbled in hot, dry weather or disintegrated in rain and frost. So I talked the problem over with a professional thatcher I had got to know quite well: what would he recommend? I thought he was going to suggest long straw, but coming from Huntingdonshire,* he was familiar with villages along the fen-edge around Willingham and Cottenham, where the cottages often have their ridges covered with saw-toothed sedge cut in what is now the nature reserve at Wicken Fen, a short distance to the east. He had some left over from last season – would I like to try it? But he warned us to use stout gauntlets. As a long-standing gardener, I'm used to cutting back pampas and other tall grasses whose leaves can give your hands deep cuts without you knowing it: they are *so* sharp. But the leaves of saw-toothed sedge were in a different class. I'll swear they could cut your hands without you touching them.

We tied the sedge into a series of bundles, which we spread and tied into place on the crown of the roof, rather like a hat, but overlapping the top tier of turves. Over the following winter it was disturbed by birds and small mammals, but it stayed in place. After a couple of years we needed to reset and repair it, but it didn't take long and was a small price to pay for such a dry roof. It also gave me an important insight into the sort of routine tasks that would have occupied people's daily lives – which was

---

* Now, like the Isle of Ely, sadly incorporated into the enlarged modern county of Cambridgeshire.

one of the main reasons we erected the house in the first place.

While we were working on the roof, I got to thinking about the roof space beneath the turf and sedge. In the past I had simply ignored it; after all, it would have been filled with smoke, fuggy and altogether pretty unpleasant. At about this time I had just discovered Manx kippers and traditional East Anglian bloaters from Great Yarmouth.[11] A few years later, I also came across the produce of traditional English smokehouses. A Mr Enderby of Grimsby wrote to say how much he had enjoyed one of my books, and would I like it if he sent me a couple of fillets of their smoked haddock, as a thank you. Of course I said yes. When they arrived, Maisie steamed them for supper. It was quite unlike anything I had ever eaten before: Mr Enderby's smoked haddock hadn't been dyed yellow and had a superb flaky texture, but it was still moist and had a captivating smoky/salty taste. Served with a knob of butter and home-grown leek and potato mash, it vanished from my plate in seconds. I've since formed a small group of archaeological Enderby fish fans and every Christmas we order hundreds of pounds' worth of fish from him – and it's all prepared in the last traditional fish smokehouse in Grimsby.[12] We tend to forget that proper traditional artisanal English food can be every bit as good as anything from France. So what would have hung in that smoke-filled roof space in the Bronze Age?

When I learned about round-houses in the mid-1960s, the first reconstructions were just being built. In those days, most of what we knew about Iron Age round-houses and settlements came from excavations carried out in the last years before the war by an exiled German professor of Jewish heritage, Gerhard Bersu, at Little Woodbury, in Wiltshire. In many respects I think it was one of the most influential prehistoric digs ever undertaken in Britain; although partly written in an internment camp over eighty years ago, the report looks and reads like something prepared yesterday.[13] It was Bersu who pointed out the significance of post-holes and how they allowed the accurate reconstruction of buildings. One member of the digging team, who was later to become a leading professor in his own right, Stuart Piggott, illustrated possible reconstructions of the buildings. Bersu's meticulous excavations suddenly brought British prehistory to life – even if most people didn't realize what he had achieved until very much later, in the late 1960s.

The first serious attempt to reconstruct life in an Iron Age round-house, using high standards of experimental archaeology, was organized in 1970 at Little Butser, in Hampshire. It was run by Peter Reynolds, a very charismatic archaeologist, who gave the project the high profile it needed in order to survive. I visited Little Butser many times and my wife, Maisie, worked there twice in the mid-1970s.[14] While she was there, she was gored by a bad-tempered Dexter cow – the small traditional Irish breed whose bones closely resemble those found on Iron Age sites. Three years later, the same cow featured in the BBC television series *Living in the Past*, where to everyone's surprise it also caused endless disruption.[15] I hope Peter hadn't lent her to them mischievously; I wouldn't have put it past him – especially if the Beeb hadn't offered him a decent price.[*]

Most people who have worked with experimental reconstructions acknowledge that the roof space would have been hung with the odd ham, fish fillet or eel, and when one visits reconstructions it is not unusual to see such things suspended above one's head. But when I started work on the turf roof of the Flag Fen house, I was very struck by the smoke in the roof space: it really was very dense and intense – and even when the fire was out, it smelled incredibly strongly of smoke. I suspect this was because Bronze and Iron Age householders would have taken enormous pains to burn nothing but dry seasoned wood,

---

[*] Peter Reynolds died in 2001, aged sixty-one.

whose smoke is less visibly dense, but is far more concentrated in smell and also, I suspect, in its ability to cure food. In effect, this meant that every household also comprised a self-contained smokehouse – which is not to say, of course, that in certain places, such as seaside or fishing villages, there weren't also specially built smokehouses, complete with racks – like their medieval and modern counterparts, but on a smaller scale.

In the modern world we take the preservation of food for granted, whether frozen in packs, dried in packets, canned or bottled. Traditional methods of preservation, by smoking and curing in salt, are reserved for ham, bacon and various rather exotic lines on delicatessen counters. Today, such techniques are more about adding flavour than extending shelf life. I love such food and am frequently to be found in our local Polish shop, where the variety of delicious cured meats is endless. So I wondered about that late prehistoric roof space: would it *really* have been the scene of a few rather forlorn dangling bits of meat and fish, or would it not have been far more populated – with every rafter festooned with eels and fish and racks full of hams and cheese? Jacqui Wood's cooking opened my eyes to the possibility of tasty food in prehistory, but the trouble with good-tasting food is that once you've tried it, you want it again – and again. We know for a fact that in the Bronze and Iron Ages Britain was home not just to pigs, cattle, sheep and goats, but also to salmon, trout, eels and even more exotic delicacies, such as sturgeon.* The roe of sturgeon is the basic ingredient of caviar, which is cured in salt – and sometimes smoked.

Would it be taking things too far to suppose that prehistoric families might have eaten caviar? I don't think it is. I can remember that mealtimes in my childhood often seemed

---

* We found Iron Age sturgeon bones in our excavations at Fengate. They could have been caught in a local river, or out in the Wash.

very adventurous: my parents enjoyed many exotic things, in retrospect as a reaction to the rather dull food of wartime rationing. Along with other grown-ups, they loved fresh oysters and squid, complete with tentacles, for example, which I detested at first, but eventually got to like and then to adore. I suspect that many Bronze and Iron Age children might have been on similar journeys themselves. Eating food has never been just about acquiring nutrition: delight and revulsion have always been involved. That is why I firmly believe that life inside a round-house would have been both interesting and exciting – and not just for adults. That mention of caviar, however, raises another important ingredient, which we take entirely for granted today, but which would have transformed life in later prehistoric times. It is time to step outside the round-house.

Scene 11

Prosperity from Mud and Mire
(1200 BC–AD 300)

The 'Red Hills' of Essex – Northey and Fengate – Tetney
and the Lincolnshire Marshes – Cowbit and the Fens

I think it's widely appreciated today that salt was very important in the past. The most frequently quoted example of this is the word 'salary', which derives from the Latin word for salt – *sal* – and reflects the fact that in medieval times certain people were paid, wholly or in part, in salt. It was a much-needed and valuable commodity.

My personal interest in salt goes back to 1977 when our team was excavating at Fengate, in eastern Peterborough. In those days, Peterborough New Town was expanding rapidly and all the local gravel pits were working flat out to provide developers and the New Town Development Corporation with aggregates and concrete. One medium-sized pit was located on the far side of Flag Fen on the edges of the large natural 'island' of Whittlesey. I knew most of the pit managers and had their permission to walk through the quarries from time to time – today, of course, such a casual attitude would be impossible.

One sunny afternoon I took a stroll through the Northey quarry, where to my great delight I spotted what looked like the distinctive U-shaped profile of two ditches, whose slightly pale, rather washed-out-looking filling was identical to that of the Bronze Age field boundary ditches we had been excavating at Fengate, for the previous six years. I immediately ran across to them. Happily for me, the quarry's mechanical excavator hadn't done a particularly tidy job and much of the Bronze Age ditch filling had been dumped to one side. Of course, I looked at it closely. In my experience it's always best to examine the surface of such deposits very carefully before you produce your trowel or spade. Very often, tiny pieces of pottery or flint tools will show up quite clearly, having been washed by many showers and morning dews. At first I could see nothing, but then I spotted something paler, and about the size of my thumb. At first glance it looked fairly straightforward. It was probably a piece of coarse Bronze Age pottery, just like the stuff we had been finding in the ditches at Fengate.

I pulled my trowel from the back pocket of my jeans, but then I hesitated. There was something odd and formless about it: it didn't resemble any pottery I'd ever seen. I laid the trowel aside and leaned forward for a closer look. Yes, it was pottery – or perhaps fired clay – but its shape was all wrong; it didn't seem even slightly pot-like. Normally, pots of this period are bowls or jars, with well-made sides, distinctive rims and good, flat bases. But this was very different and hard to describe. It looked more like somebody had squashed a bit of clay and then fired it. I pulled out my trowel and carefully cleared the soil around it. Then, very slowly, and with both hands, I lifted it out of the ground.

While I was trowelling, the thought occurred to me that it might turn out to be a broken weight from a prehistoric weaver's loom; we'd found several of these in earlier years and they often proved to be quite fragile and crumbly. But when I held it up, it seemed quite firm – even hard. It had obviously been heated deliberately: it wasn't something made of clay that had somehow fallen into a hearth or bonfire. And my first impression was right: it did look like a piece of squeezed clay, with slightly flattened ends. The more I turned it over in my hands, the more I thought I might know what it was. Slowly, it was starting to look more familiar – or was I deluding myself? I think archaeologists quite often have moments like that.

That piece of fired clay remained in the back of my mind for some time. Then one day I was sitting in the pub with some archaeological colleagues and we were discussing the first digs we had been on. I told them about my time on one of the longest-running 'rescue' excavations of the day, at the huge gravel pits overlooking the Thames Estuary at Mucking, in Essex. I think a couple of the others had been there too and we had a few laughs – the way ex-students do. Then, while we were chatting away, everything suddenly fell into place. I knew exactly what that piece of fired clay was all about.

The piece of fired clay we had found in that gravel pit at Northey was part of what archaeologists refer to as '*briquetage*'. This is a French word used to describe bits of rather shapeless, brick-like fragments of fired clay. These had originally formed a series of basins and their supports to hold seawater, which was then heated up to make salt. The particular piece from Northey would have been one of several lumps of clay that had been hand-squeezed to prop up an evaporation vessel over a kiln-like fire. This would explain its flattened ends.

The reason the mention of a well-known site in Essex made me suddenly remember what salt-extraction debris looks like is quite simply that Essex has a very long coastline to the north of the Thames Estuary. It's a flat landscape, subject to frequent tidal flooding, and is intersected by numerous creeks and pools. In certain areas, usually set slightly back from the lowest-lying tidal mudflats, are a series of low mounds, known locally as Red Hills.[1] These are all that remain of ancient salt-extraction sites, which got their name from the distinctive red colour of the burnt clays and silts that accumulated on them while they were in use. Red Hills extend along the Essex and Suffolk coasts and up into East Anglia. They can be dated from the Bronze Age, through the Iron Age and into Roman times. The briquetage from Northey was dated to around 1200 BC, which would place it at the very start of the sequence.[2]

I have always found that one of the most appealing aspects of archaeology is that it can reveal remarkable stories not just about great sites, but about humdrum, everyday objects too. One find I will never forget was revealed in a very ordinary ditch just a short distance from Northey. It was also part of the salt-making process, but it had a unique story that still has the power to fire my imagination: I would so like to meet the person who made and intended to use it.

At the same time that Northey was being excavated, we also started to find evidence for salt extraction in two of the Bronze Age field boundary ditches at Fengate, about half a mile to the south-west, on the other side of the Flag Fen basin.[3] This time we found six pieces of briquetage, but also two unusual pieces of pottery. One was a substantial fragment from a large, flat-sided vessel that had deliberately been snapped off along one edge, which also showed clear evidence for a saw-like cut.[*] Sawn vessels like this are known from salt-production sites elsewhere. Near it was a small flat-bottomed round bowl of about 95-millimetre (4-in) diameter. It was quite competently made, with thin walls, but no care whatsoever had been taken over its appearance: it

---

[*] Toothed metal saws didn't appear until a millennium later. The cut was possibly done with an abrasive, such as coarse grit or sharp sand, and a tough fibre or skin twine.

was poorly finished, with a very irregular rim – quite unlike other pottery of the time. One got the firm impression that this was a disposable vessel – the equivalent today of a supermarket yogurt pot. Again, similar containers have been found on other prehistoric salt sites.

Complete pots are very rarely found on prehistoric settlement sites, because what generally survives are the remains of domestic or farmyard rubbish – and as a rule, people in the past, just like today, don't discard unbroken pots. If the Fengate pot had been intended as a container, then it would have been filled with salt that had been freshly removed from the evaporation pans and was still slightly damp. It would have been packed in and then allowed to harden, thereby becoming more stable and easier to transport. Today, we take powdery table salt for granted, but it only remains pourable and loose through additives[*] and because modern houses are warm and dry. Take some unadulterated ground sea salt on a camping holiday to the Lake District, and you will soon discover how it behaves when even slightly damp.

If the salt in the moulds was indeed in a block, then it would make sense to break the jar to remove it. I would suggest that the salt used in the preparation and consumption of food would have been kept in a lidded container close to the kitchen hearth. Small blocks could be split off, as and when they were needed. That unused, rather hastily made pot lying in a ditch near the Fengate briquetage and the large sawn-through sherd reminded me very much of the debris that lay around the back yard of Truman's Brewery in Brick Lane, in East London, where I took my first full-time job, shortly after leaving university. The yard was by no means an untidy mess, but it was somewhere people worked and the debris of daily production was all around us: broken pallets, leaky wooden casks and faulty bottles. At the

---

[*] Known as 'anti-caking agents'.

end of the day they'd be tidied away into skips, or onto heaps to be burned at the weekend.

Traditionally, beer is brewed in batches, known as gyles, and material would often be left over at the end of a batch. It was stored carefully to be used in the next gyle, but I wonder what would happen if brewing, like salt extraction, was seasonal: something that only happened in the warmer months of summer? Maybe that explains why the pottery salt container wasn't used. At the end of the summer, when the weather became colder and damper, it was swept into a nearby ditch, whose sides and bottom were probably thickly lined with grass, cushioning its fall and preserving it for posterity. I wonder if the people who made the pot and had the task of clearing the season's rubbish had any idea that we would be thinking about them, over three thousand years later.

Peterborough is about 56 kilometres (35 miles) from the coast as the crow flies, and I wouldn't have expected to find evidence for salt extraction there. But even today the River Nene is tidal as far inland as the wonderfully named Dog in a Doublet sluice, midway between Whittlesey and Thorney, just 8 kilometres (5 miles) east of Peterborough. Sea levels in the Bronze Age were 2 or 3 metres (6–10 ft) lower than they are today (rising sea levels are not a modern phenomenon), but the region had not been subject to the extensive drainage and flood-protection measures that were introduced in medieval times, and later. Were it not for these many high banks and deep ditches, large areas of the western Fens should have been flooded by the sea many centuries ago. By the Bronze Age, the area around Fengate and Northey, a short walk east of Peterborough's Eastern Industrial Area, would have been a landscape of seasonally flooded tidal creeks and mudflats.[4] I suspect that in particularly active seasons, tidal floods would have reached Peterborough by flowing up the various winding courses of the River Nene. Peterborough-on-Sea is an interesting thought – and maybe one that might become reality again, before too long.

The presence of tidal waters so close to Peterborough would explain why there was evidence for salt extraction, but it was clearly on a fairly small scale – and for quite a short time. Water levels continued to rise slowly throughout the Bronze and Iron Ages. By the start of the Iron Age, however, there was less salt in local water; marine tides were confined closer to the coast, which would help to explain the growth of huge peat beds in Whittlesey Mere, the great freshwater lake that had formed directly south of Peterborough. This was one of the largest lakes in England, prior to its drainage in 1852.[5]

While a few people were starting to extract salt from brackish (semi-salt) water at Northey and Fengate, some 1,500 kilometres (930 miles) to the south-east, at the lakeside location of Hallstatt in the Austrian Alps, Europe's first large-scale salt mine was coming into operation. There is some evidence that people had been extracting salt from Hallstatt in a small way since Neolithic times, but after 1200 BC the pace started to quicken; from 800 BC until about 500 BC, the mines were a major enterprise. Salt doesn't just pickle onions and bacon. It also preserves anything in close contact with it, like the superb pieces of fabric worn by the Bronze Age miners at Hallstatt – and even a three-thousand-year-old wooden staircase leading from one gallery to another. It is the oldest staircase anywhere in the world.[6] I mention this partly because I'd hate you not to have the chance of seeing such a remarkable structure when you next find yourself in the Alps, but also because it shows that from the start of the first millennium BC, salt was playing a major role in the European economy.

Britain is an island surrounded by sea, so it is not surprising to discover that salt was being extracted quite widely by coastal communities. The presence of rocks and cliffs makes salt extraction more difficult – what is required is easy access to less turbulent waters. Quiet tidal ponds and lagoons where you can erect your heated evaporation dishes are ideal – and these are most readily found along Britain's east coast. Sadly, these coastal mudflats are under serious threat from climate change and rising sea levels. It is therefore essential that sites similar to the Red Hills of Essex are surveyed and mapped, so they can be protected when new coastal wetlands are constructed during the process of what used to be called 'Managed Retreat'[7] – but which today we would see as controlled coastal flooding.

I think it is inevitable that the world we inhabit will colour, if not actually shape, our view of the past, which is why I have taken readers to places they may not be very familiar with. When Britain was held in the grip of the Ice Ages, sea levels were very much lower, largely because so much water was locked up within enormous ice sheets, some of which partially covered Britain. The land that would later become the island of Britain was then an integral part of the European mainland. As sea levels rose, the North Sea began to be recognizable as such from about twelve thousand years ago. It is generally thought that land to the south – now beneath the sea – in what one might term the North Sea basin was quite well populated.[*] It was a very rich environment for hunters and fishers, with quantities of shellfish, waders and eels, as well as vegetables such as marsh samphire. There were even low hills and areas of woodland. People would probably have regarded what are now the countries of Denmark, Germany, Holland and Britain as a slightly hostile hinterland – until, that is, they were forced to move there, as water levels rose even higher, from about 6000 BC. The reason I mention this is that it suggests to me that people then would have had a very different

---

[*] Prehistorians call it 'Doggerland', see Scene 1, page 9.

cultural 'mindscape', or sense of social history, compared with how we see ourselves today.

Our world is essentially landlocked and increasingly urban, whereas their populations were mainly centred on coastal places. Although societies were to change quite radically with the arrival of farming shortly before 4000 BC, I believe that many communities would have continued to have strong links to the coast and the sea. Salt would have played a major role in maintaining those links. Some recent surveys are now showing that the extent of salt extraction along the coasts of eastern England was far more intensive than we had once supposed. Salt must have been traded with inland communities in considerable quantities; and as we all know, once you have tasted salted food, there is no turning back – you are hooked. Indeed, as with all pleasurable addictions, you will be happy to spread the good news. Like sugar very much later, salt was a commodity whose success was inbuilt and guaranteed.

I've already suggested that my interest in the prehistoric salt trade was first kindled by our relatively minor finds at Northey and Fengate. I say minor, because we never discovered an actual place where salt was extracted (these, incidentally, are known to archaeologists and historians as 'salterns'). I would dearly have liked to have found one, but it was not to be, because the salterns close to the edge of the Fens, at places like Fengate, would almost certainly have been ploughed flat by centuries of farming. If they do survive, they'll lie in buried landscapes, such as the newly revealed complex at Must Farm. While we were excavating in the Cambridgeshire Fens during the last three decades of the twentieth century, fellow archaeologists were surveying for new sites just across the county boundary in Lincolnshire. They were working closer to the coast, in areas where medieval and recent farming had been less intense – and what their work revealed was truly remarkable.

In the early 1990s, a subsurface geophysical survey was carried out ahead of the construction of a new sewage treatment works at Tetney (see map, Illus. 11.1, page 213), not far from Cleethorpes on the north Lincolnshire coast.[8] The survey was done because the area was known to have been the site of many medieval salterns, thirteen of which were recorded in the Domesday survey of 1086. The industry thrived throughout the Middle Ages and into the sixteenth century, when Lincolnshire salterns were put out of business by competition from Scotland and north-eastern England.

The survey at Tetney revealed what looked like a classic set-up: a medium-sized natural pool, about 16 metres (17 yd) across, with a spread of occupation debris to one side and two dense patches of salt-making briquetage fragments along part of the edge of the pool. Immediately next to the larger spread of briquetage, and also alongside the pool, was a fire pit, where clay pans of salt water from the pool were heated up to extract the salt. These pans were raised above the fire using clay supports similar to the ones we found at Fengate and Northey. The pottery was broadly similar and also came in two distinct forms: thick- and thin-walled. Then the results of radiocarbon dating came through and the Tetney site was securely dated to between 845 and 745 BC. So it was firmly Late Bronze Age.

Our understanding of salt extraction has been transformed by a series of discoveries made during the course of the English Heritage Fenland Survey of 1981–8.[9] It had long been realized that the archaeology of the Wash Fens was very rich and well preserved; but it was becoming increasingly apparent that this valuable resource was rapidly being destroyed and seriously damaged by drainage and intensive arable agriculture – hence the need for the survey. While it was taking place I was carrying out active research in the Fens with my team, and we helped the Fenland surveyors whenever we could. At first I found their discoveries very exciting, but as time passed and more and more sites were drying out, and the extent of plough damage became evident, I found the survey was starting to depress me. This was despite the huge amount of work they did, and their scrupulous attention to detail. They were certainly revealing superb and unexpected sites. Indeed, amazing new discoveries, such as the waterlogged Bronze Age settlement at Must Farm, are still being made as a direct consequence of the survey's pioneering research.

It was something deeper that was upsetting me. It felt as if a lot of what was being done – what we were all trying to achieve – was to no avail. Somehow we were failing to get across to the wider public. Sure, our conferences, lectures and seminars were well attended, but their audiences were mostly elderly and I recognized many of the faces as long-term archaeological enthusiasts. I remember giving a talk once and having to stop because of the high-pitched noise given off by so many of the audience's hearing aids. It seemed to me that the scale of the damage to our most important and best-preserved archaeological sites demanded a new audience – preferably of younger people. In retrospect, we would have welcomed a Greta Thunberg – but even as recently as thirty years ago, such a youthful figure would still have been regarded as suspect and unreliable. So our message remained – and I fear still remains – unappreciated outside archaeological circles. The public at large don't realize just how much of our archaeological heritage has been destroyed since the war – and why we must take urgent measures to protect what little is left. Sadly, when politicians want to stimulate economic development, archaeology is usually seen as an impairment to growth, because a dig or survey might delay a project by a few months.

Today, there is widespread – and entirely justifiable – concern over the largely man-made climate emergency and the damage it is doing to the environment. Some of us have been very worried about it since the 1970s. The pollution scares of that decade and the 1980s frightened everyone. I recall reading Rachel Carson's *Silent Spring*, a pioneering classic of environmental science first published in 1962.[10] The book's title refers to the lack of birds of prey, killed off by accumulating DDT and other pesticides – many of them synthetic organic compounds that became concentrated in animals at the head of the food chain (and whose use is now banned in many countries). When I was a child, growing up in the countryside in the 1950s, you never saw sparrowhawks or kestrels, let alone buzzards, kites or harriers. I can well remember seeing the first buzzards circling above their nest in the wood we planted on our small farm. That was around 2010. It took almost twenty years for them to find us, but as they wheeled high above my head, exchanging their distinctive 'mew-mew' calls, I thought of *Silent Spring* and how Rachel Carson would have welcomed them.[*]

I seem to be witnessing history repeat itself. Just as in the 1980s, when archaeology was never mentioned in any discussion of pollution, today all we hear about is the climate emergency. But the wholesale destruction of ancient landscapes by intensive modern agriculture, across lowland Britain and western Europe, is an integral part of the process. At the same time, archaeological sites are being trashed by wars and antiquities traders in the Middle East. Yet even this wanton vandalism fails to raise public awareness. For most British people, the words 'archaeology' and 'history' are still synonymous with hoards of buried treasure,

---

[*] Carson died in 1964, just two years after her landmark book's publication.

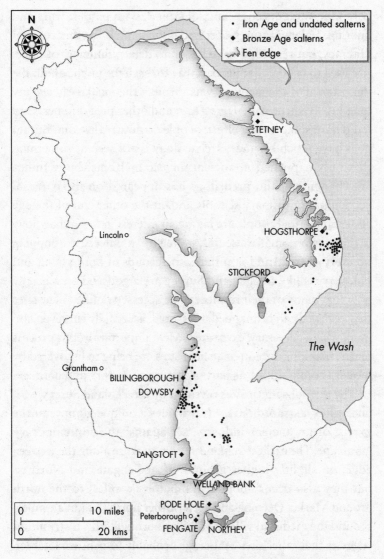

11.1 A map showing the distribution of Bronze and Iron Age salt extraction sites (salterns) in the Fenland region. The Bronze Age sites mostly date to the period 1300–700 BC. The majority of sites belong to the later Iron Age (from about 300 BC into earlier Roman times).

with kings and queens – and, of course, with battles, wars and fighting. I blame ratings-obsessed TV channels for this cultural illiteracy, but recently I have begun to detect glimmers of hope.

I used to believe that the best way to teach the public about the importance of archaeology was through the media – hence my long involvement with *Time Team* and other programmes. And it did have some lasting effect: people do now realize that Britain does have a rich heritage; archaeology is not seen as something that only happened in ancient Greece or Rome. Now things are changing again: prehistory has appeared on the national curriculum of primary schools and, at the other end of the age spectrum, retired people are taking an interest in the archaeology of their region. Small museums, staffed by volunteers, are popping up everywhere. And for enthusiastic groups of both young and old, surveys like the Fenland Survey are a godsend – especially now that many of their results can be accessed online.[11] The sites they revealed can be mapped, measured, accurately surveyed and even, where necessary, excavated. Most importantly, this process means that long-forgotten ancient sites are being rediscovered by modern communities, as part of their local history and heritage.

The map of saltern sites revealed by the Fenland Survey was, and still is, extraordinary.[12] It provides a unique glimpse of the extent of an ancient industry, set against the contemporary landscape. The earliest Fenland saltern sites are along the western edge, on slightly higher ground, as at Fengate and Northey, but they also occur about 8 kilometres (5 miles) to the north around Market Deeping and even further north (24 km/15 miles) around the medieval village of Billingborough. This distribution suggests that other sites of this age probably lie beneath later fen deposits a short distance to the east. These few sites aside, the vast majority of Fenland sites belong within the Iron Age and into Roman times, from about 500–400 BC probably through to the second and third centuries AD.

We had long suspected that there was more to the production of salt in prehistory than just the boiling-up of water. The problem is that seawater isn't *that* saline: 1 litre (1¾ imperial pints) produces just 3.5 grams (0.1 oz) of salt. And it takes a lot of heat to boil off a litre of water – just to produce a bit less than a teaspoon of salt. So it seems very likely that one of the reasons why salterns were located at places like Tetney was the natural tidal pools that occurred there. These were sometimes enhanced by temporary dams, perhaps built up in late spring when the weather calmed down and water levels were still high. They would then be left alone for the seawater within them to heat in the summer sunshine – day after day. People sometimes laugh at the idea of hot weather at places like Skegness – 'It's SO bracing!' – but as someone who has lived near the Wash coast for a long time, I am only too aware how hot it can become on long summer days. I've seen permanent grazing die back and turn brown after a hot July, and it would have been no different in the Bronze Age.

Eventually, in late summer or early autumn, people would head out into the marshes and scoop what was left of the water in tidal pools into the evaporation dishes. It would have been quite muddy, but very salty. As part of the baling-out process, the water would have been filtered, initially through reeds or straw, but later through woven fabric. This was probably the part of the process that involved the larger pottery vessels. Experiments have shown that heating the water also makes it easier to filter out mud and clay particles. Eventually, the damp salt would be packed into pottery containers, which were then loaded onto carts or barrows and taken inland. It all sounds quite simple, but as ever, excavation reveals a more complex story.

Cowbit (pronounced 'Cubbit') is a medieval village built on one of the dried-out courses of the River Welland, just south of Spalding. Today, the landscape is quite dramatic, with the great

PLAN

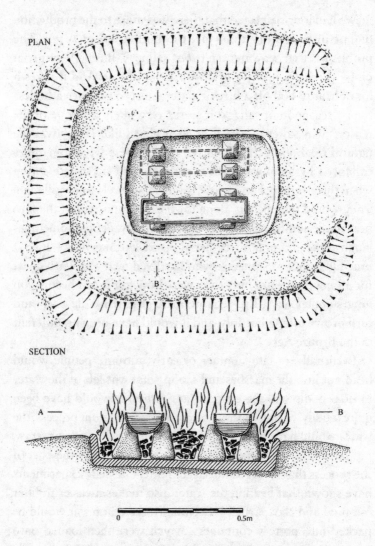

SECTION

A —

— B

0   0.5m

11.2 Reconstruction of a traditional Iron Age open, tray-like
saltern hearth, where two gutter-shaped troughs are raised above
the hot charcoals on pyramid-shaped clay supports.

flood banks of the modern river and huge areas of intentionally flooded 'washland' between them. I said 'modern', but in reality the great Welland Washes were created in 1664 – one of many major fen drainage schemes of the seventeenth century. As part of the Fenland Survey, a series of about thirteen salterns was found near the village in Cowbit Wash; sadly they were now very dried-out and had been quite badly damaged by ploughing.[13] Despite the dryness and damage, in 1986 it was decided that one site should be excavated. It turned out to be a very wise decision.[14]

Radiocarbon dates suggest the Cowbit site was in use towards the latter part of the Iron Age, during the last two centuries BC.[15] There is evidence, however, that it was almost certainly visited on several occasions. There were not many traces of domestic rubbish or other signs of permanent settlement, which perhaps suggests that the saltern was worked by a small group from a nearby community. A broadly similar pattern was observed at other salterns of this period in the Fens, which might imply that salt extraction was something carried out by local communities not so much to earn a living as to supplement their lifestyle. There is evidence to suggest that a few centuries later, in Roman times, the production of salt had gradually intensified to become a true industry and one that supported the families living close by the salterns, full-time.

The Cowbit dig revealed the bottom of a saltern oven. The walls were of clay and the base led off the stoke pit, where the hot draught from a covered fire was conducted into the oven along two grooves in the base. The grooves were bridged by four slabs, which carried a series of short clay supports for a large evaporation tray. A series of troughs were raised on slightly taller clay supports above the tray. It was important that hot air from the hearth and stoke-hole was able to circulate freely – hence the many supports – around the evaporation vessels, which were

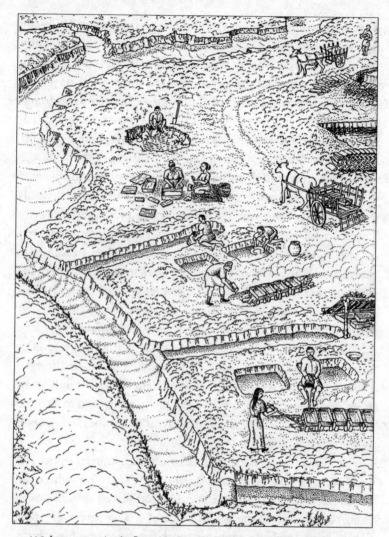

11.3 A reconstruction by Dave Hopkins showing life on a Lincolnshire Fenland saltern at South Drove, in Morton Fen, about 6.5 km (4 miles) west of Spalding. The scene is based on excavations of a site that was in use in the late first to early second century AD, in early Roman times, although the people and the techniques they employed were firmly based on earlier, Iron Age, practices.

formed from stiff clay, before the oven was fired up, and were then discarded when it was emptied.

The enclosed oven-like salterns at Cowbit were rather unusual and would not have been found on earlier sites of the Bronze and Iron Ages, where the evaporation vessels that contained the concentrated brine were heated over a fire, held in a pan-like open hearth, beneath them.

The fen around Cowbit has been drained and farmed for many centuries, which is why the archaeological remains had been damaged. But head north for a couple of miles, into Spalding, then turn left towards the western fen-edge and after about 6.5 kilometres (4 miles) you enter Morton Fen, which was drained far more recently. The saltern site at Willow Tree Farm in Morton Fen lies close to the new nature reserve at Willow Tree Fen.[16] The site was well preserved and the excavators were able to piece together how the whole complex would have worked.

Although the Willow Tree Farm saltern was in use in the transition from the Iron Age to Roman times – in other words, it's slightly younger than the site at Cowbit – most of the techniques used there were traditional. The tidal mudflats at Willow Tree Farm were capped in many places by layers of peat, which were cut and placed in stacks to dry. This would provide fuel for the salterns – and indeed for the neighbouring settlement (which would have been placed on less flood-prone land). The excavations revealed that tidal creeks had been extended by artificial canal-like cuttings, which were further lengthened by shorter spurs that ran up to, and alongside, the salterns. Once filled, they were blocked off and this was where the initial, sunlight, evaporation took place. Smaller, roughly square, steep-sided tanks were cut between the spurs and the actual saltern ovens. Slightly more concentrated water was scooped from the spurs into the tanks, where it was allowed to settle and evaporate further. It was then poured directly into the troughs on their supports above the unlit fire.

The evaporation troughs and their clay supports were all made on site, and when the heated evaporation had been completed, the salt-filled troughs were allowed to cool. They were then loaded onto carts and taken back to the settlement.

We tend to think of families as closely knit small groups – so-called nuclear families – of parents and children. In the modern world, grandparents frequently live on their own, in separate houses, often in different towns or cities. It's a very self-contained existence, where individual identity and freedom are most important. But in the relatively recent past, households were generally much larger, with grandparents, not to mention various unmarried or widowed aunts and uncles, sharing the same roof as the main nuclear family. In these larger households, it was not uncommon for members of the family to move elsewhere for extended periods: young men would accompany herds or flocks to distant summer grazing, and in more elite families young men and women would spend the summer season attending balls in fashionable Bath or London, while older people would retreat to the comfort of spa towns such as Buxton or Cheltenham.

My point is that family ties provide both the emotional and social support together with the networks needed for people to be very independent at certain times in their lives. I don't think for one moment that complete nuclear families would have decamped from their farms on natural 'islands', or from villages around the fen-edges, to spend time at places like Cowbit, firing up salterns. It seems far more likely that this would have been done by selected members of several related families, undoubtedly under the close supervision of a recognized salt-maker, who may also have been a senior member of one of the families. I would guess that many of the people in these groups would have been young adults and they almost certainly would have visited the salterns for several years in succession, because the skills required of them were considerable – and acquiring them would have formed an important part of their education. If one considers salt-making in this light, it might well have been a very congenial occasion: the close rules of domestic life could be set aside in this wilder marshy environment, where younger people could relax and take the time to discover themselves, away from the constant supervision of their parents.

Today, the process of acquiring knowledge and experience of life when young is seen in two quite distinct ways. First, there is Education (with a capital 'E'); this is a process where children and young people are lectured by an older teacher, often aided today by online support and specially written textbooks. The pupils who prove quick to learn are regarded as successful and are then moved into Higher Education (again with capital letters), followed by entry into a Profession (ditto). The other route is known as training or apprenticeship and is reserved for those with 'practical skills'. These people might find writing essays or learning languages difficult, but can often do impossible things with wood or metal. Like most field archaeologists, my working life has been spent among both groups of people. I cannot discern any qualitative distinction between Education and training. They are both part of the same process: learning.

I have often been asked if there is any evidence for education (without a capital letter) in prehistoric Britain. The short answer to that is both Yes and No. No, there are no identifiable schools or classrooms, but Yes, it took huge skill to build round-houses, or shrines like Stonehenge, whose builders understood both the lunar and solar calendars and probably many other complex astronomical phenomena as well.* Those skills and that background information *must* have been passed on from previous generations. Much of this education would doubtless have been provided informally, within a family setting: one can

---

* See Scene 4, page 64.

imagine a grandparent teaching a circle of younger children. But most information would have been passed on at work, when younger people were learning new skills, out on the farm, or in the round-house kitchen. I suspect that the late summer trip to the tidal salterns would have been another learning opportunity, but one experienced away from home and the reproachful gaze of disapproving parents. I had a similar experience when I was sixteen and spent many hard-working weeks at harvest time, driving tractors on a large Shropshire hop farm. The evenings were very convivial indeed.

The Fenland Survey has shown that those salterns out in the tidal mudflats around the Wash were not as lonely as we once believed. I would not be at all surprised if the people working them did not get to meet up with others, like them, working nearby. Hard work does not have to be dull and I suspect that the people working the salterns would probably have seen their time in the marshes as something of a holiday: a refreshing break from the routines of the farming year. Who knows, maybe they would meet a future partner there? And when it was over and they all returned to their families, they brought with them the basic ingredient of many delicious pickles and tasty meals. I bet they were given a very warm welcome home.

Scene 12

Living near Water (1000 BC–AD 200)

*Atlantic Britain – Fenland Farmers –
Loch Tay and the Isle of Skye*

We Britons are used to getting wet. This reflects the fact that we live in a group of islands on Europe's north-western edge, at the brink of the Atlantic Ocean. Thanks to the revolution of the Earth, our weather systems move from west to east, with greater or lesser energy, depending on the time of year. The ceaseless passage of storms, rain and shower clouds from off the sea ensures that our islands are constantly supplied with rain. The western approaches to the British Isles, especially Ireland and the highlands and islands of Scotland, are the wettest places, but parts of Wales, south-western and north-western England are only slightly drier. These are all areas where rain-fed blanket bogs of acid peat were able to form naturally.* But the water couldn't stay on land for ever: it had to continue on its journey back to the sea by way of countless streams, rivers and brooks. This constantly renewed cycle of rain and drain has given Britain a uniquely complex set of landscapes, where natural watercourses, ponds and lakes have played a major role in the development of local settlements and economies.

---

* See Scene 8, pages 150–2, for more on blanket bogs.

Anyone who has ever taken part in an excavation on a wetland, such as the Fens, is soon struck by the extraordinary way in which people in the past learned to cope with their often difficult and dangerous surroundings. Inevitably, we tend to concentrate on the problems people faced and we often downplay the brighter side of their lives: their productive farmland, or the ready supplies of fuel and winter protein. I have long tried to avoid it (not, I must confess, always successfully), but there is a natural tendency to dwell on the way that these often harsh conditions determined how ancient regional economies and communities developed. It might seem like everything was about response and adaptation. Archaeology and history, however, show that the reality was very different: people were prospering and in time they would actually gain control of their surroundings, to such an extent that many of Britain's largest wetlands, such as the Fens, the Somerset Levels and Romney Marsh, have been drained. Mindful of rising sea levels and climate change, it would now appear that much of this drainage was almost certainly a long-term mistake. But the fact remains that the development of recent and ancient societies has never been determined by environmental conditions alone. It was always a two-way process in which human culture, imagination and inventiveness played an equally influential part. We can catch glimpses of that ingenuity and creativity in the superb conditions of preservation that can be found on many waterlogged prehistoric sites.

Although the eastern side of Britain has less than half the annual rainfall of the west, much of the rain that falls over west-central and central Britain finds its way into rivers that flow eastwards, into the North Sea. These landscapes are drier than their western counterparts. Rain-fed acid blanket bogs, for example, are very unusual in all but the lowest-lying, wettest parts of these regions, where drainage is naturally impaired.[1]

The largest of the eastern wetlands are the Fens, the low-lying landscapes that surround the Wash.

I have spent most of my professional life working in the Fens, excavating sites in a landscape that has changed beyond recognition over the past four centuries, when wholesale drainage converted a complex network of shallow lakes, slow-flowing rivers, marshy meadows and lush willow and alder woodland into a series of huge rectangular arable fields defined by deep ditches and dead-straight tracks. Soon, however, history will be reversed and the featureless fields will start to be replaced by new wetlands, as levels in the North Sea rise and the costs of maintaining such deep drainage become prohibitive. So what would it have been like to have lived in such a watery landscape in prehistory? More importantly, what can our pre-Roman ancestors teach us about daily life in a wetland? The lessons we learn from them will almost certainly come in useful in the near future.

First, however, I must quickly dispel some commonly held myths.[2] Wetlands have had a very bad press over the years. They are often portrayed as thinly populated, disease-ridden and impoverished. In the popular imagination, the Fens and other wetlands were seen as lawless places where thieves and outlaws ruled the roost and where the few small and isolated communities lived in constant fear of attack. Archaeology and local history, however, have shown that the reality was altogether different. There were some places where it was too wet to live permanently, but they were rich in other resources that could be exploited by people living on slightly higher ground nearby. The supposedly empty and hostile wetlands were abundant sources of hay, thatch and grazing in the drier months of summer and autumn, while the rivers and lakes within the marshes sustained huge populations of fish, eels and wildfowl that provided a seemingly infinite supply of that most sought-after commodity in the ancient world:

protein-rich food to take people through the lean months of winter and early spring.

Archaeological research over the past four or five decades has revealed that the land surrounding the seasonally flooded wetlands was densely settled, as were the many natural islands within them. Far from being lawless, wetland communities were tied together by a net of mutually agreed rules and regulations that controlled hunting and fishing, together with the seasonal exploitation of grazing and the gathering of hay. Flood-free land was also carefully managed for the production of cereals. We know that such rules were in existence long before the Norman Conquest of 1066 and similar laws must have existed in prehistoric times – otherwise such a successful network of arable fields, pasture, farms and settlements would not have been possible.[3]

In the modern world, we have grown used to the fact that the laws that govern our daily behaviour are passed by politicians and are then subsequently modified – even improved – by lawyers. It's a process with a long and often rather chequered history, but its roots lie deep within the prehistoric world, many millennia before the emergence of ancient Greece or Rome. There is no written evidence for these early laws; so we must turn to anthropology for clues as to how they would have worked. Anthropology is the study of humanity. Physical anthropologists research into the development of the human body from early prehistoric times to the present;[*] social anthropologists study the organization of, and the philosophies behind, the world's many cultures and societies. The discipline of prehistory combines many of the features of both physical and social anthropology, together with the research techniques of archaeology. It was social anthropology that gave us the ideas we needed to unravel

---

[*] See Introduction, page xx.

the organization of the prehistoric Fenland landscape – and how it would have been run and managed from one day to another. What I hadn't anticipated was how these insights into the remote past would profoundly change the course of my own life. The study of the past is never a one-way process.

The flood-free, drier land around the edges of the Fens was often heavily settled in later prehistoric times. During our excavations at Fengate, on the eastern side of Peterborough, we revealed a system of long, straight ditches that had been laid out sometime after 1900 BC, very early in the Bronze Age, and which continued in use for about a millennium.* These ditches marked out (and helped to drain) a complex system of fields and droveways that ran along the edge of the fen for many square kilometres. Much of the system still lies buried beneath thick accumulations of later fen and flood deposits between modern Peterborough and Whittlesey. It's a large area, covering about 10 square kilometres (4 sq miles). Viewed from the surface, the land seems flat and until very recently it was dominated by two large medieval churches: Peterborough's massive twelfth-century cathedral and St Mary's, the parish church of Whittlesey, with its soaring fifteenth-century spire. Both buildings symbolized the wealth of the Fens in the Middle Ages.

My attention was first drawn to Peterborough when in 1970 I read a news piece in a recently launched archaeological magazine called *Current Archaeology*, which I'm delighted to say is still thriving.[4] The author was clearly very worried about the proposed expansion of Peterborough into a New Town because of the archaeological destruction that would inevitably result. At

---

* See Scene 10, pages 186–95.

the time, nobody had made any plans to do anything about it and this was particularly regrettable, because just three years earlier an authoritative survey had revealed the area's extraordinary archaeological potential.⁵ At the time I was looking for what was to be my first research project, so I decided to visit Peterborough and do what today would be called a 'scoping exercise'. I was mindful of the great archaeologist Sir Mortimer Wheeler's famous advice: 'Time spent in reconnaissance is never wasted.' So I spent the summer and autumn of 1970 on excavations in the low-lying Nene Valley, just upstream of the city, and was able to do research in various libraries, in Peterborough Museum and, most rewarding of all, in Cambridge University's extensive aerial photographic archive, where I ordered a set of prints of the fields and farms that run along the Fengate fen-edge, a mile or so east of the magnificent cathedral – which I also visited for the first of many times. By the end of the process, I had put together the bare bones of the Fengate Project, which began in the spring of 1971 and didn't end until 1980, by which time we were discovering new prehistoric sites and landscapes in nearby parts of the Fens.

The photos I'd ordered from Cambridge revealed a series of dark lines that were only visible in growing cereal crops in years with a damp spring and a dry early summer. These marks are known to archaeologists as cropmarks and they are often highly distinctive; in certain very dry summers, such as that of 1976, they can reveal extraordinary details, such as the door post-holes of buried Iron Age round-houses. It's just a matter of knowing where, and when, to look – wherein lies the skill of a good aerial archaeologist. Happily for us, the gravel subsoil at Fengate was ideally suited to the formation of cropmarks.

To my absolute delight, the marks on my new set of prints were amazingly clear. The edge of the ancient fen showed up as a dark area, where all the cropmarks ended. Just above it, the drier, flood-free gravel soils of the fen-edge were much paler; this was where the cropmarks became very distinct. The ones that interested me were a series of dark lines, which we knew were formed by the naturally filled-in courses of ancient ditches. In these ditches, the layers of soil that filled them retained water better than the loose gravel surrounding them. This dampness encouraged the crops on the surface to grow more lush – and this lush growth showed up from the air as a dark mark. The cropmarks showed clear evidence for Iron Age round-houses, Bronze Age barrows and even a possible henge, but we decided not to investigate them at first – after all, we knew very broadly what we could learn from them. Instead, we opted to examine a series of rather mysterious straight ditches that ran more or less parallel with each other, straight across the gravel terrace, down to the fen-edge, where they terminated. By the autumn of 1972 and the end of our second season of digging, we knew we had discovered one of the earliest field systems in England.

Our first three seasons' work had revealed many acres of prehistoric fields, thanks to the large earth-moving machines we'd used to clear away the topsoil, and I could see from their layout that the long straight ditches had been laid out to manage livestock – and the many sheep and cattle bones from our digs supported this. Droveways divided the system into separate holdings, which my rural background and knowledge of anthropology suggested were probably divided between different clans or families. One other point seemed obvious to me: nearly all the fields were entered by way of corner entranceways. Anyone who has ever tried to drive a herd of cattle or a flock of sheep from one field to another will know that the gates have to be at the corners. Put them in the middle of a long side and the animals won't go through them: they'll often bunch up, panic and seem to go a bit mad. But drive them to a corner gate, using the sides of the field as a natural funnel, and everything will run smoothly.

Medieval town planners were also aware of this simple expedient and always had roads enter the town's marketplace at its corners.

I can remember going to a market in southern Ireland with my mother's family (who farmed in County Carlow) sometime in the late 1950s, and all motorized traffic had to give way to small herds of cattle and sheep being driven back to their farms in the country round about. Looking back on those Irish farmers, the main focus of their lives appeared to be on livestock: principally dairy cows, sheep and pigs. Yet I was well aware, from living on my grandmother's farm, that they also grew wheat, barley, oats and of course potatoes. I didn't realize it then, but the physical measures needed to keep animals are far more prominent than those for growing crops: gates, byres, droveways and markets last longer in the archaeological record than a few ploughshares, millstones or plough-scratches at the base of the topsoil. That is why our first two decades of research at Fengate, and later at Flag Fen, placed so much emphasis on sheep and cattle. We now know, from preserved pollen and other evidence, that prehistoric Fenland farms actually combined livestock herding with crop-growing. It was an arrangement that gave them the flexibility they needed to exploit the many resources of their rich natural surroundings.[6]

The life of a full-time field archaeologist in the late 1970s wasn't particularly easy or secure; in such circumstances, mortgages are hard to come by. But eventually we got one and Maisie and I moved into our new house early in 1980. It was a farmhouse built in 1907 and, unlike other buildings of the early twentieth century in many parts of the Fens, it wasn't subsiding. It also came with a paddock, a large abandoned yard and one or two ageing outbuildings. The farmer who'd sold it to us suggested we keep some animals there. At first we dismissed the idea, as we were far too busy, but after a few weeks we started to change our minds. A month or two later we discussed it with him again and he said that his father used to keep a few sheep there. So we bought three or four ewe lambs from another farmer, down the drove. Soon we had put them to a neighbour's ram and the following spring we welcomed our first lambs.

For some reason, sheep-keeping suited us. For a start, it provided a contrast with the intense activity of a large excavation. During lambing, you spend long hours on your own, with only ewes and lambs for company – plus the occasional visiting barn owl. I suppose today these would be seen as Mindfulness Moments, but there is something so calming and kind about the sight of a ewe nuzzling her drowsy lamb to wake up and take another feed.

My dual life as an archaeologist and sheep farmer gave me the inspiration to write a book on prehistoric farmers: *Farmers in Prehistoric Britain*, which was published in 1998.* The preparation of a non-fiction book isn't a less creative process than the writing of a novel; in fact, sometimes it can make extraordinary demands on one's imagination. It can also involve some remarkable surprises. I can't remember the precise moment when it happened, but at some point when I was thinking about the new book I happened to visit a local sheep farmer. We used to help local farmers – as they did us – at certain busy times of the year. We had worked on this particular farm many times, but on this occasion we had come to give them a hand with sheep-dipping. The flock was quite a large one – maybe 300 animals – and it was a two-stage process. First the sheep were run through a narrow drafting race where they could be inspected and any lambs that were ready for slaughter could be removed. The chemicals used in the sheep dip were highly toxic, which was why the fat lambs ready for butchering had to be taken out.

---

* A revised second edition appeared in 2006, published by Tempus Publishing, Stroud, Gloucestershire.

I had just bought my own drafting race the previous summer at the East of England Show (the display model was sold off cheap) and I wanted to understand how to work it. Essentially, it consisted of two ultra-long hurdles, which confine about five sheep in a tight line, nose to tail. At one end of the race is an up-and-down guillotine-style gate, and at the other there's a three-way drafting gate, which can be moved from side to side to send individual sheep left, right or straight ahead. In this particular set-up, the drafting gate sent sheep into two holding pens (to right and left), while straight ahead was the sheep dip. The two side pens were for holding fat lambs and elderly or sick animals, neither of which should be dipped.

People stood on each side of the drafting race, checking udders, teeth and ear tags. I think I'd just nipped behind a bush for a pee, but I can remember returning to the race and as I approached it the people standing on either side suddenly reminded me of the animal-handling landscapes we'd revealed at Fengate almost twenty years earlier. I must have been thinking about the book subconsciously, because I couldn't help reflecting that there must have been similar scenes in the Bronze Age (but without the nasty chemicals), when people sorted through their livestock at the beginning and end of the long summer season. Every spring and autumn – and at least once in the summer – we had to use our drafting race. It was hard work and we always tried to enlist as much help as we could find. Even so, it could be very exhausting. But aching muscles don't feel half so bad if there's plenty of banter and good-natured teasing.

We ate our sandwiches with lanoline-covered fingers and our clothes reeked from that moment on, but my sheep-keeping had now acquired a new dimension: instead of just my friends and helpers, my mind's eye could see, smell and hear people in Bronze Age clothes, all with the same smelly fingers and slices of crusty bread. Certain tasks are timeless – as are the ways we perform them. I don't know whether my imagination was playing tricks, but sometimes I'll swear those Bronze Age farmers were laughing about the shape and behaviour of their sheep, and how they resembled certain friends and relatives. I wouldn't admit for one moment that we would ever have behaved so inappropriately ourselves – perish the thought! – but the knowing looks I saw those tired men exchange told me much about Bronze Age humour – and our shared humanity.

Water has been a recurrent theme throughout these Scenes from prehistoric Britain, but this doesn't simply reflect the fact that the British Isles have a wet climate. Water is just as important – maybe even more so – in the Near East or in sub-Saharan Africa, for the simple reason that it is essential to the maintenance of life. This fundamental truth has been evident to humans since earliest times and it would help explain why springs, rivers and lakes have always been treated as special places. It would also explain why water has traditionally played such an important part in rituals surrounding the anointing of new chiefs or leaders – and of course at the very start of life, when families gather around a water-filled font to welcome a new baby into the world and the church. We saw at Blick Mead* how water can be seen as a symbol of life, when you glimpse your reflection on the surface – and of death, when you pass through it and drown. And it's this reflective, symbolic aspect of water that I want to touch on now.

If you require a spectacular, uplifting landscape setting, most people would probably opt for hills or snow-capped mountains. Such thoughts surely lay behind the selection of the locations of places like Edinburgh Castle and Lincoln or Durham Cathedral.

_____

* See Scene 4, pages 65–8.

But flat landscapes too can have an openness and breadth that allows the imagination to ascend into the sky and escape the grip of life here on Earth. As I write this, we are passing through the peak of the first Covid-19 lockdown and I concede that when I have woken in the depths of the night it has often proved hard to return to sleep: there are so many people and things to worry about. But as soon as I get up and draw back the curtains, the sight of our garden, wood and the flat fields of the surrounding Fenland landscape, emerging from the mists of morning, has an immediate calming effect. Reality and a sense of proportion returns: yes, the pandemic is bad, but it could be a lot worse and (so far) British society is coping – if not always very efficiently. Personally, I find comfort and reassurance in old buildings and enjoy spotting the numerous medieval church spires that still adorn the Lincolnshire Fens. Indeed, many of these were built in years of far more deadly plagues.

I was pondering these matters while standing at the edge of our garden pond. Below me in the water were two smooth newts. Every so often their tails would wiggle and they'd swim rapidly to the surface, where they'd grab a mouthful of food and a lungful of air, before returning to the depths. Their lives were completely unaffected by the horrors of coronavirus. As humans, we take the world as we find it – the spires on the horizon, the newts in the pond – and then we make it ours. In prehistoric times, the spires might have been lone oaks or huge barrow mounds, but those newts would have been the same. If you were born into a family that lived near water, wildlife and nature would have been integral parts of your existence. You weren't concerned with notions of symbolism or aesthetics, because they were irrelevant. People had more sense than to analyse their behaviour. For the residents of the Fens, or the lochs of the Scottish Highlands, the water, like the hills or the flatlands, was just there, an essential part of their lives. Sometimes it would have been comforting, at other times threatening; but it was never taken for granted.

There is a tendency to exaggerate the importance of spectacular scenery. I suspect this may partly have arisen from the rise of the Romantic view of the Lake District landscape, as taken by the Wordsworths, closely followed by Burns, Scott and others in Scotland.[7] I love both areas, but even Lake Windermere or the charming Scottish Borders market town of Peebles can be somewhat uninviting on a cold, foggy day. Perhaps it's too easy to overestimate the importance of such iconic scenery to our daily lives.

I remember meeting a delightful, smiley elderly gentleman visitor when I was a curator at the Royal Ontario Museum in Toronto. We got to chatting and it turned out he was the owner of a small farm near the town of Welland in the Niagara Peninsula. A few weeks earlier I had driven close by Welland on my way to visit the Niagara Falls, where I had been almost blown away by the scale, energy and deafening din of the massive waterfalls. I told him how impressed I had been, and he smiled. 'You must visit the whole time?' I asked. Again, he smiled and shrugged. It turned out he sometimes took young visitors to the Falls, but only if they asked him specially. Niagara was just a part – and not a very large part – of his life as a farmer, which he found far more absorbing.

While we were chatting, I couldn't help reflecting on my years as a student at Cambridge. Had I ever visited King's College Chapel during that time? I realized that I had not done so until five years after I graduated. Or the Fitzwilliam Museum? Again, no – that took slightly longer, maybe seven years to happen. So, despite society's fetishizing of the spectacular, we tend not to get too excited by the dramatic views, sites and monuments on our doorsteps. Indeed, I can remember being far more moved when I discovered the parish church, windmill and lovely Georgian houses of the little Fen village of Moulton than when I first encountered the magnificence of Lincoln Cathedral. I suspect this disparity was a result of my growing interest in Fenland history and it illustrates well how knowledge, relevance and setting have always been more important to us than visual impact alone. A memorable scene involving water, for example, can be achieved by contriving unusual or striking foreground interest against a contrasting background. In such instances, scale doesn't matter: it could be a tub on a balcony, a garden pond, a Highland loch or a goldfish bowl; you don't need to own an island in the Bahamas to enjoy the restorative powers of water. The complexity of our relationship with water is well illustrated by the way our understanding of prehistoric life near rivers, lakes and on islands has been transformed over the past 170 or so years.

In 1854, engineering work to improve the lakeside harbour at Zurich, in Switzerland, led to the discovery of the first 'Lake Village', which was excavated by Ferdinand Keller, a remarkable man who was an excellent writer as well as a gifted archaeologist. Keller's reports on Swiss 'pile dwellings' (stilt houses) reached a huge audience right across Europe.[8] I even have a few dusty volumes of his on my own shelves. Soon, new sites were being found elsewhere in the Alps and also much further afield, in Holland, Scandinavia, Ireland, Scotland and England.[9] The sites fired people's imaginations. Waterlogging meant their level of preservation was superb: wooden tools, baskets, fabrics and even items of food in remarkably good condition were found within the timber and woven-wattle walls of buildings, excellently conserved in the muds of the lakebeds.

The two major sites revealed in England were at Glastonbury and Meare in the Somerset Levels.* In Scotland, public and academic interest was fuelled by the influential Rhind Lectures given in 1888 by Dr Robert Munro on 'The Lake-Dwellings of

---

* See Scene 8, page 154.

Europe'.[10] I have a copy of the book that was published two years later, in 1890.[11] It's a weighty volume – not the sort of thing you'd take with you on the train – but beautifully bound and printed on top-quality paper. Munro's style is authoritative, but refreshingly light, and his voice has a distinctive ring to it. He deserves to be better known. His book is also packed full of excellent illustrations, which I still find inspiring. Soon, 'lake-dwellings' were being discovered on the shores of many of Scotland's lochs. Lake dwellings dating from early medieval times, when they acquired their Celtic name 'crannog', had been known about for some time.* Today, the word is used to describe all lake dwellings in Ireland and Scotland.

Crannogs and other houses and settlements built over water are usually thought of as defensive structures. But just like castles or those imposing gateways through town walls in medieval times, or even hillforts in the Iron Age,† there was far more to them than that. They could also have been about the conspicuous display of wealth and power, but I believe that more often, like hillforts, they were symbols of regional identity, both for the benefit of locals – for whom they would have provided a sense of belonging – and for visitors from outside. They are saying that this is our area and we, its inhabitants, welcome you to it.

The people who actually lived in the house or houses on the crannog might well have been the family of the local chieftain. Dwellings were never just a reflection of an individual's wealth and prestige, because all societies in pre-Roman Britain were structured around family, clan or tribal ties.[12] So the head of the clan, dwelling in his or her crannog, was a symbol of the communities living in the area, most of whom would have been related by blood or marriage.

---

* The word derives from the Irish Gaelic for a timber dwelling.
† I cover hillforts in Scene 14.

12.1 A view of the reconstructed Iron Age (500 BC) house excavated in Loch Tay at Oakbank Crannog. This reconstruction is at the Scottish Crannog Centre, also in Loch Tay, near Kenmore, Aberfeldy, Perthshire.

I don't know whether it was because of the revival of a general interest in history, which was a prominent feature of the nation's cultural life at the turn of the twenty-first century, but some twenty years ago I found I was becoming increasingly interested in viewing the past as an unfolding, interconnected narrative.[13] In contrast, at this time history at school was starting to be taught as a series of isolated snapshots – a trend that was made worse by countless television shows centred on the lives of various kings and queens (all too often Tudor) and much historical 're-enactment' (or flouncing around in pretty dresses). My growing interest in the gradual evolution of British prehistory and early history led me to write *Britain BC*, *Britain AD* and eventually *The Making of the British Landscape*, a project that took me some five years to finish. It was while I was taking pictures for this book that I decided to visit the reconstructed crannog at the Crannog Centre, on the edge of Loch Tay, about 8 kilometres (5 miles) outside the small town of Aberfeldy, in Perthshire. The date of that visit was 26 July 2008, and it was an experience that still lives with me.[14]

The focus of the Crannog Centre is an accurate reconstruction of the Iron Age crannog at Oakbank. The site was first revealed by its excavator, Nick Dixon, during a survey that uncovered a total of eighteen crannogs in what is admittedly a large loch. The excavations took place in 1981 and 1982 and revealed a substantial Iron Age round-house, constructed around 500 BC.[15] It had a solid wooden floor of alder and stood at the end of a substantial wooden walkway.[16] The approach was clearly intended to impress – and it succeeded.

As I worked on *The Making of the British Landscape*, I was becoming increasingly aware that its shaping and creation was about more than the construction of impressive buildings, or indeed the need to grow crops, mine coal or conduct trade through large ports. These are all good practical reasons for shaping urban and rural landscapes, but they are only telling a part of the story. Other, more complex and certainly more profound motives were also at work.

I can remember leaving the crannog and starting to walk back towards the car park, when for some reason I turned off the path and found myself heading down the slight slope leading to the lake shore. My photographer's instincts were telling me that I had to place the crannog in a wider setting: that view along the walkway was great, but my readers would want more.[17] And when I got down to the lakeside, this is what I saw:

12.2 A reconstruction of the crannog at Oakbank (500 BC) in its setting in Loch Tay, Perthshire.

For a moment, the house and the walkway leading up to it were more real than the loch and the mist-shrouded hills of the opposite shore. It was a case of our world, on the lakeside, and other worlds in the loch and beyond. Never had anywhere felt quite so on the edge of reality, so liminal, as that Iron Age reconstruction did at that moment.

Finds of butchered bones suggest that feasting took place in crannogs; peculiar Bronze Age objects known as flesh-hooks may well have been used to lift and display the meat. These are found on crannogs and other wetland sites, such as Flag Fen.[18] But there are also hints that music may have been involved in these, or other, ceremonies. The site at Oakbank Crannog, for example, produced two fragments from wooden objects: one with notches that (with the eye of faith) look a bit like the notches on a lyre bridge, the other resembling part of a small wooden 'penny whistle'.[19]

In 2005, an Iron Age (*c.* 300 BC) burial of a young woman was found at the entrance to High Pasture Cave on the Isle of Skye.[20] This was clearly a place of great significance. The young woman had been buried in a stone-lined grave that formed an integral part of deep blocking deposits, which had been deliberately placed near the entrance to prevent access.[21] Within the cave, the archaeological layers were somewhat earlier and had accumulated over several centuries. One of the most remarkable finds from the hearth deposits inside High Pasture Cave was the charred remains of a notched wooden bridge for a stringed instrument.[22] The distinguished prehistorian of music, Dr Graeme Lawson, who also happens to be our neighbour across the Fens, is convinced it's part of the bridge of a lyre, an ancient stringed instrument that can be either strummed or plucked – or both.[23] I have heard Graeme play one of his reconstructed ancient lyres and it completely transformed my notions of prehistoric music, which up until then I had rather patronizingly assumed was loud, simple and brash. When Graeme played his lyre, the music could be complex, tranquil, lively and even raucous. In the right hands, the instrument had extraordinary versatility, producing solo melodies, dance rhythms and accompaniment to singing. The Iron Age Celts also possessed a trumpet-like horn – the carnyx – fragments of which have been found in locations as far apart as the south of France and the north of Scotland. Carnyces – today we would refer to them as 'brass' – were very carefully fashioned to produce music rather than just the braying, hunting-horn-like sounds we are treated to in so many historical dramas.[24]

So we must never make the mistake of thinking that pre-historic people who were born with musical gifts were not capable of producing wonderful sounds from their instruments. Indeed, there is no other way of explaining why ancient lyres were constructed with such extraordinary skill and care. It was because the musicians expected it. I would love to have shown Graeme's reconstructed Iron Age lyre to Stradivarius. I'm sure he would have been very impressed.

Scene 13

Of Trees, Carpenters and Wheelwrights:
The Growing Importance of Woodworking Skills
in the Bronze and Iron Ages (1500 BC–AD 43)

Buckets from Thorney – The Fengate Wooden Stake –
Woodland Management – The Flag Fen Wheel

It would be so exciting if the Indiana Jones image of archaeology were true, with world-changing discoveries being made every day, and at high speed; but I'm not sure I could stand the pace, nor indeed the constant tension. Hoards of treasure don't excite me; I'm not interested in things for their saleroom value alone. I want to know where items originated, who might have made them, who would have worn or used them – and when.

Above all else, I'm profoundly fascinated by what finds, however ordinary or humble, can reveal about people's lives in the past. Even pieces of shaved wood can give a hint of what it might have been like to have lived in the Iron Age. So in this Scene I will steer clear of the very considerable skills of prehistoric goldsmiths and jewellers and instead turn my attention to those skills – today we often refer to them as 'trades' – of the men and women who worked with wood.

Most archaeological sites are on dry land, where conditions of preservation are poor. This usually means material that cannot decay any further, such as flint, pottery and often bone and metalwork, is all that survives. We tend to forget about all those items made from rot-prone organic materials, such as wood, leather, fabrics and fibres. The recent discovery and excavation of a short-lived settlement of five Bronze Age buildings on a pile-built platform at Must Farm, on the southern side of the Flag Fen basin, near Peterborough, has provided us with a very important inventory of items that were used in the settlement before its collapse, following a disastrous fire, after just one year of occupation.[1] Wooden artefacts were at the top of the inventory. There were 160 of them. There were 120 pottery containers, 90 pieces of metalwork and 80 glass beads.

I have always enjoyed doing a bit of carpentry, but I freely confess I'm not very good at it. Somehow, I can never get joints to fit together snugly. Mine tend to wobble a bit and have to be secured with an additional tack, screw or hidden dribble of wood glue. I have friends who can build boats and do things with wood that simply amaze me and I admire them immensely, but there's a difference between being a talented amateur and a true professional. My boatbuilding friends tend to work only when they're feeling in the mood. But professional carpenters turn up for work every day and their standards don't slip. They would never use a naughty dribble of glue.

I first began to understand professional carpenters when we were building our house, back in 1994. Of course, I had seen them at work many times throughout my life, and I'd admired what they were doing, but I was never closely involved; I was always something of a spectator. But when you design and build your own house you are constantly having to make decisions: do you want this sort of skirting board or that type of door surround? And your bookcases (we have many of them): do you want them a certain size and what sort of depth? We soon appreciated the difference between carpenters, who assembled the timber-built barn and the timber frame of the house, and joiners, who worked at a later stage of the project on bookcases, banisters, stairs etc. We worked together for about a year and got to know each other very well. At the time, Maisie was excavating and studying the Bronze Age timbers from Flag Fen and our carpenters and joiners provided us with many very useful insights, particularly as regards the uses and strength of various joints and fixings.

It was while we were sitting with the builders during tea breaks inside the frame of what was slowly becoming our new home that I began to think about crafts in the past. Would there have been professional specialists? Certainly, the standards of prehistoric woodwork were well up to professional standards, but we must be careful about judging prehistory using modern values. Today, for example, we have very different ideas about what constitutes 'normal' when it comes to practical, hands-on skills. Most people might be prepared to turn their hands to home improvements, but this is more likely to involve the assembly of a flat-pack desk, table or bookcase than the shaping of actual wood, required by true carpentry. By the same token, our prehistoric ancestors wouldn't know what to do when confronted by a sheet of fake, lookalike wood, such as MDF.* Judging by the timbers, the joints and the assembly of Bronze and Iron Age houses, now being so vividly rediscovered at Must Farm, most ordinary men and women would have been very skilled with axes and chisels.[2] It's worth remembering that the hours in the day that we devote to reading books and looking at screens could have been spent very differently in the distant past – either developing practical skills, attending to the family or just thinking. Even in pre-literate days, people would have needed time for thought.

---

* Medium Density Fibreboard.

When we showed professional carpenters and woodworkers some of the Bronze Age woodwork at Flag Fen, they were very impressed by the standards of its execution and by its obvious practicality and utility. Everyone who saw it agreed: this was work to a professional standard.

Our knowledge of prehistoric woodwork has advanced by leaps and bounds over the past four or five decades. This largely reflects the rise of sometimes very large-scale excavations ahead of commercial developments such as housing estates, roads or gravel quarries. My own projects at Fengate and later at Flag Fen were a response to the expansion of the industrial areas of Peterborough New Town, in the 1970s and 1980s. We knew that factories had deep foundations and that everything in their path was inevitably going to be destroyed. So we learned to be quite adventurous in the way we used mechanical excavators. We tried not to leave any area of clay or silt uninvestigated. We'd drop quite deep trenches into anything that looked even slightly promising – and surprisingly often, it paid off. We found several well-preserved Bronze and Iron Age wells in this way.

A regular supply of clean water is essential to all human life and there is good evidence that people knew how to control and channel water and how to store it in tanks and communal reservoirs, from the earliest times. Indeed, water management was an essential component of Bronze Age salt-extraction processes.[*] But as the environment becomes more controlled, and as fields, farms and settlements spread across the landscape, ready supplies of water may be harder to come by. In low-lying areas such as the fen-edge to the east of Peterborough, the permanent groundwater table, or 'sock' as it is still known to many farmers in the region, lies about 2 metres (6 ft) below the surface in summertime – and much higher in wet winters. Large-scale field systems began to

---

[*] As we saw in Scene 11.

be laid out along the Fen margins in the centuries after about 1800 BC and this is when we start to find the first wells being sunk down to the 'sock'.

The sinking of numerous wells down to the 'sock' ensured that every house in every farm and village would have had ready access to a reliable source of water. Consequently, it was no surprise that when we were excavating Bronze and Iron Age settlements at Fengate, we frequently came across hand-dug wells. In most cases they were 2 or 3 metres (6–10 ft) deep and their sides were often reinforced against collapse by a woven lining of willow or hazel wattle-work. The ground they were dug through usually consisted of quite loose sand and gravel. This meant that the sides of the well would rapidly have collapsed without the lining, which was remarkably strong in compression; it was also very porous. So these wells would have produced good, clean, naturally filtered (by passing through sands and gravels) water. In some instances, people would have climbed into them, down a notched-log ladder, removing the water when they could reach down to it, using two-piece wooden buckets. It's their superb conservation allied to their very ordinariness, and the direct light they throw on a routine daily task, that gives these buckets their fascination. It's as if there was a direct link between the splash as a bucket hit the water in the Bronze Age, followed by over three millennia of silence. And then archaeologists are privileged to come along and witness the ripples.

Although we never found any ourselves at Fengate, a number of Bronze and Iron Age buckets have been found during pre-development commercial excavation on Fenland sites. One of the earliest (c.1400 BC), and best preserved, was discovered lying at the bottom of a well during excavations ahead of gravel extraction at Tower's Fen, Thorney, about 5 kilometres (3 miles) east of Peterborough.[3] The well had been positioned at the side of a Bronze Age field and there were clear signs that it had been redug, probably several times. This would suggest that it had been used regularly and doubtless frequently. Water for animals would have been tipped into wooden or clay-lined troughs, although sometimes disused gravel pits were converted into watering holes that could be visited by livestock. We know that gravel was spread on house floors and along the slippery surfaces of wooden planks at Flag Fen, and we revealed some Bronze Age hand-dug gravel pits, one of which still had its notched-log ladder, upright in the ground.[4]

The Tower's Fen bucket had been made by hollowing out a log. The outer bark and sapwood had been trimmed off to give a smooth outside finish and it had a single carved handle just above the rim. Other Bronze and Iron Age wooden buckets usually have two slightly smaller loop-like handles on opposite sides of the rim, sometimes with rope still attached to them. Such buckets were for lowering into deeper wells. The base of the bucket was carefully shaped, with a cleanly cut slot below a sloping flange. This would allow a baseplate to be snugly fitted from beneath. There was evidence that some form of resin or fat had been applied to the inside surface, to make the bucket watertight and to prevent seepage. The bucket was carved from a log of alder (*Alnus glutinosa*), a wet-loving tree and one of the few native British species that is capable of actually growing in water. We grow alders on our farm and the wood is quite soft and relatively easy to hollow out. It's also quite reluctant to split and doesn't readily rot when wet, unlike so many other trees. All in all, alder was an excellent and well-informed choice for a bucket. I suspect that Iron Age people would have had a depth of knowledge and experience of trees, wood and carpentry that would amaze us today, living as we do in such environmentally impoverished surroundings.

The fact that nearly all prehistoric wooden buckets are found in fens and bogs, or at the bottom of disused wells, is no accident.

Most carved wooden water containers will very soon split and cracks will appear if they are stored in the open air and allowed to dry out. The same can also be said for canoes and other craft carved from single logs. So they are best kept somewhere dark and damp – like the bottom of a well.

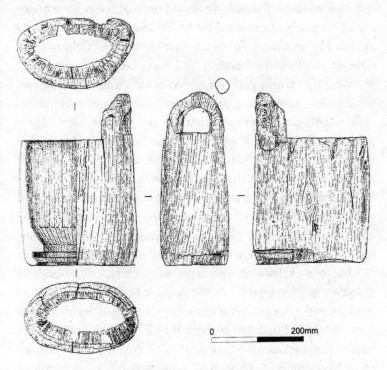

13.1 Wooden two-piece bucket from Tower's Fen, Thorney.

Very often when pottery or wooden vessels are found on waterlogged sites, they have scraps of food adhering to their surfaces. This doesn't indicate prehistoric slovenliness so much as the events leading up to the vessel's final moments – like the collapse of a house into a lake. To gain a better picture, we should consider what mealtimes would have been like in an

249

Iron Age household. We know that buildings were carefully laid out and that a good deal of care was taken in the growing and preparation of food. Iron Age pottery is of high quality, with a fine, smooth finish. So far as we know, ceramic plates had yet to appear, but we know wooden bowls and platters existed, and these were also well made. We also know that feasts were major social events, accompanied by much ceremony and probably attended by musicians. Given what we know about Celtic society, with its emphasis on ancestry and local heroes, it seems very probable that family gatherings took place regularly. Mealtimes would have provided a daily opportunity for households to come together, to cement relationships and provide discipline for growing children. So it seems to me inconceivable that people would willingly have eaten their meals off dirty or fly-blown platters. I am sure our Iron Age forebears would have done the washing-up! But now I want to look at another find from a well on the edge of the Fens, this time from our excavations in the 1970s at Fengate. The person who excavated it was my wife, Maisie Taylor, and she was quick to recognize its importance.

Maisie is a leading specialist in prehistoric wood and woodwork. Her interest in the subject began when she was working in the Fengate team while still a student at the Institute of Archaeology in London (now part of UCL). Her imagination was inspired by a small oak stake that she discovered at the bottom of an Iron Age well. There is an unwritten law in archaeology that the most interesting and difficult finds are invariably made right at the end of a dig, when most of the students and staff have returned to university and when the weather is starting to look grim. And that's what happened in this instance. We only recognized the well for what it was very late, and we knew the site was going to be developed – and therefore destroyed – shortly. By now, everyone had departed except for Maisie and myself. So we excavated it ourselves, and I'm so glad we did.

What made that particular stake so unusual was that one side had been shaped into in a very distinctive, under-cut socket. Maisie worked out that it had to have once formed part of the socket, or housing, of a dovetail joint.[5] At the time, dovetail joints were not known on Iron Age timbers, so the discovery caused much interest. I can remember being very impressed by the standard and confidence of the woodwork when I first saw it. But I didn't realize that the well-executed joint cut into the wet stake in my hands would be the first of a train of discoveries that would change my perception of prehistoric craftsmanship for ever.

Prehistoric Britain is sometimes portrayed as a thickly wooded and very empty place, where people would have journeyed for days through dark forest paths linking far-flung settlements. I hope this book may already have dispelled some of these myths. For a start, the woodlands that covered the British Isles in post-Ice Age times were far from blanketing: certain river floodplains would have been naturally quite open, and on thinner, often sandy or limestone soils, a variety of heath-like plants, including shrubs, heather and bracken, would have formed a more open environment. And individual woodlands themselves would have been very different in nature: dominated by beech in the chalk landscapes of the south, by oaks in the Midlands, and by wet-loving species – such as willow, poplar and alder – in lower-lying areas of the Thames valley, Lincolnshire and East Anglia. To modern, urban eyes, woods are woods, but to people who truly understood their surroundings, these different types of woodland would have seemed very different: chalk and cheese.

The 'clearance' of trees and woodland has formed a major topic in many books devoted to landscape history. Indeed, the choice of the word is interesting, because it implies that people wanted to 'clear', or get rid of, trees, as if they were somehow

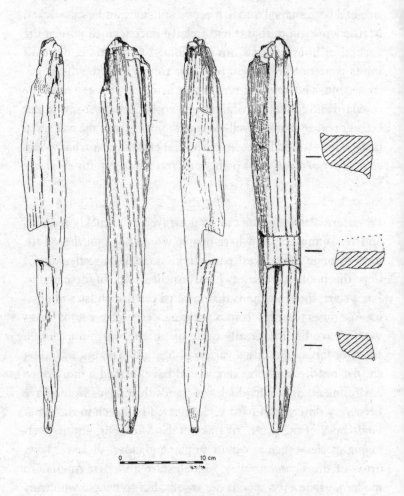

13.2 *Four views of an oak stake from an Iron Age well, at Fengate, Peterborough. Note the dovetail housing joint cut into one side.*

in the way. Often, landscape historians have assumed that the aim of such clearances was to achieve open arable landscapes, which have since developed into the prairie-style 'grain plains' that have become such a sad feature of modern Britain. It's a view I have never shared.

Having tried using them many times, I honestly don't believe that early flint, stone or bronze axes were ever intended to 'clear' large forest trees. They're simply too light and small for such heavy work. If large, well-established trees needed to be removed, their bark would have been detached in a ring around the base of the trunk (something light axes are well shaped to do). The tree would then die and eventually blow over. Pigs and grazing animals such as sheep are also very good at bark-ringing, which they do by nibbling away at the bark to enjoy the sweet sap beneath. It's also worth pointing out that felled or ring-barked tree stumps will re-sprout vigorously, as coppiced stools. So 'clearance' would never have been a simple matter, though again, pigs and other grazing animals would have helped the process by munching on the fresh shoots.

Archaeologists approach prehistory through studying pottery, metalwork, flints, bones and other things that survive in the drier conditions found on most archaeological sites. But if through great good fortune you are able to work with waterlogged organic material, such as wood, you soon find yourself taking a rather different position from your colleagues. I firmly believe, for example, that much of the forest clearance that we know took place in later prehistory was a by-product of other activities such as the keeping of livestock, the search for coppice products (for use in hurdle-making), for fuel and timber for construction. Once the trees had gone, then the land could be ploughed and used to grow cereals. This way of viewing woodland 'clearance' sees the process as a natural by-product of the gradual growth and expansion of the population, the rapid decline of wooded areas in the later Neolithic and Bronze Age Britain (between *c.* 3000 and 1000 BC) reflecting the rise of local human populations.*

The idea of woodland 'clearance' makes the assumption that prehistoric communities somehow turned their backs on the woods. But we know that in the Middle Ages, communities treasured 'their' woods as a valuable resource, not just of firewood, but of sturdy poles for building and of hazel rods for hurdles, willow for baskets – and many other things. Oak for use in buildings would have been felled in older woodlands, probably reserved for hunting, and often part of the estate of an abbey or local aristocrat. I am convinced that broadly similar attitudes to trees and shrubs would have existed in the Bronze and Iron Ages. We can see this, for example, in the straightness and high quality of the roof timbers used for houses at Must Farm. This timber must have been grown and set aside for building purposes – people didn't just stumble upon such well-formed young trees by accident. There is now abundant evidence that prehistoric woods were being carefully managed as long ago as 4000 BC, with the arrival of farming in the Neolithic period. As time passed, it is noticeable that huge, slow-grown oak planks, doubtless split from the massive trees that were still growing in the primeval post-Ice Age forests, were being used in certain important structures.[6] They do occur occasionally at Flag Fen (1300–900 BC), but by the Iron Age, such planks had become very rare indeed, and instead we find narrower boards split from trees that had been deliberately encouraged to grow faster. This would suggest that stands of primeval forest had been progressively reduced; maybe by the Iron Age some would have been protected, perhaps as massive trees of special importance to the spirits of the ancestors.

---

* Sadly, this is a process that we can witness to this day in places like the Amazon Basin, although in Brazil it has recently been hastened by some disastrous political decisions.

Careful woodland management leads to better timber and higher-quality carpentry. But trees and shrubs have to be managed for other things as well. Indeed, some would see such management as a variant of farming; take the production of hazelnuts. We know from numerous excavations that hazelnuts were an important food to the pre-farming, Mesolithic hunter-gatherer communities, some ten thousand years ago. Small pits filled with hazelnuts occur quite frequently on Mesolithic settlements and charred nutshells are often found in and around hearths. Clearly, hazel bushes must have been important, because we also know that pliable rods of hazel were used in the construction of house walls.

Over the past twenty-five years I have planted and grown about 400 hazel bushes in both woodland and hedgerows. The bushes that are surrounded by tall trees deeper in the wood grow long, straight rods when they are coppiced. They produce very few nuts. But the hazels around the edges of the wood and in hedgerows are best managed in a different way. Their stems are pruned back, rather than being simply coppiced to the ground, and in the sunshine they tend to branch out. These bushes produce a wealth of nuts, which can be picked, either off the stem or off the ground when the plant is given a good shake. Over the past ten years, nearly all our hazelnuts have been taken by grey squirrels in July and August – long before they are ripe. But the point is that hazel must be grown in different places and managed in contrasting ways to produce nuts or rods. I can't prove it, but I have a strong hunch that this was something hunter-gatherer communities understood fully, back in Mesolithic times – many millennia before the first 'real' farmers arrived in Britain.

The working of wood and the management of woodland are among the oldest and most important skills we humans possess and yet today they are largely ignored in favour of two much cruder, bipolar opposites: fell trees and farm the land, or plant trees everywhere to mitigate climate change. Both are overreactions. Clearly, the latter would be preferable, but it is also very destructive to traditional landscapes. I would suggest instead a more considered approach and with it a real process of reskilling: we must reacquire woodland management skills and return to traditional materials, such as wood, or indeed to its modern variants, such as MDF, if we are to cut down on our use of plastics. Above all else, we must have the humility to learn from the past, if we want to enjoy a civilized future.

The discovery of the dovetail housing joint late in the Fengate project slipped into the background quite rapidly, as the team turned its attention to other threatened sites in the Peterborough area. Indeed, I had almost completely forgotten about it when in 1994 our excavations at Flag Fen revealed one-third of a Bronze Age three-part wooden wheel, dating to about 1300 BC.[7] Technically speaking, such wheels are known as slab wheels because they are made from three shaped wooden planks, or slabs, which are held together by braces slotted into dovetail housing joints and by pegs or dowels, fitted into sockets in neighbouring slabs. This arrangement allows wheels to flex slightly, yet remain robust and secure.

The wheel fragment had been beautifully made, and although some of the pieces had shrunk after some three thousand years in the ground, it was clear that all the joints fitted together snugly and that the wheel would have been very functional – but also good-looking. All the wood used in its construction had been carefully selected, without knots and with good, straight grain. The choice of the woods used for its various components was very well informed and was clearly based on knowledge passed down from previous generations. The timber selected for the main

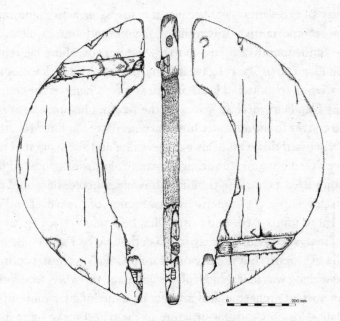

13.3 Three views of one slab from a Bronze Age three-part slab wheel dating to about 1300 BC, from Flag Fen, Peterborough.

slab or plank was alder. Unlike oak, alder is reluctant to split and although it isn't as strong as oak, it is resilient and resistant to wet rot. The two dovetail braces that joined the three slabs together were made from oak sapwood, with the bark still intact. They would have looked very striking. The oak tree selected was young and straight-grained. Oak sapwood (the wood below the bark that carries the vessels that feed the tree and its roots) is far more flexible than the much harder heartwood that forms at the centre of the tree (from old sapwood) and provides the trunk and larger branches with a near-rigid internal frame. Both oak sapwood and alder would have benefited from occasional wetting, which would have helped maintain flexibility. The two dowels were made from carefully shaped oval pegs of ash. Ash was an excellent choice because it is strong, easy to shape and – most importantly – it is resilient, flexible and wears well.

In the months leading up to the publication of the big report on Flag Fen in 2001, I gave dozens of lectures to archaeological societies, schools and local organizations. Whenever the slide of the Flag Fen wheel appeared on the screen, I had trouble trying to convey to the audience how the wheel actually fitted together. I discussed this with Maisie one evening and she suggested that we asked our resident draughtsman, Colin Irons, who had just completed a course in technical drawing, whether he would like to draw up a 3D isometric reconstruction of the wheel and the various joints used. And this is what he produced (see fig. 13.4).

It was so vivid and easy to grasp that we had to include it in the big report, but the reason I found Colin's reconstruction so absorbing was that it suddenly reconfigured the wheel from being an ancient archaeological artefact to something far more up to date. Not only did the structure of the wheel make immediate sense, but you could think about it as if it were something that needed fixing in the garage, or out in the garden shed. I remember consulting the handbook of my first chainsaw, when the chain needed tightening, and I was struck by the similarity of the diagrams in the manual to Colin's clear, concise drawing of the Flag Fen wheel. The past and the present had merged into one.

Not far from the wheel, but at a slightly different level, we found part of what had once been an oak axle, for a wheel of about the same size. It looked as if the vehicle to which the axle had been attached had been overloaded, because it had broken at its weakest point, a few inches in from the wheel at the place where the body of the vehicle would have been joined to the axle. After it broke, the axle had been removed. Then the broken end was very roughly chopped, to form a rather crude point. Finally, it was driven into the ground as one of the many stakes along the Flag Fen causeway. A square-section pin was found close by.

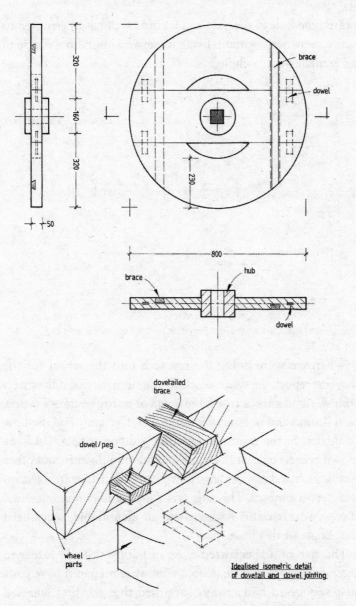

Labels visible in the drawing: brace, dowel, 320, 160, 320, 50, 230, 800, brace, hub, dowel, dovetailed brace, dowel/peg, wheel parts

Idealised isometric detail of dovetail and dowel jointing

13.4 An idealized drawing of the Flag Fen three-part wheel with a central hub inserted. Note the two dovetailed braces and the two locating dowels.

It fitted the hole in the axle and it could well have been used to secure the wheel, or more likely its separate hub, to the axle in the manner of a lynchpin.*

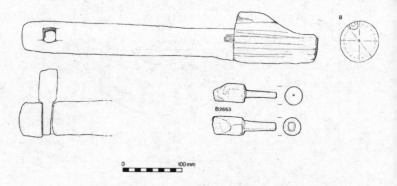

13.5 *Part of an oak axle with two views of a possible lynchpin, which retained the wheel, or its hub, on the vehicle. The axle broke in antiquity and was then roughly sharpened and reused as a stake or a peg.*

When we were doing the research into the wheel for the Flag Fen report, we were struck by the similarity of slab wheels from wetland sites across large areas of north-western Europe, from Britain and Ireland to Scandinavia, Germany and the Low Countries, in the centuries on either side of 1000 BC. All the known wheels exhibit the same careful manufacture and other details, such as dovetail joints, dowels and the deliberate selection of different timbers. This suggests a degree of communication. Maybe wheelwrights had become an identifiable, specialized craft at about this time.

The rise of a specialized class of highly skilled craftsmen suggests that there were people who were prepared to pay for their services. I had always supposed that the first wheeled

---

* A pin through the end of an axle to keep the wheel in position.

vehicles would have been rather crude, probably used for carting hay or straw on farms, and with big wheels and heavy superstructure. But the trouble is, there's no archaeological evidence for such vehicles. When hay or straw needed to be moved, it was more likely to be carried to stacks by people with forks, or by oxen pulling sledges or slung containers. The vehicle used by our friends* *The Flintstones* featured wheels made from slices sawn off from large, round tree trunks. It's an appealing idea, but unfortunately wheels of that sort would split wide open after a few days of use. All the careful carpentry found in Bronze Age wheels is about avoiding such splitting. In other words, it's impossible to fashion easy-to-make, heavy-duty wooden wheels. So what sort of vehicles were the Bronze Age wheels made for?

A similar, but complete, slab wheel was found near Flag Fen at Must Farm, in 2016.[8] It dated to around 1100 BC and was about a metre (3 ft) in diameter – slightly larger than the Flag Fen wheel, but certainly not cart-sized. Other European Bronze Age wheels are of comparable size. This suggests that they were intended for vehicles smaller than farm carts. I had been pondering these questions while writing the Flag Fen report in the later 1990s, when in 1997 I was hired (I was rather broke and very freelance at the time) to direct excavations at an expanding gravel pit a few miles north of Peterborough, just across the county boundary in Lincolnshire, at Welland Bank Quarry. The site was perched on the gravel soils along the edge of the Witham Valley fens and it had produced good evidence for a farming settlement of the later Bronze Age.

One Friday, as we were returning to the site in relaxed mood after a lunchtime visit to the local pub, it started to rain quite hard but then, after a few minutes, began to ease off. I could see

---

* See Scenes 2 (page 25) and 9 (page 172).

the black rain-bearing cloud heading in the direction of the site, which we reached about ten minutes later. A couple of diggers had a problem and they wanted my advice. We spoke for about fifteen minutes and once we had finished, I decided I should start making plans to expand the dig into an area of featureless silt, which my experiences at Fengate had taught me not to ignore. By this time, it was almost half an hour since the rain shower had passed over, and it struck me that any deep pits hidden below the silt patch might start to show through as the silt dried out after the sharp shower.

When I arrived at the silt, I couldn't believe my eyes. There weren't any dark marks that might have revealed buried pits or wells, but instead I was able to glimpse something unique – and far more exciting. Running across the silt in a gently curved line were two absolutely parallel dark marks, each about two inches wide. About 20 metres (22 yd) away I could just make out two other parallel lines that seemed to cross and intersect with the main set. And I knew exactly what they were. I called over a couple of experienced excavators and together we outlined the edges of the marks with the tips of our trowels. As the marks started to fade, we found they could be brought back using sprinkler watering cans.

The marks were clearly the ruts made by a two-wheeled vehicle and the thickness of the wheels was about the same as the Flag Fen wheel.[9] The two wheels were about 1.1 metres (3½ ft) apart, which would suggest a small cart or carriage, appropriate for a single person. At one point, the vehicle had got stuck in the mud and we could see how it had been rocked forwards and backwards to release it. There was no possibility that it had been a four-wheeled cart-like vehicle. The silts in question had probably been laid down by the River Welland flooding at various times between about 800 and 600 BC.

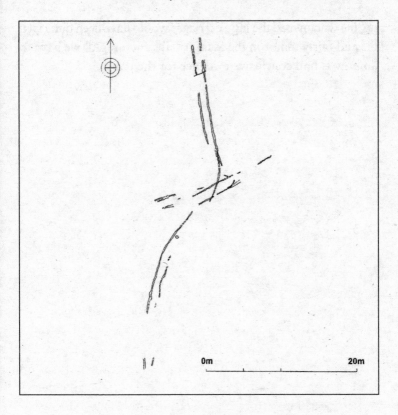

13.6 A plan of later Bronze Age (800–600 BC) wheel ruts at Welland Bank Quarry, near Market Deeping, Lincolnshire.

When I was a boy in the 1950s, I can remember seeing similar-sized vehicles being towed by donkeys (always known as 'asses') in the Irish village in County Carlow where my mother's family lived. They were used to take their owners to the village pubs and it was said that the asses knew the way home without being driven or steered. I think the Bronze Age vehicles were used in a similar way, mainly to transport light goods and people. The wheels could not have been cheap to make, so I suspect the people who owned the little carriages would have been quite well off and fairly senior in the local tribal structure. All we have to do now is find conclusive evidence for the pubs.

Scene 14

Life in the Sky: Hillforts (1200–100 BC)

Maiden Castle – Danebury – Dorset Hillforts –
Pen Dinas and Cardigan Bay

Exciting archaeology is about great sites and great archaeologists – and in some happy instances it can be about both. There are, however, dangers in linking certain people with particular places for too long. Ideas about the place that were expressed during their lifetime can become fossilized and fixed. Up-and-coming younger people tend to hesitate before offering alternative views and interpretations, which may often be based on good, solid evidence. I have seen this happen in my own area of expertise – indeed, I have sometimes been a bit of an old fossil myself – until the emerging facts forced me to change my ways. Old ideas can sometimes prove hard to dislodge, because they can be so comforting – and they are often linked to good friends and colleagues who are no longer with us. So simply to discard them would seem somehow disloyal. Indeed, the relationship between prehistorians and the sites they are trying to untangle can be as complex as the lives of the people being investigated. As time passes, I find this complexity both exhilarating and humbling. It's what keeps me going.

Britain's best-known Iron Age site is undoubtedly Maiden Castle, the imposing Dorset hillfort just over 3 kilometres (2 miles) outside the county town of Dorchester. The decades after the last war saw the rapid rise of television and the creation of a new cluster of celebrities. Quiz shows were a popular feature of early post-war television and one of the best-known and most widely watched was *Animal, Vegetable, Mineral?* It was broadcast from 1952 until 1959 and by far the most popular of the panellists was the strikingly handsome archaeologist and soldier Sir Mortimer Wheeler. Wheeler was undoubtedly a remarkable man with a very strong – some would say domineering – personality, which was matched by his considerable archaeological achievements, both in Britain and across the territories of what was then still the British Empire. He also had a distinguished military career, which probably explains his impressive moustache. He was elected BBC Television Personality of the Year in 1954 and it's fair to say that his influence still lives on.[1]

Wheeler's best-known British excavation took place between 1934 and 1937 at Maiden Castle and the report appeared in 1943. It had been assembled and largely written during the darkest years of the war, when the author admits his mind was largely elsewhere, for entirely understandable reasons. There is also a tragic backstory to the project: the field team was run by three archaeologists, including Wheeler and his wife Tessa. Two years into the project, Tessa Verney Wheeler died and the volume is dedicated to her memory; she is now widely regarded as a pioneering female archaeologist.[2] Her death meant that she wasn't able to take part in the writing-up and the volume's interpretations are very much framed within Wheeler's world view, which is perhaps best described as militaristic and Empire-based. Tessa's influence would undoubtedly have softened it. Having said that, he did publish it, quite promptly (by the standards of the time) and under extremely difficult circumstances.[3] The report is certainly well organized and clearly written. Most importantly, and in common with all good excavation reports, it can be reinterpreted and reworked. In other words, no data have been removed that might undermine the explanations proposed by the author. It's fair and balanced.

The big problem with Wheeler's view of Maiden Castle was that he placed huge emphasis on a story that made good reading, and which appealed to the soldier side of his personality and background, but which can now be proved to have no basis in reality. As Wheeler saw it, the massive build-up of defences that happened later in the Iron Age was a direct response to the rise of the Roman Empire and the threat it posed to Britain. I can completely sympathize with that view, given the fact that in the late 1930s, while he was carrying out much of the later work in the report's preparation, the Nazi threat to the peace of Europe was growing as Hitler's regime became increasingly militaristic. By 1940, when Wheeler must have been writing or editing the final chapters, attacks on Britain had begun in earnest. So I don't find it even slightly surprising that he made the climax of his Maiden Castle story centre on the growing threat from Rome and its conquest of Britannia, culminating in a final battle and the creation of a war cemetery within the hillfort's eastern entrance.

With their enclosing ramparts of massive banks and deep ditches, hillforts are undoubtedly the most spectacular of prehistoric monuments and they dominate the landscapes around them. Maiden Castle is one of the most impressive examples, but there are others in Dorset that can rival it. Some 32 kilometres (20 miles) to the south-east, the imposing ramparts of Hambledon Hill – like those of Maiden Castle – completely surround and seem to take over the hill itself, while the spectacular so-called promontory fort at Hengistbury Head, on the coast near the Dorset/Hampshire border, would have been visible from a great distance, both inland and across the sea. Given the prominence of their locations, it is easy to see why these monuments demanded that epic histories, involving identifiable tribes and individuals, attach to them. Anonymous terms like 'the Bronze Age' or 'Iron Age hillfort' may be fine for archaeologists or prehistorians, but they hardly fire the popular imagination. To do that, you need names.

The earliest recorded British names appear in the writings of Roman authors, such as Tacitus. Tacitus (*c.* AD 56–*c.*120) was writing in the late first and early second centuries AD and one of his books was the *Agricola*, a biography of his father-in-law, who was governor of the Roman province of Britannia from AD 78 to 84.[4] Tacitus gives us the names of the late Iron Age tribal kingdoms, many of which (but not all) fought to repel the Roman conquest of AD 43. The most famous tribe of all were the Iceni of East Anglia, who rebelled against the injustices of Roman rule in AD 60–1, under perhaps the best-known pre-Roman monarch[*] of the day, Queen Boudicca, or Boadicea, as she was known in Victorian and Edwardian times. A famous statue of her in her chariot (complete with revolving knives) marks the entrance to Parliament Square from Waterloo Bridge.[5] The most celebrated late Iron Age kingdom of southern England was that of the Durotriges, who have been very closely identified with the enlargement of the Dorset hillforts at Hod Hill and Maiden Castle. This was the explanation favoured by Wheeler in his report on Maiden Castle, and by the distinguished Romanist and archaeologist Sir Ian Richmond, excavator of Hod Hill in the 1950s. Richmond was Professor of the Archaeology of the Roman Empire at Oxford University.[6]

It used to baffle me that the two leading archaeological authorities of the time, Wheeler and Richmond, should be so completely won over by the idea that hillforts were a response to an impending threat from the growing Roman Empire across the Channel. That, however, was before the Covid-19 pandemic. Now,

---

[*] Perhaps chieftain or 'tribal leader' would be a better term.

having lived for many weeks under lockdown, I am beginning to understand how the appearance of a new, external threat can influence one's judgement. Wheeler and Richmond lived through a brutal era in which mass slaughter had become routine. And it didn't end with Victory in Europe Day in 1945: Stalinist repression continued in the Soviet Union and eastern Europe well into the 1950s and beyond. Britain must have appeared to be an island of peace and calm at the centre of a raging storm. So I can see why, in a Second World War and early Cold War context, these men placed so much emphasis on such a ruggedly pro-Ancient British and anti-Roman interpretation of two iconic hillforts. In theory, we should protest at the 'distortion' of objective truth in this way, but on the other hand we can never remove all subjectivity from a discipline of the humanities such as archaeology. The skewed interpretation of the hillforts provides us with a clear example of the extent to which everyone, including intelligent, highly educated people like Wheeler and Richmond, can be affected by the events of their time. Maybe that simple observation provides us with a lesson that is just as significant as the importance of objective truth. Interpretations, like the archaeological sites themselves, must always be seen in context.

There has always been a tendency in the world of archaeology to isolate and categorize different types of sites and finds. Hillforts were an early example of this trend. Some eighty were excavated in the 1920s and 1930s during a surge of research known by some as 'hillfort mania'.[7] The approach was overwhelmingly focused on hillforts as defensive military constructions. This view remained fashionable in the 1940s and then, after the war, in the 1950s and early 1960s. The researches of people like Wheeler and Richmond belonged to this general tradition; there was a great interest in hillfort defences and the details of their construction, which sometimes involved quite complex internal timber reinforcements.

The complex layout of hillforts' defended entranceways, with their many blocking banks and other diversions, led to a lively debate on how they might have developed through time. These debates continued into the 1960s. It was all very interesting (although I must confess that as a student in the mid-1960s, the intricacies of hillfort defences never floated my boat even slightly) and it did advance the story to a certain extent, but while it continued we were losing sight of the more general questions, such as: what were hillforts used for? And were they all the same? To find answers to these and other problems, hillforts had to be examined in their settings. It was time to return them to their contexts; to see them as places inhabited and built by human beings, rather than military artefacts: the prehistoric equivalents of tanks or guided missiles.

One or two younger archaeologists working in the 1960s were keen to approach hillforts from such a broader perspective. Principal among them was Barry Cunliffe, whose long-term (1969–88) researches at Danebury, a hillfort on the edges of the Test valley, near Stockbridge in Hampshire, have had a profound influence on our understanding of these extraordinary places. He was able to demonstrate that the interior of the hillfort was very carefully laid out, with well-defined roads, often lined with houses or other buildings.[8] I visited Danebury while it was being excavated and it undoubtedly exerted a big influence on the way my own researches were heading. But when it came to hillforts, I have always found there was something special about those spectacular ramparts at Maiden Castle. Maybe, too, my interest was heightened by the memory of Sir Mortimer – and by the association with the war. I don't know why, but the place has always fascinated me.

In the mid-1980s I was frantically busy running excavations

at Etton, while simultaneously starting work at Flag Fen, so I couldn't find the time to visit some new research that was being organized at Maiden Castle by English Heritage.[9] I knew many of the archaeologists involved and I was getting word that the project was producing amazing results. But it was all coming through to me second-hand, which was very frustrating. The fieldwork took place over two seasons, in 1985 and 1986, and readers will have noticed that I refer to it as 'research' or 'fieldwork' rather than the more usual 'excavations'. Yes, excavations did take place and they were extraordinarily productive, but the whole project was very carefully planned from the outset and the dug trenches were just part of a much larger programme of work. I think history will judge this Maiden Castle project as one of the best planned and executed pieces of archaeological research of modern times.

Detailed field surveys were carried out after ploughing and included the plotting and collecting of thousands of pieces of pottery, flints and other artefacts. These clearly showed that the landscape around the hillfort had been settled from Neolithic times; this coincided well with the construction and occupation of a double-ditched causewayed enclosure that is located in the eastern half of the later hillfort and can be dated to the early third millennium BC. A distinctive kink in the layout of the massive ramparts in both the north and south sides of the hillfort shows where the Iron Age defences were slightly diverted to respect the ditches and banks of the earlier site.

The trenches were carefully positioned to avoid those of Sir Mortimer Wheeler – the idea being to build on and enhance what he had already revealed. This also meant that they could test and verify many of his conclusions. The dig was also planned and laid out in ways that amplified the experiences and research carried out by Barry Cunliffe at Danebury. The two projects were intended to be closely comparable, which indeed they were. The excavations at Danebury and Maiden Castle both showed clear evidence for a slightly smaller early phase in the fifth and sixth centuries BC, followed by massive enlargements and developments in the Middle Iron Age, from about 300 to 100 BC.[10] Thereafter, the use of both sites is at best casual, or non-existent. So there is absolutely no evidence whatsoever for them being built to repel Roman invasions. If we transpose the Roman conquest to modern times, so that AD 43 becomes 1943 (coincidentally, the date Wheeler published his Maiden Castle report), then most hillforts would have been abandoned by 1800: several years before the Napoleonic battles of Trafalgar and Waterloo – a long time previously.

These early dates also suggest that most hillforts could never have been built by the famous pre-Roman tribal kingdoms, people like the Durotriges or the Iceni. Instead, we must seek their origins in much earlier times, possibly even in the final centuries of the Bronze Age, from around 800 BC. So could these early hillforts have arisen as a result of certain tribes becoming richer or just being militarily successful? That would be the obvious inference but the trouble is, it makes the assumption that all hillforts were essentially the same: regional defended centres for larger or smaller populations. It's a nice, simple explanation, but sadly it's also probably wrong.[11] Later projects that investigated hillforts followed the lead of Cunliffe at Danebury and the English Heritage team at Maiden Castle: they shifted their gaze away from the massive ramparts to the large area of land they enclosed and to the landscape that surrounded them. With a little help from modern science-based technology, these broader approaches have opened our eyes and provided some remarkably exciting new discoveries, which have transformed our understanding of life in Iron Age Britain.

★

We know about the existence of some thirty-five hillforts in the county of Dorset. About a third of them were examined in one way or another during the pre-war 'hillfort mania', but only four have so far been subject to proper archaeological excavation and even at Maiden Castle the area of the interior examined has been very small. This partly reflects the expense of modern research excavation, but it also demonstrates the legal protection provided by the Ancient Monuments Acts in action: these sites are safeguarded for the future and they must not be unnecessarily damaged – even by well-meaning archaeologists. One way round these problems is to use techniques that do not disturb the ground. Fans of Channel 4's *Time Team* will recall that we always relied heavily on John Gater and his small team of 'geofizz'* professionals, whose futuristic instruments used electronics and radar to look at what lay hidden below the surface. The hundreds of detailed surveys John's team produced have proved of enduring value to archaeologists and are still regularly consulted today.

Since 2009, archaeologists and geophysicists based at Bournemouth University have been carrying out a detailed survey of prehistoric and Roman sites in Dorset, including about two-thirds of its known hillforts.[12] It had traditionally been assumed that most of the large areas enclosed by hillforts remained essentially unoccupied: open areas of grass, perhaps used as grazing. These were, after all, sites placed on the tops of high hills and the prehistoric inhabitants, just like the geophysicists carrying out the survey, would have been frequently battered by strong winds and driving rain. Even in sunny Dorset, high hilltops are not the kindest of environments. But the geophysical plots showed a very different picture. Their surveys have been remarkably complete, revealing the extent of occupation across

---

* Or geophys (geophysics).

the large areas enclosed by the ramparts. Hod Hill provides a particularly clear example.

The Hod Hill survey revealed the outline of over 200 ring-ditches surrounding Iron Age round-houses, whose diameter was about 10–15 metres (11–16 yd); they mostly feature a single entranceway, which often faced south-east, towards daytime sunshine. I know from round-houses I have reconstructed myself that you need an outer ditch to catch run-off from the conical thatched roofs, which would otherwise wet the mud-plastered walls and cause them slowly to collapse (waterproof plaster was not introduced in Britain until Roman times). The geophysical data also showed clear evidence for storage pits and/or hearths within each building – which would suggest they were used by people rather than animals.

One of the most striking features at Hod Hill (and also at Maiden Castle and other sites in the survey) was the clear evidence of roads heading towards the entranceways through the defences. A few smaller lanes can be seen to branch off them. Houses and other structures cluster along the roads and lanes, frequently overlapping with each other. This would suggest that many were rebuilt and that the site was occupied for quite an extended period. Each of the 200 or so round-houses would have been large enough to have accommodated a family of perhaps six to ten people, but we know they could not all have been occupied at the same time. If we also include the many smaller houses and other possible structures that were revealed, we might well be looking at a population certainly of hundreds, if not of a thousand or two, at certain times.

The geophysical plots at Hod Hill revealed some fascinating details that provide hints that the settlements were probably controlled by a centralized authority, or authorities – most likely tribally based. For example, some of the roads and lanes appear to have been bounded by ditches along their edges. On closer examination of the plots, these ditches can be seen to have been formed by joining up a series of neighbouring house ring-ditches. This new ditch would also help the houses stay dry, it would clearly edge the road – and also help reduce mud. As we would say today: a win-win situation, brought about by close co-operation and a positive attitude. But it didn't happen in only one instance, which is why I think it was about more than just happy coincidence and friendly neighbours. I am convinced it was symptomatic of something far more profound.

At some points along the edges of Hod Hill's internal roads, the ring-ditches of houses are replaced by a series of four-post structures, which have been interpreted, very convincingly – and helped by experimental work – as raised grain storage silos. Inside houses, grain was stored in pits, possibly lined with basketry or fabric, but the family's top-up supply would have come from the line of raised silos further along the road. It is hard not to see such a short supply chain as being organized collectively by the tribal authorities, on behalf of the people who would have both consumed and grown the grain. When Barry Cunliffe's excavations started to reveal grain storage silos at Danebury, I can remember being fascinated by the discovery; there was something very immediate about it. Throughout my childhood I had lived in an agricultural village in north Hertfordshire, surrounded by grain stores and combines. The Christmas turkey came from my uncle's farm and after the festivities we cut sprigs of hazel from a nearby wood for the next season's peas and runner beans. Our 'supply chains' were all very local and they were still largely family-run.

There is a tendency to see local, or family-based, networks as being just about economics, but there was also another side to them. During the Great Depression of the 1930s, for example, my grandfather helped organize the digging of a large pond, which still exists today and is home to a huge population of vociferous frogs in springtime. The creation of that pond gave employment to many men in the village in wintertime, when rural work was hard to find. Socially altruistic schemes such as this were not confined to the 1930s; in late Victorian times, a soup kitchen was built in an outbuilding on one of the farms near the centre of the village. Our village wasn't unique: similar rural soup kitchens were built elsewhere to help feed the hungry in hard times.

The emergence of more centralized systems of governance, as witnessed by the organization of hillforts in the Iron Age, was not just about command and control. A gradual centralization of local governance will not necessarily give rise to powerful chiefs or egotistical Big Men – Iron Age equivalents of ex-President Trump. Yes, powerful individuals would sometimes have taken advantage of the system, but there were always checks and balances, because the system was based on family ties and family values, which have always included a strong element of social care for the elderly and vulnerable. I strongly suspect these very ancient and deep-rooted traditions of local supply and demand, of social control and humanitarian welfare, will be fundamentally important in the third decade of the twenty-first century.

When we think about hillforts and defensive sites in general, we naturally tend to focus on their military aspects: the ramparts, entranceways, strategic positioning and so forth. People also get rather excited about the discovery and location of weapons and ammunition: swords, spearheads, arrowheads and slingstones. The bodies and graves of fallen warriors are treated with enormous care and possible wounds are studied under the searching beam of high-powered microscopes. Such things may provide us with glimpses of how people conducted the brutal business of hand-to-hand fighting in the ancient past, but do they really tell us very much about how people might have viewed defensive sites such as hillforts and, later, castles? It's worth bearing in mind that imposing structures have also to be seen and thought about when the local people are living their daily lives and the community is not at war.

Fighting is an expensive business and very disruptive; anthropological research has shown that in many tribal societies the actual process of killing, or being killed, was sometimes limited to certain individuals – 'champions' who would represent a particular powerful person, or community.[13] The biblical fight between David and Goliath (a Bronze Age memory?) is a good example of this. Another way to minimize the economic impact of conflict was to confine it to times of the year when younger men were less heavily occupied doing useful, productive tasks on the land and in the community. After harvest, in the autumn, is such a time and further economic and social damage can be constrained if attacks are limited to certain types of raids, such as rustling for livestock. Prehistoric people may well have talked or sung about wholesale slaughter and bloody battles, but very rarely actually engaged in such mayhem. Our ancestors were not stupid. We would do well to heed their example, in a modern era that has seen two blood-soaked and astronomically expensive world wars.

As people went about their daily lives below the towering ramparts of the local hillfort, did they gaze up at them as glorious symbols of military prowess? Maybe sometimes, just as some people might gaze on the White Cliffs of Dover as a symbol of Britain's wartime resistance to the Nazi threat. But thoughts like that are relatively rare. Even when I see a Spitfire or a Lancaster bomber – and both iconic planes are quite frequent visitors to the skies above our farm, because the RAF Battle of Britain Flight is based at RAF Coningsby, on the edge of the Fens, a few miles to the north of where I'm writing this – I don't see them as symbols of the Battle of Britain, nor of the carpet-bombing of German cities. I look at them as superb pieces of engineering and I thrill to the sound of their roaring Rolls-Royce Merlin engines. Other people may think of wartime personalities as the planes fly past: Churchill, perhaps, but more likely Vera Lynn or my mother's huge favourite, Tommy Handley, the comedian star of the highly successful BBC Radio wartime show *ITMA* (*It's That Man Again*).[14] And then there are those unexpected thoughts and coincidences that arise when you think about any historical topic: the last episode of *ITMA* was broadcast on my fourth birthday, in January 1949.

So we should be very careful about attributing simplistic motives when we ponder the significance of certain sites and monuments to people in the past. Our own thoughts about such things can be complex, confusing and plain inexplicable – so why cannot theirs have been, too? This morning I woke up at about 3.30 a.m. and soon I became conscious that my brain was worrying about – surprise, surprise – Covid-19 and the pandemic. As time passes, I find I am getting better at managing these early morning anxiety attacks – to such an extent that I now find I have nights of decent sleep, when I wake up feeling rested. These good nights happen about five times a week. This morning was one of the other two, poor-sleep nights. So I did what I always now try to do in such moments: I decided to think about this book, or my blog or possible garden improvements. Anything is better than anxious worrying. And this time my subconscious decided to ponder the hillforts of Cardigan Bay.

The previous morning I had been researching future topics for this book and those Welsh hillforts did seem very appealing. For a start, they're not widely known and their landscape settings can be astonishingly spectacular. I had visited them during filming for *Time Team*, when I had stayed with our old friend and leading expert on henges, the late Geoff Wainwright. It was Geoff, incidentally, who played a major part in organizing the 1985 excavations at Maiden Castle. As I lay there trying to work out what I would write when I returned to the book after getting up in a couple of hours' time, I realized that I had actually answered one of the questions that was intriguing me: namely, why did people build those extraordinary monuments? Yes, of course they were about defence and they were symbols of strength and tribal authority, but they also represented the community, the life and thoughts of the people living within and around them. You can witness something similar today, when religious belief has ceased to be relevant to so many people, yet our great medieval cathedrals are being visited by ever-increasing numbers of people. They are now regarded as symbols of local pride and identity, but also of something else: call it a sense of serenity or mysticism, but it's something that we all need to help us manage the tensions, fatigue and sheer hard work of daily life. So to get an idea of why hillforts were built in the first place, I want to head west, to the port of Aberystwyth, midway along the westward-sweeping shoreline of Cardigan Bay.

There are about a hundred hillforts down the western side of Wales and their development doesn't seem to have followed the pattern observed in southern England, which we saw, for example, in Dorset. They do, however, seem to have originated at around the same time (1100–800 BC), in the late Bronze Age. A recent study of the hillforts of Cardigan Bay by Toby Driver has clearly demonstrated that they were constructed to be seen in two different ways, probably by different groups of people: local residents and people either passing by or visiting the area from outside.[15] This arrangement is very clearly seen at one of the most spectacular hillforts in Britain, at Pen Dinas, which lies on a hill immediately to the south of Aberystwyth.[16]

14.1 The hillfort of Pen Dinas, immediately south of the port of Aberystwyth. The hillfort is crowned by a stone monument to the Duke of Wellington (erected 1858). Just beyond the main ramparts, to the north, and joined to them by two extended banks of another enclosure, is a second, circular enclosure, which was probably an earlier version of the hillfort.

The hillforts inland from Cardigan Bay seem to make no attempt to blend into the landscape. Everything about them is spectacular, with steep banks, often originally built up behind a high drystone wall. Incidentally, like plaster, cement or mortar wasn't introduced to Britain until Roman times. The focus of these hillforts was always inland, away from the sea, and they were obviously constructed to impress people living across large tracts of the countryside, because visibility from a distance was plainly a dominant feature. They were also sited to overlook important features in the landscape that tribal leaders might want to control, such as the confluence of two rivers or the foothills of a mountain range. If the need to dominate from a distance was a primary strategic concern, they were also carefully sited and laid out to impress local people and to overlook the features in the landscape that affected their daily lives.

The massive ramparts at Pen Dinas, for example, dominate the river valleys and coastal lowlands behind the modern town, but there are also two attached – I am tempted to say subsidiary – enclosures beneath the main, or South fort. These comprise a large circular enclosure (the North fort) of comparable size to the South fort and another, the Isthmus enclosure, which linked the two with a substantial curved drystone rampart along its eastern side; the wall and rampart along its western, or seaward, side is much slighter and clearly not built to impress.

The North fort at Pen Dinas resembles some of the larger fortified farmsteads that were a feature of late Bronze Age and Iron Age Wales. It pre-dates the main South fort, but continued in use throughout its existence, attached to it by the Isthmus fort. The three enclosures were linked together by an internal road and there were houses, usually within their own smaller enclosures, in both the North and South forts. The whole complex was approached from the east (inland) by a road that entered an impressive gateway in the large drystone rampart of the central, Isthmus enclosure. Recent excavation has shown that the gateways and other components of the three enclosures were repeatedly modified and rebuilt. The layout of the Pen Dinas hillfort clearly shows this dual focus on both local people and the broader picture, but I don't think that the two were competitive or non-complementary in any way. I believe it reflected the way that the Iron Age people of western Wales viewed their world.

We used to believe that much of the work of building hillforts was probably carried out by captured enemy warriors, essentially working as slaves. Indeed, a set of Iron Age iron slave collars to go around the necks of five slaves, which were linked together by lengths of chain, was found during preparation work for a wartime bomber airfield, in former lake deposits at Llyn Cerrig Bach, in Anglesey.[17] The old lake had been used as a special place to make offerings for about five hundred years, starting around 300 BC. The slave chains dated to the first century BC. The presence of slaves, who may well have been prisoners of war captured from neighbouring tribes, does not necessarily mean they were used to perform tasks in Britain. They could equally well have been taken abroad and sold within the Roman Empire, where there was more wealth to pay for them.

The most reliable evidence from excavations suggests that the Welsh hillforts were generally constructed with some care and were regularly and well maintained, which might argue against the use of unwilling slave labour. There can be no doubt that they were built as military structures, since their gateways were frequently altered and improved and often featured robust timber walls and other structures. It also seems likely that the 'military' action did not involve fighting between rival armies, but skirmishing between raiding parties and defenders – and mostly in the autumn and quieter times of the farming year. Although the defensive works of these Welsh hillforts were clearly very functional and well-constructed, they seldom encircled a hilltop with the same completeness that we saw, for example, at Maiden Castle and other Dorset sites. This suggests that attackers were not expected to approach from the rear and that their assaults were as much displays of valour, to be witnessed by a frightened audience of local people, as they were attempts to capture the fort. These hillforts would not have been subject to prolonged, drawn-out sieges, as happened, for example, to castles in the Middle Ages.

For many years, archaeologists, like the general public in Iron Age times, were attracted by the obvious, spectacular military posture of these hillforts. But when they are examined closely, and are seen in the context of the settlements and landscape around them, they can be appreciated for what they are: symbols of power and stability. They would have provided much comfort and security for the people living in the area. I often think of them as emblems of civilization and civic life in an Iron Age culture that was about to be traumatized by the Roman conquest. I sometimes wonder to what extent their continuing dominating presence in the landscape ensured that Celtic culture was not destroyed, and continued to flourish in post-Roman Britain.

Scene 15

And What Then? Daily Life in Roman Times (AD 43–410) and Later

Rural Roman Britain – West Stow – Canterbury – Brixworth

Few periods in British history have been misrepresented quite as much as the almost four centuries when we were a part of the Roman Empire, from AD 43 to about AD 410. It's not that ancient historians and archaeologists have got things wrong: far from it, they have spent vast amounts of effort working out the dates of coins and in reconstructing details of when and how different units of the Roman army were moved from one fort to another. The main problem has been that the role of pre-Roman British communities – the Celts, or the native Iron Age British, call them what you will – has been greatly underestimated, leading to massive distortion. Furthermore, the way the period has traditionally been taught has led to an unhelpful separation of the incoming Romans from the native Iron Age Britons. Prehistory is considered to be a branch of archaeology and anthropology, whereas Roman archaeology has strong links with ancient history – and in most universities the two are taught in separate departments by staff who often have very different backgrounds.

The Romans undoubtedly brought to Britain some very

important technical innovations, ranging from the first use of new ploughs that actually turned the soil over (earlier ones had simply cut deep channels in it), to the introduction of cement and plaster, bricks and tiles. The Romans also introduced writing and efficient systems of governance suitable for nation-sized populations. But the fact remains that the number of actual Romans who invaded was very small. Most of the troops who came to Britain were not Romans at all; they would have been recruited from other parts of the Empire. When the Roman army conquered a new territory, the forces that opposed them would subsequently be recruited into the army and then sent far away, to new areas of conquest. It was a simple but very effective method of avoiding rebellions in newly won territories.

The Romans would not have conquered Britain had there been nothing in it for them. Although not united as a single nation, the British were a long way from being a chaotic, squabbling group of tribal kingdoms – as they have sometimes been portrayed. For example, the different parts of the British Isles had long been connected by a system of roads and tracks, and the landscape was organized into a complex network of farms, hamlets, villages and larger settlements, although true towns had yet to appear. Farming in pre-Roman Britain was well organized and very productive. Most importantly, there is little evidence that fields or farms were abandoned after the Roman conquest. The vast majority continued in use and became even more productive as money-based markets were set up in the newly established towns that grew in prosperity in the second and third centuries AD.

The layout and development of ancient field systems can reveal much about past farming practices and they have long fascinated prehistorians who have studied and surveyed them, both on the ground or from the air, for well over a century.[1] When Roman field systems were studied, it was often as part of a prehistoric or regional survey. Only occasionally, the Fens being a notable exception, were Roman field systems studied in their own right and there was certainly no attempt to draw them all together into a coherent picture.[2]

We saw in the previous chapter how the military-focused approach to the Roman conquest caused problems with the interpretation of hillforts such as Maiden Castle. Similar approaches – almost amounting to an obsession – dominated studies of Hadrian's Wall and other Roman military installations throughout the 1950s, 1960s and into the 1970s. I suspect the failure to consider fields of the Roman period in Britain as a unified topic was another outcome of this overemphasis on military and other history-based issues, together with a disproportionate emphasis on the archaeology of Roman villas, towns and roads. (The study of Roman roads could, of course, also be readily linked to the military.)

The field systems of Roman Britain were only considered as a unified topic as recently as 2007, in a remarkable atlas compiled by Jeremy Taylor.[3] This study draws extensively on a mass of unpublished data, housed in local council offices – the result of excavations and surveys carried out in advance of development projects. The Roman fields of England were based upon (and developed out of) the fields that were being used in the late Iron Age, at the time of the conquest, in AD 43. The families who farmed them were the families who ran them before the Roman invasion. As a general rule, there was little or no disruption when the Roman army arrived. Farming landscapes in the north and west tended to be more open, with larger fields and grazing areas and with more dispersed and smaller rural settlements than those in the south and east, where greater emphasis was placed on the growing of crops.

The big change in Roman times came in the later second and third centuries, when trading networks opened up and farms and other rural industries became more prosperous. I have always found this particular period fascinating. The conquest had happened, and people accepted it; but they were still British, they still had Celtic (i.e. British) names and they probably still spoke a Celtic language, but by now they would have understood Latin and maybe, too, some of the contemporary languages of Germany and the Low Countries, with which trading links were becoming better established. Europe was in a state of flux; this was a period of rapid change. So are there signs in the archaeological record of how people were able to adapt so rapidly to the new reality of Roman rule – in the course of just two or three generations? At the time of writing, we are living through a period of extraordinary uncertainty both at home and abroad: Brexit still looms darkly over the horizon, the Covid pandemic continues its unpredictable course, Trump lost the election but was reluctant to accept the result, and China is growing increasingly menacing. Talking to friends, relations and colleagues, it is clear that we are all seeking stability in our lives, and we find it in different ways and in a variety of activities. I find myself spending most days out in the garden, either weeding borders or planting a huge selection of fruit and vegetables. When Maisie isn't in the garden with me, she occupies her time sewing or cooking – but she doesn't restrict herself to old favourites. We have both found that we can enhance the interest of whatever it is we are doing by venturing into unexplored territory, whether that be new fabrics or patterns, or new recipes involving previously untried vegetables. Tenderstem broccoli and home-grown and dried cannellini beans have recently become firm favourites, both in the vegetable garden and on the dinner table.

I think I might have found evidence for a similar enjoyment of new food fashions and other innovative personal experiences during politically or socially difficult times in the finds we came across when we dug the ditches of a farm dating to the early Roman period at Fengate in Peterborough.[4] I confess they didn't make much sense to me when we excavated them in the late 1970s, but I think they are beginning to do so now. The farm in question was erected on the site of a later Iron Age hamlet that had been in existence for some three or four centuries. At any one time, it would have consisted of about a dozen houses, plus shelters and small barns for livestock. This was quite a substantial and prosperous community in the later Iron Age, but it seems to have been abandoned at about the time of the Roman conquest. We don't know why its inhabitants left, but it seems to have been a peaceful process. The site of the deserted hamlet was then reoccupied about a century later, in the third quarter of the second century AD. This reoccupation made use of many of the earlier site's ditches, but this time for a farm rather than a settlement. The farm was based on livestock, probably cattle and sheep (to judge from the bones found). It lay at the wetland edge and was accessed by way of a wide, ditched droveway, which would have been used to drive livestock to and from the higher land of the fen margins, now beneath the city of Peterborough.

The conventional picture of the Roman conquest features blue-painted Ancient Britons facing the uniformed might of the Roman army.* In reality, the distinction between the two sides was not as stark. Many of the well-established British tribal kingdoms had good relations with Rome and certainly in better-off parts of south-east England people from richer families drank wine and used olive oil imported from the Mediterranean. In the late Iron Age, many more people began to use a type of sprung brooch, which closely resembles a large modern safety pin. These so-called *fibula* brooches are decorative, but they are essential for securing Roman-style toga-based clothing. So the evidence

---

* The blue face-paint was made from a dye extracted from the leaves of woad (a plant of the cabbage family, *Isatis tinctoria*), which was grown in the Fens until the 1930s.

seems to be suggesting that many in the upper echelons of Iron Age communities in southern Britain were starting to adopt aspects of Roman culture about a century before the conquest of AD 43. The excavations of the Fengate settlement, prior to its abandonment at the time of the Roman conquest, revealed some thirteen fibula brooches.

The recut ditches of the second-century AD settlement at Fengate produced large quantities of pottery made in the semi-industrial workshops of the nearby Roman town of Durobrivae (modern Water Newton) just 11 kilometres (7 miles) to the west. In among the pottery were a few pieces of Samian ware, glossy and finely finished red pottery that was made in central Gaul (France). This was very upmarket stuff and would have made quite a statement when placed on a dinner table. The dig also revealed about a dozen pieces of hard ceramic kitchen mortars, including one example that was half-complete. These mortars look remarkably similar to modern ones and feature strong, wide rims that were easy to grip. Many were well-worn and some had been burned. Their importance lies in the way that they were used: most mortars were, and are, used to grind or powder spices. So far as we know, the use of spices was unknown in British prehistoric kitchens. The grinding of spices for food was a Roman practice, and yet here is good evidence of its adoption by Late Iron Age Britons in a Fenland farm kitchen.

It seems to me that the local British population adapted to the challenges of what was rapidly becoming a new order by changing with the times, but they would have done it in their own way – and that's why I am prepared to bet good money that even the spiciest food prepared in a Fenland farmhouse would still have had a distinctively British flavour. People were adapting to the changing world around them in their own, distinctive fashion.

The two or three centuries that followed the withdrawal of the last Roman troops from Britain, in the years around AD 410, have often been described as the Dark Ages – an inaccurate term that I detest, mainly because it suggests that the Romans brought light, which then vanished when they withdrew. These centuries were traditionally seen as very bleak: civil governance broke down, farms and fields were abandoned and countryside that had been cultivated returned to dense woodland. And as if things couldn't get any worse, this grim and lawless landscape was then invaded by successive waves of Anglo-Saxon brigands and warlords from the other side of the North Sea. That at least was the conventional wisdom in the decades before and just after the last war; but it was largely based on misreadings of later accounts of the period, which were not trying to portray objective history and were all written for their own, rather different motives.

Then in the 1960s, at places like Mucking in Essex* and elsewhere, archaeologists returned to the excavation of early post-Roman sites, but at a much larger scale than had been possible previously; what they revealed was very different from the, by then, widely accepted view of an anarchic age of darkness. Their findings have been enhanced and confirmed by research in subsequent decades and we now see the post-Roman Anglo-Saxon period as an exciting time of change and innovation. A coherent group of regional kingdoms emerged, and – after a period of several centuries during which the balance of power shifted between them – eventually came together into a single nation and identity, that of England and the English.

The change from a more Romanized way of life was not as dramatic as used to be believed: entire field systems were not abandoned overnight. Naturally, there were some changes: there

---

* See Scene 11, page 203.

was no Roman army, for example, that needed to be supplied with British grain, and there was a move towards the keeping of more livestock, but scrub and then woodland did *not* take over the British landscape. As for the human population, there is genetic evidence for an influx of people from continental Europe, but there is also evidence that British people moved across the Channel.[5] In other words, it was a two-way process. The population movements were probably rather slighter than we are currently witnessing in the early twenty-first century. The change in language took place over several centuries. The language brought to Britain by Germanic settlers in the fifth century, known as Old English (or Anglo-Saxon), became the dominant tongue spoken in England and the south of Scotland, gradually replacing Brythonic and Latin, the languages of Roman Britain – although Latin would remain the language of scholarship and the Christian church (present in Britain since mid-Roman times). Brythonic would eventually retreat to the western parts of Britain – to Wales and Cornwall – while in northern Scotland and Ireland other forms of Celtic were spoken. Many communities across Britain would have been multilingual, however, as indeed are significant numbers of people in north Wales, the Scottish Isles or western Ireland, today.

We know from sites in the Somerset Levels and at Flag Fen and Must Farm in the Fens that the prehistoric inhabitants of Britain were very good at woodwork.* It would seem that these traditions of craftsmanship continued to develop through Roman times because they again became evident in the early post-Roman Saxon period. This was the time when timber buildings became more popular, following the widespread use of brick and stone that had become so fashionable in Roman Britain. Surviving early Saxon timberwork is still quite rare, but excavations have

---

* See Scene 13.

revealed the ground plans of many buildings. Using their ground plans as a basis, experimental archaeologists have worked out how these timber structures were assembled and erected.

A village of reconstructed Saxon buildings has been painstakingly recreated at West Stow in Suffolk.[6] Over the years I have visited many ancient timber buildings and I am always slightly disappointed that they have completely lost their smell of 'woodiness'. The sap and oils that give oak and pine their light but very distinctive smells have long since dried up. As we saw at Seahenge, the smell of tannic acid is very strong indeed shortly after the oak timbers have been cut and split[*] and tannin continues to scent the air for a long time afterwards. Many of the reconstructed buildings at West Stow have already been standing for the equivalent of a human generation (say thirty years), yet when you're inside them, they still retain a distinctly woody atmosphere. It's what you would have experienced had you been living there in Saxon times – together, of course, with the usual household smells of fires, cooking, laundry and babies.

The second and most famous conquest of British history after the Romans was, of course, that of the Normans, in 1066. We always think of the Normans as being French, whereas the truth was far more nuanced. At the time, western Europe had been forming many new identities, which were in the process of settling down. The Normans were becoming French, but their roots are revealed by the dictionary definition of the name, Norman: 'one belonging to the mixed Scandinavian and Frankish race'.[†] Britain was going through similar changes, which were probably hastened

---

[*] See also Scene 9, page 175.

[†] *The Shorter Oxford English Dictionary*, vol. II (Clarendon Press, Oxford, 1978), p. 1413.

by the arrival of the new elites from across the Channel. As with the earlier Roman invasion, history has tended to overemphasize the new, in favour of what had gone before. The process was actually begun by the Normans themselves, who set about an extraordinary programme of building, or – more importantly, sometimes – rebuilding. Most of the surviving Norman buildings are castles, monasteries, cathedrals and, of course, parish churches. England has one of the largest and finest collections of medieval churches anywhere – and about a quarter of the eight thousand or so that survive are Norman. But closer inspection usually reveals a more complex story. Nowhere is this better illustrated than at Canterbury, where the first church of post-Roman Britain was established by St Augustine in 597.

It is believed that Augustine might have used an earlier Roman church or some other building for the very first cathedral, but soon work began on a new structure, which was revealed when Kevin Blockley and his team carried out detailed excavations ahead of the re-flooring of the nave between January and June 1993.[7] They uncovered evidence for an earlier building, which had been constructed in at least four phases.[8] The first church, which may or may not be that of St Augustine (the dating is still too imprecise to be certain), was considerably smaller than the rebuilding that happened later. It was undoubtedly post-Roman, because its walls were cut into a layer of Roman soil. The second phase saw the demolition of the first church and the construction of a larger and longer building, perhaps in the seventh century.

The third phase saw a rebuild of the second structure, but we don't know why this happened. In the fourth and final phase, we are presented with one of the largest Saxon cathedrals in England and undoubtedly one of the finest of its time in Europe. Any developing structural problems were sorted out by enlarging and thickening walls. Two substantial six-sided towers were added at the west end, which also featured a rounded apse, like that at the

15.1 A reconstruction of Canterbury Cathedral as it might have appeared before the Norman Conquest, around AD 1000. The drawing is by the archaeologist Kevin Blockley, who co-directed extensive excavations of the cathedral between January and June 1993.

east end. Rounded, or apsidal, church ends developed in Roman times and were an important component of early post-Roman Byzantine churches. They became common across most of Europe in early medieval times.[9]

I love to visit ancient buildings and I'm usually equipped with my mobile phone and, of course, a copy of the relevant Pevsner county-by-county guide. These sources tell me in great detail about the various phases of each building – how this window was reframed and that doorway blocked or moved – and I can usually absorb myself in such things for about an hour, before my head begins to swim and I start to crave a cup of tea, or something a bit stronger. It's then, when I'm sitting down, either within a restaurant or tea room or outside, that I start to contemplate what might have happened and what life would have been like there in the past.

Sometimes in these circumstances, well-known historical events come to dominate one's thoughts. In the case of Canterbury, it has to be the 'martyrdom' of Archbishop Thomas Becket, who was murdered in the north-west transept of the cathedral in 1170.[10] I say 'martyrdom', because his murder could also be seen as a straightforward piece of power politics gone wrong. The subsequent elevation of the victim into a saint was more about the reputation of Henry II than Becket. I was pondering such themes when I came across what in many ways was a far more memorable event, which had taken place 159 years previously, in that now vanished, pre-Norman cathedral.[11]

The many Danish raids of the tenth and eleventh centuries AD were often led by men with wonderful names. The devastating raid on Canterbury by the brothers Hemming and Thorkell the Tall in 1011 reduced the cathedral to ashes. The then Archbishop of Canterbury, Alphege, was bound and taken prisoner to their camp at Greenwich. He refused to be ransomed, so the furious Danes murdered him by pelting him with ox bones during a drunken orgy. Following the raid and the withdrawal of the Tall Vikings, the shrine of the martyred archbishop drew many pilgrims to the city. And the story of his murder continues to fascinate me. On digs I have dealt with many, many bones, so I often find myself wondering about the ones those Vikings drunkenly hurled at the unfortunate archbishop: had they been kept to one side, following the butchery process earlier? Or were they thrown at the poor bishop only when the meat had been gnawed off them? The latter would have resulted in a much more protracted, if slightly sweeter-smelling, demise.

In these Scenes I've tried to capture snapshots of the past, rather as an archaeologist does on an excavation. Most of a digger's day is lived firmly in the present, wheeling barrows, sipping mugs of tea or looking for mislaid finds trays, trowels or labels; but every once in a while one is brought face to face with the past. Almost invariably, that moment happens when one is alone, but not always: I recall the day on a *Time Team* excavation of a Victorian railway navvies' camp at Risehill, high in the Yorkshire Dales, when my digging companion, Raksha Dave, and I simultaneously sniffed the dark, peaty-looking stuff that we were gingerly scraping with our trowels and realized that it wasn't peat at all.[12] It was human excrement and we had located the latrine site. Normally, cesspits and latrines lose their smell quite fast, as soil fungi and bacteria break them down in a few years, but that excavation was quite literally up in the clouds, at an altitude of some 365 metres (1,200 ft), and the thin soil was very acid indeed. So the micro-organisms couldn't get a grip. The smell was made more poignant by the knowledge that the Population Census of 1871 had noted that one of the navvies in the camp had taken his own life in the latrines. So we were sniffing precisely what he would have been smelling in his final minutes on this Earth. That moment still haunts me.

As readers will no doubt be aware, I do like to visit old buildings. Over the past two decades, Maisie and I have taken our breaks and holidays in Britain, partly because we both dislike crowded airports and beaches, but mostly because we love Britain and the extraordinary variation you can experience in its landscape over quite small distances. Having lived in Canada, where you can sit in a train for whole days while vast, identical tracts of plain or prairie glide past the windows, the only relief being provided by the occasional group of grain-storage silos, I love the fact that every British country station and each parish church or nonconformist chapel has a different story to tell, and they're all so close together – even in such supposedly 'lonely' parts of the country as the Black Fens or the Lincolnshire Wolds.

So we have tended to take our vacations in holiday cottages and converted old buildings that allow us to gain a sense of place. Neighbours are best avoided. We have had some wonderful breaks: in an old Tudor banqueting house, in a couple of medieval gatehouses, in a gardener's cottage built on Lord Byron's estate at Newstead Abbey[13] and, perhaps most memorable of all, in a holiday flat built into the ruins of a medieval Carthusian monastery at Mount Grace, in the North York Moors.[14]

Carthusian monks lived in solitary, self-contained cells and it was marvellous to be able to walk through and around the buildings in the late evening, when all the tourist parties and visitors had gone home. I've always been a fairly sociable sort of person and I couldn't even begin to understand the appeal of a hermit's life. But our stay at Mount Grace has subtly changed my attitudes. Maybe I've become a little less sure of things. I think I can now sort of understand why somebody would choose to opt for a solitary life – even if I would never do it myself in a thousand years. I actually think my stay at Mount Grace might have helped me cope a bit better with the imposed solitude of the Covid pandemic lockdown. Carthusian monks led extremely ordered lives; that was the key to their success. Mount Grace was certainly an experience to treasure. But I've left the best until last.

When you live and work in such a distinctive regional landscape as the Fens, it's very easy to become introspective and to see the relatively specialized landscapes that our long history has bequeathed to us as being somehow typical – which they're not. No landscape is typical: all are unique, just like the communities who created and inhabited them. That's why I also like to study, visit and think about the counties that border Fenland. It's rather like people at a party: you can soon spot groups of friends and in time you can identify what it is that unites them. Some may be old pals from school or college; others might share hobbies or professional interests, such as lawyers, writers or musicians. But the really interesting time for any avid people-watcher is when a few drinks have been taken and one or two brave individuals start to venture outside their groups. Usually these adventurers are the prominent, perhaps more self-confident members of a group.

In the Middle Ages, the equivalent of the confident social adventurers were the merchants who travelled between market towns, selling their wares. As time passed, the scale of such deals increased and long-distance trade links between the different regional economies of England became more firmly established. The process was further strengthened by the success of certain abbeys and priories that had built up substantial farmed estates, which were managed by paid agents, who were often known as the abbot's or prior's man – and hence the long-forgotten medieval origins of my own family name. Peterborough Abbey was very prosperous indeed, possessing substantial estates along the Nene Valley,* which runs like a spine down the centre of Northamptonshire. In the 1980s I was becoming increasingly interested in the links between the Nene Valley and the Fens in the Middle Ages and how they subsequently developed in early industrial and modern times. For me, the past only comes into its own if somehow you can relate it to the present. That, at least, was my theoretical justification for many journeys down the Nene Valley into the heart of rural Northamptonshire. But

---

* Upstream of Peterborough, the River Nene is known as the River Nen.

then I discovered something remarkable that made all such justifications irrelevant.

Northamptonshire is sometimes known as the county of spires and squires and I have long been an admirer of its many fine country houses and churches.[15] I had just driven past the superb Saxon church at Earls Barton and was sitting in the car with my sandwich and a copy of Pevsner's *Northamptonshire*, when the book fell open at the entry for another village church nearby. I glanced at it, the way one does, but there was something about the entry that held my attention. The more I read, the more excited I became. I honestly can't remember if I even finished my lunch, because the next thing I knew I had set off at a cracking pace through the outer suburbs of Northampton; then north for about 5 kilometres (3 miles), to the small town, or large village, of Brixworth. In retrospect, it seems odd that I had hurried so much to get there, as of all British churches, that at Brixworth had been there for a very long time indeed – and it was certainly not about to go anywhere.

My version of Pevsner then was an older edition with just one black-and-white photo of the interior of Brixworth Church, which didn't really do it justice. It was the exterior, without any of the thick mask of whitewash that so disfigured British church interiors in the late nineteenth and twentieth centuries, that made such a strong impression on me. It was quite unlike any other church I had ever seen. By now, I was walking along the tarmac path towards a plain wooden door, set in a double-arched doorway, on the south side.

To many people with an archaeological background, the bricks and stones of a wall are like the layers of a ditch or a pit: they preserve the story for posterity. To read that story, you have to work in reverse. So the highest things are usually the most recent, and original structures tend to lurk below, or behind, newer ones. Two clear examples were evident as I walked up that path. The upper part of the tower, from about a metre (3 ft) below the clock face, was clearly much later, as was the Lady Chapel, which had been built on to the south-west end. But everything else seemed consistent, although quite unlike other Saxon churches I was familiar with, such as Earls Barton, nearby, or Barnack on the very edge of the Fens, in south Lincolnshire.

I walked round the outside twice, before venturing inside, where the dreaded whitewash was much in evidence, but there could be no doubt that this was a very early church indeed. My copy of Pevsner suggested that the main body of the church had been constructed in the late seventh century, but a series of excavations between 1972 and 2010 have clearly shown it was actually built about a century later: towards the end of the eighth or the beginning of the ninth century.[16] All Saints' Brixworth is the largest and among the earliest of Anglo-Saxon churches surviving in Britain, but it was originally even larger, with a series of side chambers on either side of the nave. These had been demolished by the time the Lady Chapel was added to the south side, in the thirteenth to fourteenth century, but their existence probably explains the height of the arches over the ground-floor doors and windows in the main body of the church.

Much of the masonry struck me as odd. It was a bit of a jumble, with what looked like reused Roman bricks, which were sometimes laid in a herringbone pattern in imitation of Roman walls. One or more courses of reused Roman bricks formed the arches over doorways and window openings, but they weren't laid in a methodical way, with firm, buffer-like ends and a central wedge-shaped keystone piece to hold the arch together. They had been placed in the wall to look good, rather than to carry a load.

Recent excavations have shown that the Roman bricks didn't come from any local villas but had been brought to Brixworth from the neighbouring Roman towns at Towcester

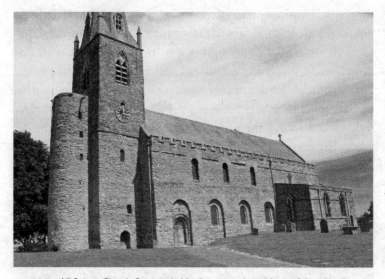

15.2 All Saints Church, Brixworth, Northamptonshire. Much of this church was built in the late eighth or ninth century. It is the largest and finest surviving Saxon church in Britain and indeed Europe. Note the apsidal end to the left (west). The tower is Saxon to just below the clock, as are the nave and eastern apse (not visible here); the small Lady Chapel to the south-east is later (thirteenth/fourteenth century). Note the distinctive thin Roman bricks re-used in the arches over the doors and windows.

(about 24 kilometres/15 miles to the south) and Leicester (some 42 kilometres/26 miles to the north). This suggests that even four centuries after the Romans had departed, their town buildings were being used as sources of building materials – and in quite an organized fashion. The quantities are remarkable and the condition of the bricks is good. Incidentally, Brixworth isn't unique in reusing Roman bricks. The tower of St Albans Abbey (Cathedral) contains vast numbers of them, removed in the later eleventh century from the ruins of the abandoned town of Verulamium, very close by.

When I first learned about the reuse of Roman building materials in the early post-Roman centuries, we were told it was a sign of the poverty that prevailed in Saxon times. In effect, people were eking out a grim existence by pilfering the buildings of the past. But we now realize that most post-Roman houses and other buildings were made from timber. Bricks and masonry were ideas imported from the Mediterranean, along with towns, most of which didn't thrive for very long after the Roman withdrawal. The British had returned to using what they were familiar with: building materials and carpentry that had mostly been developed in later prehistoric times. But people hadn't forgotten about the Roman buildings. They had largely been abandoned, but everyone knew where they were, so when building in stone was starting to come back into fashion, in the seventh and eighth centuries (which is also when the earliest true towns of the post-Roman period were being established), Roman bricks were in effect being quarried for use elsewhere. The scale of their reuse in St Albans, and indeed at Brixworth, is remarkable and suggests that traders and dealers were probably involved. It certainly wasn't just casual pilfering.

Whenever I visit Brixworth and look at the bricks above those arched windows, I can't help wondering whether the people who quarried, traded and then relaid them were aware of what they were doing. There is a tendency when we think about the post-Roman centuries to suppose that people were ignorant of their own past; that once the Roman army and civil servants had gone, people simply forgot about them. But if I have learned anything from a life spent scraping through the debris of the past, it is that people have long memories.

History survives among ordinary folk in tales and stories, so I would be very surprised indeed if the Saxon masons who removed, traded and then relaid those bricks at Brixworth were in any doubt at all about what they were doing. I don't think of them as vandals or pilferers, and they certainly wouldn't have felt any guilt: they were recycling – which is something we must all be doing today, if, that is, we are to moderate the impact of climate change and the threat of irreversible environmental damage that currently confronts us. But it will require humility. We could learn so much from those skilled Saxon tradesmen.

Acknowledgements

The writing of this book has been a work of two parts: before and after Covid-19, which struck in March 2020, more or less when I was making the transition out of the Neolithic and into the Bronze Age (Scenes 6 and 7). Subsequently, I have been in self-imposed isolation and while I have lacked for few comforts, thanks to a productive vegetable garden and a very proficient cook (my lovely wife, Maisie), the lack of other close human contact has been palpable. This has meant that the writing of this book has played an important part in preserving some sense of 'normality' in a world that was becoming increasingly unstable not just due to the pandemic, but to other widespread problems, such as the rise of populist politicians and 'fake news', civil unrest in parts of the Middle East and the emergence of China as a world power. So I am more than usually grateful to the many people who went to such trouble to help me in so many ways, with pictures, with information and with editorial advice. Thank you all for doing it so well and with such kindness. I hope you benefited from the experience as much as I did.

I owe a special debt of gratitude to Marion Dowd, for providing me with copious information on Irish cave sites. Thanks are also due to Kevin Blockley (Canterbury Cathedral), Andy Richmond (Tower's Fen bucket) and Dave Stewart (Dorset hillforts). I have received continuing help and advice from

Chris Evans, Mike Parker Pearson, Maisie Taylor and Michael Bamforth. The editorial team at Head of Zeus have been superb throughout. In particular I have received clear guidance from Anthony Cheetham and from my editor, Richard Milbank, who has been most helpful and understanding. His expertise in the development of Old English was particularly useful; he kindly, but ruthlessly, exposed my hopeless attempts to make sense of a difficult subject, in Scene 15. Copy-editing was by Jenni Davis, design by Ben Cracknell, index by Ben Murphy.

Notes

Introduction

1 Chris Scarre (ed.), *The Human Past: World Prehistory and the Development of Human Societies* (Thames and Hudson, London, 2005). This huge and beautifully illustrated book provides a remarkable overview of world prehistory, set against environmental change.

2 *Farmers in Prehistoric Britain* (Tempus Books, Stroud, 2006) and *Home: A Time Traveller's Tales from Britain's Prehistory* (Penguin Books, London, 2014).

3 Brian Fagan, *A Little History of Archaeology* (Yale University Press, London, 2018), chapter 9.

Scene 1

1 Brian Fagan, *A Little History of Archaeology* (Yale University Press, London, 2018), chapters 7 and 8.

2 Clive Waddington, 'Battling the Waves', *British Archaeology*, November/December 2014, pp. 34–9.

3 N. Pevsner and B. Watson, *The Buildings of England. Norfolk 1: Norwich and North-East*, 2nd ed. (Yale University Press, London, 2002), pp. 539–42.

4 A. D. Mills, *A Dictionary of English Place-names* (Oxford University Press, Oxford, 1991), p. 324.

5 S. Parfitt, N. Ashton and S. Lewis, 'Happisburgh', *British Archaeology*, September/October, 2010, pp. 14–23.

6 www.selrc.org.uk/maplocation.php?location_id=38

7   'First Impressions: Discovering the Earliest Human Footprints
    in Europe', *Current Archaeology*, 289, April 2014, pp. 12–16.
    N. Ashton, 'One Million Years UK', *British Archaeology*, March/
    April 2014, pp. 20–1. See also: http://www.britishmuseum.org/
    research/research_projects/all_current_projects/featured_project_
    happisburgh/discovering_the_site.aspx

8   B. J. Coles, 'Doggerland: A Speculative Survey', *Proceedings of the
    Prehistoric Society*, vol. 64, 1998, pp. 45–81.

9   en.wikipedia.org/wiki/West_Runton_Mammoth

10 'Colonising Britain', *Current Archaeology*, vol. 288, March 2014,
    pp. 14–21.

11 The definitive report on Boxgrove is by M. B. Roberts and
    S. A. Parfitt, *Boxgrove: A Middle Pleistocene Hominid Site
    at Eartham Quarry, Boxgrove, West Sussex,* English Heritage
    Archaeological Report 17 (English Heritage, London, 1999). For an
    excellent summary see 'Boxgrove', *Current Archaeology*, No. 153,
    July 1997, pp. 324–33.

12 paleoleap.com/eat-this-bone-broth/

13 I discuss the agricultural recession of the 1870s in *The Making of
    the British Landscape* (Penguin Books, London, 2010), pp. 492–7.

Scene 2

1   en.wikipedia.org/wiki/Homo_sapiens

2   en.wikipedia.org/wiki/William_Buckland#The_Red_Lady_of_
    Paviland

3   Adrian Desmond and James Moore, *Darwin: The Life of a
    Tormented Evolutionist* (Warner Books, New York, 1991),
    pp. 204–5.

4   For a good overview, see Stephen Green and Elizabeth Walker, *Ice
    Age Hunters: Neanderthals and Early Modern Hunters in Wales*
    (National Museum of Wales, Cardiff, 1991).

5   'How Old is the Red Lady?', *Current Archaeology*, 215, January
    2008, p. 4. See also: rcahmw.gov.uk/paviland-cave-and-the-ice-age-
    hunters/

6   Stephen Aldhouse-Green, *Paviland Cave and the 'Red Lady': A
    Definitive Report* (Western Academic and Specialist Press, Bristol,
    2000). For a useful summary of the former: Stephen Aldhouse-
    Green, 'Great Sites: Paviland Cave', *British Archaeology*, 61,
    October 2001, pp. 20–4.

7   Richard Bradley, *An Archaeology of Natural Places* (Routledge, London, 2000).

8   Francis Pryor, *The Making of the British Landscape*, p. 3, with note (Penguin Books, London, 2010).

9   The earliest Mesolithic site in Ireland is still Mount Sandel, which has produced radiocarbon dates of 9750 BP (before present), or 7800 BC. See Peter Woodman, *Ireland's First Settlers: Time and the Mesolithic* (Oxbow Books, Oxford, 2015), p. 183.

10 Marion Dowd, *The Archaeology of Caves in Ireland* (Oxbow Books, Oxford, 2015).

11 Ibid., p. 81.

12 P. Woodman, M. Dowd, L. Fibiger, R. F. Carden and J. O'Shaughnessy, 'Archaeological Excavations at Killuragh Cave, Co. Limerick: A Persistent Place in the Landscape from the Early Mesolithic to the Late Bronze Age', *Journal of Irish Archaeology*, Vol. 26, 2017, pp. 1–32.

13 Dowd, *The Archaeology of Caves in Ireland*, p. 131.

14 Ibid., pp. 85–6.

15 Marion Dowd (pers. comm.) tells me that recent trace element analysis of the bones suggests that the man ate a hunter-gatherer's diet.

16 Francis Pryor, *Seahenge: A Quest for Life and Death in Bronze Age Britain* (HarperCollins, London, 2001).

17 David Robertson et al., 'A Second Timber Circle, Trackways, and Coppicing at Holme-next-the-Sea Beach, Norfolk: Use of Salt- and Freshwater Marshes in the Bronze Age', *Proceedings of the Prehistoric Society*, vol. 82, 2016, pp. 227–58.

18 Dowd, *The Archaeology of Caves in Ireland*, pp. 143–5.

19 B. Quinn and D. Moore, 2007. mooregroup.wordpress.com/2007/10/08/the-archaeology-ireland-article/

Scene 3

1   www2.palomar.edu/anthro/hominid/australo_1.htm

2   Chris Scarre (ed.), *The Human Past: World Prehistory and the Development of Human Societies* (Thames and Hudson, London, 2005), pp. 116–17.

3   I illustrate a glaciated valley in the Scottish Borders in *The Making of the British Landscape* (Penguin Books, London, 2010).

4 For a superb account of the period, see S. J. Mithen, *After the Ice: A Global Human History 20,000–5000 BC* (Weidenfeld & Nicolson, London, 2003), chapter 15.

5 See, for example, R. Tipping, R. Bradley, J. Sanders, R. McCulloch and R. Wilson, 'Moments of Crisis: Climate Change in Scottish Prehistory', *Proceedings of the Society of Antiquaries of Scotland*, vol. 142, 2012, pp. 9–25.

6 en.wikipedia.org/wiki/Little_Ice_Age

7 en.wikipedia.org/wiki/River_Hertford

8 jncc.defra.gov.uk/page-1999-theme=default

9 My account of Lake Flixton and the sites surrounding it is based on N. Milner, B. Taylor, C. Conneller and R. T. Schadla-Hall, *Star Carr: Life in Britain after the Ice Age* (Council for British Archaeology, York, 2013), chapter 3, and N. Milner, C. Conneller and B. Taylor, *Star Carr Volume 1: A Persistent Place in a Changing World* (White Rose University Press, York, 2018), chapter 4.

10 Today known as the Scarborough Archaeological and Historical Society. Go to: www.sahs.org.uk/

11 I have discussed Star Carr in *Paths to the Past: Encounters with Britain's Hidden Landscapes* (Penguin Books, London, 2018), pp. 13–18.

12 For continuing research in the Carrs area, go to: carrswetland. wordpress.com/

Scene 4

1 For the damage in the late 1980s, see Timothy Darvill, *Ancient Monuments in the Countryside: An Archaeological Management Review* (English Heritage, London, 1987).

2 Mike Parker Pearson, *Stonehenge: Exploring the Greatest Stone Age Mystery* (Simon and Schuster, London, 2012).

3 See, for example: lbi-archpro.org/cs/stonehenge/

4 O. G. S. Crawford and Alexander Keiller, *Wessex from the Air* (Oxford University Press, Oxford, 1928).

5 I discuss the fissures in *Stonehenge: The Story of a Sacred Landscape* (Head of Zeus, London, 2016), pp. 37–8.

6 See, for example, the post alignment at Fiskerton, Lincolnshire, which I discuss in *Britain BC* (HarperCollins, London, 2003), p. 285, with refs.

7   D. Jacques, T. Phillips and T. Lyons, *Blick Mead: Exploring the 'First Place' in the Stonehenge Landscape* (Peter Lang Ltd., Oxford, 2018), p. 4.

8   Ibid., p. 113.

9   D. Jacques, T. Lyons and T. Phillips, 'Blick Mead': Exploring the 'First Place' in the Stonehenge Landscape', *Current Archaeology*, No. 324, March 2017, pp. 18–23.

10 D. M. John, 'The Cause and Significance of Crimson Flints in Springs Associated with the Mesolithic Settlement at Blick Mead', in D. Jacques et al. *Blick Mead*, pp. 122–6.

11 Tim Dinsdale, *Loch Ness Monster* (Routledge and Kegan Paul, London, 1961). The revised 2nd edition of 1972 was particularly influential. Recent research suggests the 'monster' might be a large eel: www.bbc.co.uk/news/uk-scotland-highlands-islands-49495145

12 H. H. Thomas, 'The Source of the Stones of Stonehenge'. *Antiquaries Journal*, vol. 3(3), 1923, pp. 239–60.

13 G. A. Kellaway, 'Glaciation and the Stones of Stonehenge', *Nature*, vol. 232, 1971, pp. 30–5.

14 R. S. Thorpe, O. Williams-Thorpe, D. G. Jenkins and J. S. Watson, 'The Geological sources and Transport of the Bluestones of Stonehenge, Wiltshire, UK', *Proceedings of the Prehistoric Society*, vol 52 (pt. 2), 1991, pp. 103–58.

15 I describe grey wethers in *The Making of the British Landscape* (Penguin Books, London, 2010), pp. 38–9.

16 Parker Pearson, *Stonehenge*.

17 en.wikipedia.org/wiki/Eleanor_cross

18 'Moving Monoliths: New revelations from the Preseli bluestone quarries', *Current Archaeology*, No. 345, December 2018, pp. 52–5.

Scene 5

1   A. Whittle, F. Healy and A. Bayliss, *Gathering Time: Dating the Early Neolithic Enclosures of Southern Britain and Ireland*, vol. 2 (Oxbow Books, Oxford, 2011), pp. 833–46.

2   www.nature.com/articles/s41559-019-0871-9

3   Francis Pryor, *Etton: Excavations at a Neolithic Causewayed Enclosure near Maxey, Cambridgeshire, 1982–7* (English Heritage, London, 1998), fig. 5, p. 10.

4   I. F. Smith, *Windmill Hill and Avebury: Excavations by Alexander Keiller 1925–1939* (Oxford University Press, Oxford, 1965), p. xxvii.

5   For a good example, see N. M. Sharples, *Maiden Castle: Excavations and Field survey 1985–6* (English Heritage, London, 1991).

6   David Hall and John Coles, *Fenland Survey: An Essay in Landscape and Persistence* (English Heritage, London, 1994), chapter 4.

7   Aubrey Burl, *The Stone Circles of the British Isles* (Yale University Press, New Haven and London, 1976), pp. 160–90.

8   For a clear explanation of the spread of farming, see Chris Scarre (ed.), *The Human Past: World Prehistory and the Development of Human Societies* (Thames and Hudson, London, 2005), pp. 397–401.

9   For more on their changing appearance, see L. Marchini, 'Romancing the Stones: Clava Cairns, near Inverness', *Current Archaeology*, No. 364, July 2020, pp. 16–17.

10 Bradley, *The Moon and the Bonfire: An Investigation into Three Stone Circles in North-East Scotland* (Society of Antiquaries of Scotland, Edinburgh, 2005).

11 Perhaps not unsurprisingly given its status, Stonehenge acquired a sorry record for unpublished excavations, which I discuss in *Stonehenge: The Story of a Sacred Landscape* (Head of Zeus, London, 2016), pp. 160–7.

12 Tomnaverie is open to visitors. www.historicenvironment.scot/visit-a-place/places/tomnaverie-stone-circle

13 Bradley, *The Moon and the Bonfire*, chapter 2.

14 M. Brennand and M. Taylor, 'The Survey and Excavation of a Bronze Age Timber Circle at Holme-next-the-Sea, Norfolk, 1998–9', *Proceedings of the Prehistoric Society*, vol. 69, 2003, pp. 16–17.

15 Bradley, *The Moon and the Bonfire*, p. 33.

16 Francis Pryor, *Paths to the Past: Encounters with Britain's Hidden Landscapes* (Penguin Books, London, 2018), pp. 41–2.

17 Bradley, *The Moon and the Bonfire*, p. 49.

Scene 6

1   Originally classed as Group VI. For a comprehensive review, see M. Pitts, 'The Stone Axe in Neolithic Britain', *Proceedings of the*

Prehistoric Society, vol. 62, 1996, pp. 311–72. Pitts shows the distribution under 'fine-grained igneous axes', in fig. 4, p. 323.

2   en.wikipedia.org/wiki/Langdale_axe_industry

3   For an excellent introduction, see M. Barber, D. Field and P. Topping, *The Neolithic Flint Mines of England* (English Heritage, Swindon, 1999).

4   J. M. Coles, 'A Jade axe from the Somerset Levels', *Antiquity*, vol. 48, no. 191, September 1974, pp. 216–20.

5   In Britain, the book that exemplified the New Archaeology was by D. L. Clarke, *Analytical Archaeology* (Methuen, London, 1968). The language used is almost incomprehensible and I would highly recommend the 2nd edition (Methuen, London, 1978), which was extensively revised by Bob Chapman.

6   K. Ray and J. Thomas, *Neolithic Britain: The Transformation of Social Worlds* (Oxford University Press, Oxford, 2018).

7   Mark Edmonds, 'Polished Stone Axes and Associated Artefacts', in Francis Pryor, *Etton: Excavations at a Neolithic Causewayed Enclosure near Maxey, Cambridgeshire, 1982–7* (English Heritage, London, 1998), pp. 260–8.

8   Special places in prehistory, such as Langdale, have been beautifully discussed by Richard Bradley, *An Archaeology of Natural Places* (Routledge, London, 2000).

9   I discuss the importance of family life in British prehistory in *Home: A Time Traveller's Tales from Britain's Prehistory* (Penguin Books, London, 2014). For an excellent summary of Orkney, see Ray and Thomas, *Neolithic Britain*, pp. 227–42.

10 whc.unesco.org/en/list/514/

11 www.orkneyjar.com/history/maeshowe/maeshrunes.htm

12 The two larger buildings are Structures 2 and 8. See Colin Richards (ed.), *Dwelling Among the Monuments: The Neolithic Village of Barnhouse, Maeshowe Passage Grave and Surrounding Monuments at Stenness, Orkney* (McDonald Institute for Archaeological Research, Cambridge, 2005).

13 www.nessofbrodgar.co.uk/

14 For useful summaries of the Ness of Brodgar, see Nick Card, 'The Ness of Brodgar: Uncovering Orkney's Neolithic heart', *Current Archaeology*, No. 335, February 2018, pp. 20–8. Ray and Thomas, *Neolithic Britain*, pp. 237–40.

15 Card, 'The Ness of Brogdar', Structure 10.

Scene 7

1   Mike Parker Pearson, *Stonehenge: Exploring the Greatest Stone Age Mystery* (Simon and Schuster, London, 2012), pp. 123–6.

2   www.tchevalier.com/fallingangels/bckgrnd/mourning/

3   I'm particularly fond of Louis Armstrong's lyrics (1911): genius.com/Louis-armstrong-oh-didnt-he-ramble-lyrics

4   The following account is based on Maisie Taylor's research: Mark Brennand and Maisie Taylor, 'The Survey and Excavation of a Bronze Age Timber Circle at Holme-next-the-Sea, Norfolk, 1998–9', *Proceedings of the Prehistoric Society*, vol. 69, 2003, pp. 1–84.

5   Ibid., p. 62.

6   This has been suggested, for example, for stone axes: Keith Ray and Julian Thomas, *Neolithic Britain: The Transformation of Social Worlds* (Oxford University Press, Oxford, 2018), pp. 126–7.

7   Parker Pearson, *Stonehenge*, chapter 2: 'The Man from Madagascar', pp. 9–26.

8   The modern Druid movement was born out of the emerging antiquarianism of the first half of the eighteenth century. For an excellent, detailed account, see Rosemary Sweet, *Antiquaries: The Discovery of the Past in Eighteenth-Century Britain* (Hambledon and London Publishers, London and New York, 2004), pp. 124–53.

9   Antler headdresses, worn by Mesolithic shamans around 9000 BC, have been found at Star Carr, Yorkshire. N. Milner, B. Taylor, C. Conneller and R. T. Schadla-Hall, *Star Carr: Life in Britain After the Ice Age* (Council for British Archaeology, York, 2013).

10   See Ray and Thomas, *Neolithic Britain*, chapter 5.

11   There is a press photograph of them in my book *Seahenge: A Quest for Life and Death in Bronze Age Britain* (HarperCollins, London, 2001), opposite p. 165.

12   In the account that follows, I draw extensively on my *Stonehenge: The Story of a Sacred Landscape* (Head of Zeus, London, 2016). It includes references.

13   Ibid., pp. 72–7.

14   Parker Pearson, *Stonehenge*, pp. 319–23.

15   Julian Richards, *English Heritage Book of Stonehenge* (B. T. Batsford and English Heritage, London, 1991), pp. 61–3. See also Andrew J. Lawson, and K. E Walker, 'Prehistoric Carvings', in R. M. J. Cleal, K. E. Walker and R. Montague (eds.), *Stonehenge in its Landscape:*

Twentieth-century Excavations (English Heritage, London, 1995), pp. 30–3.

16 Usefully summarised in: en.wikipedia.org/wiki/Laser_scanning_at_Stonehenge

17 See, for example: commons.wikimedia.org/wiki/Category:Axes_in_heraldry

Scene 8

1 Rosemary Sweet, *Antiquaries: The Discovery of the Past in Eighteenth-century Britain* (Hambledon and London Publishers, London and New York, 2004), pp. 93–4.

2 A. Fitzpatrick, '"The Amesbury Archer": A Well-furnished Early Bronze Age Burial in Southern England', *Antiquity*, vol 76(293), 2002, pp. 629–30.

3 Keith Ray and Julian Thomas, *Neolithic Britain* (Oxford University Press, Oxford, 2018), pp. 276–84.

4 W. G. Hoskins, *The Making of the English Landscape* (Penguin Books, Harmondsworth, 1970), pp. 242–7.

5 See my *Paths to the Past* (Penguin Books, London, 2018), chapter 15, pp. 84–7.

6 Ibid., chapter 16, pp. 88–90.

7 P. Gillingham, J. Stewart and H. Binney, *The Historic Peat Record: Implications for the Restoration of Blanket Bog*, Natural England Evidence Review NEER011 (18 March, 2016).

8 See my *The Fens: Discovering England's Ancient Depths* (Head of Zeus, London, 2019), Epilogue, pp. 395–401.

9 John Coles, *Field Archaeology in Britain* (Methuen, London, 1972).

10 John Coles, *Experimental Archaeology* (Academic Press, London, 1979).

11 vivacity.org/heritage-venues/flag-fen/

12 I draw extensively on Bryony and John Coles, *Sweet Track to Glastonbury: The Somerset Levels in Prehistory* (Thames and Hudson, London, 1986). The Sweet Track was first brought to academic attention in 1973: J. M. Coles, F. A. Hibbert and B. J. Orme, 'Prehistoric Roads and Tracks in Somerset: 3. The Sweet Track', *Proceedings of the Prehistoric Society*, vol. 39, 1973, pp. 220–93.

13 This account is based on J. M. Coles and B. J. Orme, 'A
    Reconstruction of the Sweet Track', *Somerset Levels Papers*, no. 10,
    1984, pp. 107–9.

14 Ibid., p. 109.

15 www.somersetheritage.org.uk/record/10739

16 Coles and Coles, *Sweet Track to Glastonbury,* 1986, pp. 46–7;
    plate 21.

17 See also Ray and Thomas, *Neolithic Britain*, pp. 292–5.

18 Coles and Coles, *Sweet Track to Glastonbury*, pp. 117–21.

Scene 9

1   I define the Domestic Revolution in *Home: A Time Traveller's Tales
    from Britain's Prehistory* (Penguin Books, London, 2014), pp. 168–
    71.

2   It has been said that Birmingham has more canals than Venice:
    canalrivertrust.org.uk/enjoy-the-waterways/canal-and-river-
    network/birmingham-canal-navigations

3   F. Pryor, *Stonehenge: The Story of a Sacred Landscape* (Head of
    Zeus, London, 2016), pp. 156–9.

4   The field systems on Dartmoor began around 1700–1600 BC. See
    A. Fleming, *The Dartmoor Reaves: Investigating Prehistoric Land
    Divisions*, 2nd ed. (Windgather Press, Oxford, 2008), p. 133.

5   The following account draws heavily on Peter Clark (ed.), *The
    Dover Bronze Age Boat* (English Heritage, Swindon, 2004).

6   Bayliss et al. in ibid., p. 254.

7   A. D. Mills, *A Dictionary of English Place-names* (Oxford
    University Press, Oxford, 1991), p. 108.

8   I discuss these ideas further in 'Some Thoughts on Boats as Bronze
    Age Artefacts', in Peter Clark (ed.), *The Dover Bronze Age Boat
    in Context: Society and Water Transport in Prehistoric Europe*
    (Oxbow Books, Oxford, 2004), pp. 31–4.

9   S. McGrail and E. Kentley (eds.), *Sewn Plank Boats: Archaeological
    and Ethnographic Papers Based on Those Presented to
    a Conference at Greenwich in November,* 1984 (British
    Archaeological Reports, International Series No. 276, Oxford,
    1985).

10 The film was first shown on 7 September 2014. For more on *Time Team* documentaries go to: en.wikipedia.org/wiki/Time_Team_(specials)

11 D. G. Buckley and C. J. Ingle, 'The Saddle Querns from Flag Fen', in F. Pryor, *The Flag Fen Basin* (English Heritage, Swindon, 2001), pp. 322–9.

12 See my *Paths to the Past: Encounters with Britain's Hidden Landscapes* (Penguin Books, London, 2018), chapter 7, pp. 43–7.

13 Keith Parfitt, 'A Search for the Prehistoric Harbours of Kent', in Clark (ed.), *The Dover Bronze Age Boat in Context*, chapter 11, pp. 99–105.

14 Clark (ed.), *The Dover Bronze Age Boat*, p. 10, with refs.

15 Chris Catling, 'When Britannia Ruled the Waves', *Current Archaeology*, 286, January 2014, p. 19.

16 We came across several when filming for *Time Team* on Bodmin Moor. See my *Home: A Time Traveller's Tales from Britain's Prehistory* (Penguin Books, London, 2014), p. 255.

17 See, for example, B. W. Cunliffe, *Iron Age Communities in Britain*, 4th ed. (Routledge, London, 2005), p. 557.

18 Indeed, I wrote a book about it: *Home: A Time Traveller's Tales from Britain's Prehistory*.

Scene 10

1   en.wikipedia.org/wiki/Cornish_Yarg

2   www.vegetablefacts.net/vegetable-history/history-of-onions/

3   Jacqui Wood has written two excellent books about historical cooking, complete with recipes: *Prehistoric Cooking* (The History Press, Stroud, 2011) and *Tasting the Past: Recipes from the Stone Age to the Present* (The History Press, Stroud, 2009).

4   en.wikipedia.org/wiki/PPG_16

5   F. Pryor, *Excavations at Fengate, Peterborough, England: The Third Report* (Royal Ontario Museum, Toronto, and Northamptonshire Archaeological Society, 1980), fig. 18, p. 27.

6   It resulted in my book: *Farmers in Prehistoric Britain* (The History Press, Stroud, 1998).

7   Ibid., pp. 98–100.

8   issuu.com/hspubs/docs/tan-30---scottish-turf-construction--june-06--plu-

9   John Coles, *Archaeology by Experiment* (Hutchinson, London, 1973), pp. 63–4. Coles also illustrates the experimental burning of the house at Roskilde, Denmark (plate 5).

10   en.wikipedia.org/wiki/Blackhouse

11   www.slowfood.org.uk/ff-products/bloaters/

12   For many years we have had an account with Alfred Enderby of Grimsby, where every Christmas we buy our smoked salmon, haddock – among other delicacies. alfredenderby.co.uk/

13   Gerhard Bersu, 'Excavations at Little Woodbury, Wiltshire. Part 1: The Settlement Revealed by Excavation'. *Proceedings of the Prehistoric Society*, Vol. 6, pt. 1, 1940, pp. 30–111.

14   Little Butser is still a popular visitor attraction. Go to: www. butserancientfarm.co.uk/about-us

15   en.wikipedia.org/wiki/Living_in_the_Past_(TV_series)

Scene 11

1   en.wikipedia.org/wiki/Red_hill_(salt_making)

2   D. A. Gurney, 'Evidence of Bronze Age Salt Production at Northey, Peterborough', *Northamptonshire Archaeology*, vol. 15, 1980, pp. 1–11.

3   F. Pryor, *Excavations at Fengate, Peterborough, England: The Third Report* (Royal Ontario Museum, Toronto, and Northamptonshire Archaeological Society, 1980), fig. 13, nos. 1–3, pp. 18–21.

4   M. Fulford, T. Champion and A. Long (eds.), *England's Coastal Heritage: A Survey for English Heritage and the RCHME* (English Heritage, London, 1997), chapter 2, pp. 25–49. For the Fens/Lincolnshire coast, see M. Waller, *The Fenland Project, Number 9: Flandrian Environmental Change in Fenland*, East Anglian Archaeology Report No. 70 (Cambridgeshire Archaeological Committee, Cambridge, 1994).

5   See my book *The Fens: Discovering England's Ancient Depths* (Head of Zeus, London, 2019), chapter 16, pp. 337–49.

6   en.wikipedia.org/wiki/Hallstatt

7   en.wikipedia.org/wiki/Managed_retreat

8   Colin Palmer-Brown, 'Bronze Age salt production at Tetney', *Current Archaeology*, No. 136, 1993, pp. 143–5.

9   David Hall and John Coles, *Fenland Survey: An Essay in Landscape and Persistence* (English Heritage, London, 1994).

10 en.wikipedia.org/wiki/Silent_Spring

11 historicengland.org.uk/images-books/publications/guide-to-historic-environment-records-england/

12 The following section draws heavily on T. Lane and E. L. Morris (eds.), *A Millennium of Saltmaking: Prehistoric and Romano-British Salt Production in the Fenland* (Heritage Trust of Lincolnshire, 2001).

13 Lane and Morris (eds.), *A Millennium of Saltmaking*, Fig 22, p. 56.

14 Ibid., pp. 13–97.

15 Ibid., p. 61.

16 For the nature reserve go to: www.lincstrust.org.uk/nature-reserves/willow-tree-fen. For the South Drove site, see T. Lane, *Mineral from the Marshes: Coastal Salt-making in Lincolnshire* (Heritage Trust of Lincolnshire, Heckington, 2018), pp. 79–80, with refs.

Scene 12

1 See, for example, S. Buteux and H. Chapman, *Where Rivers Meet: The Archaeology of Catholme and the Trent-Tame Confluence*, Research Report 161 (Council for British Archaeology, York, 2009).

2 See my recent book *The Fens: Discovering England's Ancient Depths* (Head of Zeus, London, 2019).

3 For a superb review of the Fens in early historic times, see S. Oosthuizen, *The Anglo-Saxon Fenland* (Windgather Press, Oxford, 2017).

4 www.archaeology.co.uk/

5 Royal Commission on Historical Monuments (England), *Peterborough New Town: A Survey of the Antiquities in the Areas of Development* (H.M.S.O., London, 1969).

6 The book that helped me revise my views is by C. Evans, *Fengate Revisited: Further Fen-edge Excavations, Bronze Age Fieldsystems & Settlement and the Wyman Abbott/Leeds Archives* (Cambridge Archaeological Unit and Oxbow Books, Oxford, 2009), chapters 2 and 3.

7 I discuss this in *The Making of the British Landscape* (Penguin Books, London, 2010), pp. 500–5.

8 I discuss the Swiss Lakes and other early 'lake village' finds in *Britain BC* (HarperCollins, London, 2003), pp. 395–405, with refs.

9   Research is still continuing today. See, for example: www. swissinfo.ch/eng/rediscovering-the-legend-of-the-lake-dwellers/ 1288560

10 en.wikipedia.org/wiki/Rhind_Lectures

11 R. Munro, *The Lake Dwellings of Europe: Being the Rhind Lectures in Archaeology for 1888* (Cassell and Co., London, 1890).

12 I discuss this in greater length in *Home: A Time Traveller's Tales from British Prehistory* (Penguin Books, London, 2014).

13 A good example of a book targeted at a new, wider, popular audience for history is Bruce Bernard (ed.), *Century: One Hundred Years of Human Progress, Regression, Suffering and Hope* (Phaidon Press, London and New York, 1999).

14 www.crannog.co.uk/

15 N. Dixon, 'Oakbank Crannog', *Current Archaeology*, No. 90, 1984, pp. 217–20.

16 onlinelibrary.wiley.com/doi/abs/10.1111/j.1095-9270.1982. tb00067.x

17 In the event we decided to use a picture of another, unexcavated and unreconstructed Loch Tay crannog at Spry Island: Pryor, *The Making of the British Landscape*, p. 153.

18 D. G. Coombs, 'Chapter 10: Metalwork', p. 264, fig. 10.5, in F. Pryor, *The Flag Fen Basin: Archaeology and Environment of a Fenland Landscape* (English Heritage, Swindon, 2001).

19 'Bridging the Gap: Exploring Evidence for Musical Instruments in Iron Age Scotland', *Current Archaeology*, No. 362, 2020, pp. 42–5.

20 www.high-pasture-cave.org/

21 'First Ever Iron Age Burial on Skye', *Current Archaeology*, No. 201, 2006, p. 456.

22 'Skye's Find of Note', *Current Archaeology*, No. 267, 2012, p. 10.

23 G. Lawson, 'The Lyre', in L. Blackmore, I. Blair, S. Hirst and C. Scull (eds.), *The Prittlewell Princely Burial: Excavations at Priory Crescent, Southend-on-Sea, Essex, 2003*. MOLA Monographs, 73 (Museum of London, 2019), pp. 231–48 and 397–402.

24 S. Piggott, 'The Carnyx in Early Iron Age Britain'. *The Antiquaries Journal*, vol. 39, 1959, pp. 19–32.

Scene 13

1   M. Knight, R. Ballantyne, I. Robinson Zeki and D. Gibson, 'The Must Farm Pile-dwelling Settlement', *Antiquity*, vol. 93, Issue 369, June 2019, pp. 645–63.

2   They have an excellent website: www.mustfarm.com/

3   A. Mudd and B. Pears, *Bronze Age Field System at Tower's Fen, Thorney, Peterborough: Excavations at 'Thorney Borrow Pit' 2004–2005*, British Archaeological Reports British Series, No. 471 (Archaeopress, Oxford, 2008).

4   F. Pryor, *Excavation at Fengate, Peterborough, England: The Second Report* (feature W17) (Royal Ontario Museum, Toronto, 1978), pp. 39–44.

5   M. Taylor, 'Early Iron Age Stake with Dovetail Housing Joint from F1551, Cat's Water Subsite, Fengate', in F. Pryor, *Excavation at Fengate, Peterborough, England: The Fourth Report* (Northampton and Toronto), pp. 175–6.

6   For example, the timber-built Haddenham long barrow. C. J. Evans and I. R. Hodder, *A Woodland Archaeology: Neolithic Sites at Haddenham* (McDonald Institute Monographs, Cambridge, 2006).

7   The wheel and associated artefacts are fully described by Maisie Taylor in F. Pryor, *The Flag Fen Basin: Archaeology and Environment of a Fenland Landscape* (English Heritage, Swindon, 2001), chapter 7, pp. 213–18. It is currently on display in the on-site museum at Flag Fen, Peterborough.

8   www.cam.ac.uk/research/news/most-complete-bronze-age-wheel-to-date-found-at-must-farm-near-peterborough

9   F. Pryor, *Farmers in Prehistoric Britain* (Tempus Books, Stroud, 2006), pp. 116–17; colour plates 11 and 12.

Scene 14

1   Wheeler's autobiography, *Still Digging* (Michael Joseph, London, 1955), is highly entertaining, but for a subtler, more nuanced biography, written by a close friend, see Jacquetta Hawkes, *Mortimer Wheeler: Adventurer in Archaeology* (Weidenfeld & Nicolson, London, 1982). https://www.amazon.co.uk/Mortimer-Wheeler-Archaeology-Jacquetta-Hawkes/dp/0297780565.

2   trowelblazers.com/raising-horizons-fervent-about-the-field/

3 R. E. M. Wheeler, *Maiden Castle, Dorset*. Society of Antiquaries Research Report, No. 12 (London, 1943).

4 T. Darvil, *The Concise Oxford Dictionary of Archaeology* (Oxford University Press, Oxford, 2002), p. 418.

5 www.speel.me.uk/sculptlondon/boadiceawestminsterbr.htm

6 en.wikipedia.org/wiki/Ian_Richmond

7 en.wikipedia.org/wiki/Danebury

8 Cunliffe's Danebury excavations have been fully published in great detail. For a useful summary of the interior layout, see B. Cunliffe, *Iron Age Communities in Britain*, 3rd ed. (Routledge, London, 1991), pp. 391–4, with refs.

9 N. M. Sharples, *Maiden Castle: Excavations and Field Survey 1985–6* (Historic Buildings and Monuments Commission for England, London, 1991). Niall Sharples also wrote a more accessible account of the excavations, *The English Heritage Book of Maiden Castle* (Batsford Books, London, 1991).

10 For an excellent summary of hillfort development, see Cunliffe, *Iron Age Communities in Britain*, pp. 378–406.

11 I review the development of hillforts in the landscape in *The Making of the British Landscape* (Penguin Books, London, 2010), pp. 124–47.

12 The following draws heavily on D. Stewart and M. Russell, 'Iron Age Interior Design: Mapping the Inside of Dorset's Hillfort Enclosures'. *Current Archaeology*, No. 336, 2016, pp. 28–35. D. Stewart and M. Russell, *Hillforts and the Durotriges: A Geophysical Survey of Iron Age Dorset* (Archaeopress, Oxford, 2017).

13 I discuss this further in *Britain BC* (HarperCollins, London, 2003), p. 287 and pp. 353–4, with refs.

14 en.wikipedia.org/wiki/It%27s_That_Man_Again

15 Toby Driver, *The Hillforts of Cardigan Bay* (Logaston Press, Hereford, 2016).

16 Toby Driver, 'Commanding the Landscape: The Hillforts of Cardigan Bay', *Current Archaeology*, No. 318, 2016, pp. 12–19.

17 C. Catling, 'The Riddle of the Lake: Llyn Cerrig Bach and Iron Age Anglesey', *Current Archaeology*, No. 273, 2012, pp. 26–33.

Scene 15

1   One of my most treasured possessions is a copy of O. G. S. Crawford and A. Keiller, *Wessex from the Air* (Clarendon Press, Oxford, 1928).

2   For Roman fields in the Fens, see C. W. Phillips (ed.), *The Fenland in Roman Times*, Royal Geographical Society Research Series, No. 5 (London, 1970).

3   J. Taylor, *An Atlas of Roman Rural Settlement in England*, Research Report No. 151 (Council for British Archaeology, York, 2007).

4   F. Pryor, *Excavation at Fengate, Peterborough, England: The Fourth Report* (Northampton and Toronto, 1984), pp. 179–96 and 227–30.

5   I discuss the Saxon period and the rise of English as a language in *Home: A Time Traveller's Tales from Britain's Prehistory* (Penguin Books, London, 2014), pp. 283–90, with refs.

6   www.weststow.org/

7   K. Blockley, 'Canterbury Cathedral', *Current Archaeology*, No. 136, October/December, 1993, pp. 124–30.

8   www.hillside.co.uk/arch/cathedral/nave.html

9   en.wikipedia.org/wiki/Apse

10   For the archaeology of Becket in Canterbury, see N. Cohen, 'England in Stone: Recounting Recent Research at Canterbury Cathedral', *Current Archaeology*, No. 364, July 2020, pp. 44–51.

11   Blockley, 'Canterbury Cathedral', p. 129.

12   I describe the Risehill dig in *Paths to the Past: Encounters with Britain's Hidden Landscapes* (Penguin Books, London, 2018), chapter 21, pp. 110–14.

13   www.newsteadabbey.org.uk/

14   www.english-heritage.org.uk/visit/places/mount-grace-priory/history-and-stories/carthusian-life/

15   www.countrylife.co.uk/property/guides-advice/northamptonshire-county-guide-163716

16   D. Parsons and D. Sutherland, *The Anglo-Saxon Church of Brixworth, Northamptonshire: Survey, Excavation and Analysis, 1972–2010* (Oxbow Books, Oxford, 2013).

Image Credits

Index

Page references in *italics* indicate images.